L. Murphy Nov '82   2-25.

CW00825744

An Unhusbanded Life
CHARLOTTE DESPARD
SUFFRAGETTE, SOCIALIST AND SINN FEINER

Hutchinson & Co. (Publishers) Ltd
3 Fitzroy Square, London W1P 6JD

London Melbourne Sydney Auckland
Wellington Johannesburg and agencies
throughout the world

First published 1980

© Andro Linklater 1980

Set in Monotype Garamond

Printed in Great Britain by The Anchor Press Ltd
and bound by Wm Brendon & Son Ltd
both of Tiptree, Essex

British Library CIP data

Linklater, Andro
  An unhusbanded life.
  1. Despard, Charlotte
  2. Feminists – England – Biography
  I. Title
  941.082′092′4   HQ1595.D/

ISBN 0 09 138310 2

Charlotte Despard (photo Hoppé, courtesy Mansell Collection)

Part of the national census protest, 1911
(courtesy of Syndication International Ltd)

Speaking in Hyde Park, 1 May 1920
(courtesy Syndication International Ltd)

Front page of *The Vote*, 13 July 1928
(courtesy Fawcett Library)

Irish demonstration, October 1924: Charlotte Despard followed
by Maud Gonne carrying placard
(courtesy Radio Times Hulton Picture Library)

With the Russian ambassador, June 1933
(courtesy Fawcett Library)

Speaking at anti-fascist rally in Trafalgar Square
(courtesy National Portrait Gallery)

ACKNOWLEDGEMENTS

In Charlotte Despard's vagabond old age many of the sources of information about her life were lost. I am, therefore, particularly grateful for the personal reminiscences of her relatives; her ward, Vere Hinton; her friends and neighbours in Northern Ireland, especially Jack Mulvenna; and former members of the Women's Freedom League.

For their professional help, which was given generously, I must thank the staffs of the Public Records Office, Belfast; the Fawcett Library and City of London Polytechnic; the Museum of London; the British Library, and the Greater London Council Records Office.

I greatly appreciated the information I received from David Mitchell about sources of suffragette history, and from James Hunt of Shaw University, North Carolina, about Gandhi's visit to London in 1909.

Finally I must acknowledge with deep gratitude my publishers' encouragement and patience.

I

Fields and gardens reach down to the black rocks of Belfast Lough on its northern and southern shores, but at its head lie the cranes and sheds of the Harland and Woolf shipyard, and beyond them the redbrick terraces of Belfast. For the most part these are utilitarian dwellings, designed only to offer shelter to people to sleep, eat and meet a few like-housed friends. Towards the city's centre, where functions, not people, are housed, the buildings become grander. Their purpose is different. When they were built it was not enough that books and papers and those who handled them should be protected from the elements; their value had to be proclaimed publicly, and in the Linen Library and City Hall might be found rolling stentorian assertions of worth and dignity. Above culture and commerce was set government, and its supreme importance was voiced by the ponderous magnificence of its home.

East of Belfast, Stormont Castle stands on a hill surrounded by green parklands. It was completed in 1931; but its Palladian style, the sweeping wings and pillared portico, is derived from an era when government was still a trust for the few rather than the representative of all. In the days when the Northern Ireland government held power, Stormont was an appropriate symbol, for it reflected that Presbyterian resolve which the settlers brought with them to Ulster in the seventeenth century and which, by the twentieth century, had calcified to an unbending determination to maintain their religious independence against the dictates of Irish geography and British politics. Set up in 1921, the Northern Ireland government, threatened, as it felt itself to be, as much by the renegades in the South as by the uncertain friendship of the United Kingdom Parliament, quickly came to epitomize the worst virtues of democracy. The majority view was deified, civic responsibility was magnified, commercial enterprise was glorified and individual conscience was stultified. All this Stormont came to represent.

Past the gate at the foot of the park drive to Stormont ran the Newtonards Road, and if the symbol at the top of the hill were in need of justification the evidence could be seen and heard in the Newtonards Road each Twelfth of July. On that day, when the Protestant community of East Belfast publicly celebrated the victory of William of Orange over King James II at the Battle of the Boyne, houses in the Newtonards Road blossomed with Union Jacks, and the birdsong whistle of fife and flute came flighting through the dark thunder of drums as the Orange Lodge bands marched down the road towards the centre of Belfast. In the wake of each band came the Lodge banner, gleaming with gold thread and motto, and behind the banner came the Grand Master, distinguished by his embroidered apron from those who followed, but like them wearing a bowler hat and a sash across his dark suit. Rank upon rank came marching by: blank, black respectability, the warp and woof of the community, showing by hat, sash and suit that they aspired to the same values as those symbolized by Stormont itself.

In 1934 Mrs Charlotte Despard came to live at 29 Newtonards Road; a frail old woman whose blue eyes were milky and half blind, and whose face was as thin and crumpled as tissue paper. She had been born in Kent ninety years before, the daughter of Captain William French of the Royal Navy and, through him, directly descended from Tierna Mor ('the Great Commander'), an earlier John French who commanded a troop of cavalry under that same William of Orange against James II. Her late husband, Maximilian Despard, came from landowning stock which, by the nineteenth century, had contributed so largely to the government based in Dublin Castle that it was nicknamed 'Castle' Irish: it provided Lords-Lieutenant, members of both Houses of Parliament, magistrates and soldiers – the scaffolding of ordered society. Its other nickname was the 'Ascendancy', and that bore with it the unspoken qualification of 'Protestant'. Although descended from the Normans, both the Frenchs and the Despards had been Protestant at least since William's reign – they would not otherwise have held their huge estates so securely – and Maximilian Despard's father, a Resident Magistrate, bore his faith and office stoutly enough to provoke a riot in Castletown when he arrested the parish priest at pistol point for the theft of eight guineas. Protected by the mob, the priest managed to escape; but in another parish, and before another, more pusillanimous, crowd, he was again arrested by a Despard, a cousin of the first, and this one had him hanged without delay in Clonmel jail. There could be no room for doubt where the Despard loyalties lay.

By blood and marriage, therefore, Charlotte Despard should certainly have been in sympathy with the religious and civil instincts of the marchers in the Newtonards Road – but no Union Jack or Red Hand of Ulster hung from her windows. Instead the blinds were drawn, and the old lady waited in the shadowed room for the noise of fife and drum to pass on down the street. She had many faiths and most of them were contradictory, but by every article in each of them she was opposed to the marchers and their music. By Catholicism, communism, pacifism and a life devoted to rebellion against a materialist, masculine society she anathematized the virtues of Stormont and the Orange Lodge. Yet, beyond question, she was 'a lady'. Of all those who remember her in Belfast, none omits to mention that she was aristocratic in both manner and speech, and the photographs of the time reveal the training which had formed her, ninety years before. Her carriage is still that of a young lady of the nineteenth century: the head is held high, the back straight, and the thin shoulders beneath the shawl are not rounded or hunched, as might provoke a governess's displeasure.

It must have been tempting for the Stormont government to dismiss her as an eccentric old woman, living out of time and social place, whose subversive opinions were a foible which might be overlooked. But they took her more seriously than that. Opposite the two policemen who guarded the entrance to Stormont Castle stood two more, guarding Mrs Despard's front gate. Whenever she was driven off in her tiny car to address a meeting of unemployed workers in Derry or Belfast, a police car followed. To Dawson Bates, the Minister of Home Affairs and the official responsible for law and order in the Province, Charlotte Despard remained a positive threat to security.

In 1934 and '35 economic hardship in Northern Ireland had intensified the bitterly high levels of unemployment amongst unskilled workers, by far the largest proportion of whom were Catholics, and the meetings which Charlotte Despard addressed were crowded with desperate, ill-fed men with little to lose. It was nothing less than revolution to which she exhorted them: the

13

overthrow of a capitalist government and the substitution of one based on brotherliness and cooperation, after the model of the Soviet Union. Nor did she offer mere words; there was money available to hire halls and to help those so minded to set up small cooperative organizations among the workless, which might become the cells and patterns for the larger revolt she had in mind. Her inflammatory speeches were not the cause of Dawson Bates' concern – indeed, it was doubtful if his informers in the audience even heard them, for her voice had become so thin with age that it scarcely reached halfway down the hall. Far more potent was her value as a symbol, since, in the eyes of the Stormont Cabinet, Charlotte Despard, for all her revolutionary sentiments, her idolatrous religion and her raffish friends, was nothing less than the sister of Sir John French.

As Inspector-General of the Army, French had in 1914 helped to scupper the Liberal government's half-formed plan to impose Home Rule on Ulster by force; as Commander-in-Chief of the British Expeditionary Force in the following year, he had been in command over the Ulster Division which later fought and died with untoward courage at the Somme; and as Viceroy of Ireland from 1918 to 1921, he had gained Ulster's favour by his friendship to the Province and his hatred of the IRA. However provoking the behaviour of his sister, it would be intolerable if she were to come to harm at the hands of some outraged Protestant; if her windows were to be broken, or her car overturned, the news would be a mockery of the Province's declared attempt to maintain law and order among its deeply divided inhabitants. Who could believe such a claim if even the sister of Ulster's staunchest friend was not immune from the violence of the government's supporters? And so the police at her gates and in the shadowing car were there not so much to spy upon Charlotte Despard as to guard her, as an ancient icon might be guarded in a museum.

Ironically, those whom she regarded as her friends looked upon her in much the same light. She was a 'grand old lady', generous to a fault, and undeviatingly compassionate to the victims of capitalism and religious intolerance, but her greatest value lay precisely in the honour due to her brother's name. If a meeting was banned, it needed only Charlotte Despard's presence to ensure that it could take place free from police interference. When four or five burly Labour leaders crowded into her little BSA car to attend such a meeting, they knew that it was her fragile body, almost crushed between them, that protected them from arrest. For that quality in her they were willing to tolerate her less happy traits.

If anything, Mrs Despard's speeches caused even more embarrassment to her Labour friends than to Dawson Bates' police. Many were covert nationalists, who dreamed that Ireland would soon be united under de Valera's Republican government; but their cause received little encouragement from her. 'As regards that government,' she said, 'I think it could easily enter competition with the South American Republicans.' No one, she asserted, was free except in a communist state, and if there was one subject on which the Catholic unemployed and the Stormont government were united, it was their common detestation of Marxist ideology. But the price to be paid for Mrs Despard's presence was to allow her to speak: she was determined to deliver her message and if she were crossed in the matter she would, with the irritable bad temper of the old, decide that the entire occasion was a failure and perhaps it was no longer worth continuing her financial and personal support. And so she spoke – a silver-haired lady, with a fine educated English accent, talking of revolution and the overthrow of government to an audience of shipyard and linen-mill workers, police spies and trade-union leaders, most of whom regarded her with either embarrassment or incomprehension.

Cut off from her friends and enemies alike, by her age, her class and her politics, Charlotte Despard seemed a lonely figure. Her interests were multifarious and ranged world-wide but there were not many in the Province who could raise their eyes from troubles at home to study the danger of fascism in Germany or Spain, solve the problems of child-brides in India or government-approved brothels in Hong Kong, or ruminate over Shelley's socialism or Krishnamurti's mysticism. Besides, her sight was fading, and she was tormented by a nagging, and occasionally paralysing, pain in her shoulder. The doctor who treated her enjoyed her company and conversation, but otherwise there was little opportunity for sociability beyond some amiable words with the policeman at her gate, or with the good neighbour who brought her vegetables from his garden. She was not at an age when new friends were easily made.

To many of her acquaintances Charlotte Despard was an object of pity. Not only was she old, in pain and half blind, but in some sinister way she appeared to have fallen into the hands of an unscrupulous couple – Molly Fitzgerald her companion and Jack Mulvenna her chauffeur. They were not a sinister looking pair. Molly was a handsome black-haired, brown-eyed girl in her twenties. She had a wide, easy smile and a direct stare. Jack, for his part, was the friendliest of young men, powerfully built and garrulously good-natured, the centre of a large group of friends. Yet the tongues wagged. What would a rich old lady, one step from her grave, want with such lively companions? The pair were 'black Irish' in the neighbours' eyes – the sort of folk from the South who would not think twice about leeching off an old woman's bounty. It was noted that the tobacconist supplied 200 cigarettes a week on the account of Mrs Despard, although she had never touched tobacco in her life. A friend who visited her had the eerie experience of gazing at a bare garden while Mrs Despard described the flowers which she imagined Molly had planted there. The RUC had little trouble in discovering that Jack had been a member of the IRA, and if they had cared to search Mrs Despard's property they might have found, in the garden, a cache of rifles, Thompson sub-machine-guns, clips of ammunition and gelignite. The neighbours would not have been surprised; it would simply have confirmed their liveliest suspicions that poor, senile Mrs Despard was being used by this extremely dangerous young couple.

But the old woman was thoroughly enjoying herself. In May of 1934 she wrote to her nephew: 'As a fact I have never been quite so well, even so young as I am at the present moment.' In her two employees she had found the companionship and high spirits which most appealed to her, and above all they held the same sort of opinions as she did. It was true that Jack had been in the IRA; but he had been expelled from its ranks for his socialist ideas and for helping to form a political party in the South dedicated to such an extreme form of worker republicanism that it had been denounced by the Catholic bishops and persecuted by de Valera. To one of Charlotte Despard's cast of thought it was hard to find better credentials. But it was Molly who won her real devotion. Molly, Irish to the marrow of her bones, breathed enthusiasm and energy – and the causes which appealed to her were precisely those which had long commanded Charlotte's support. To hear Molly on a platform, denouncing war with a vehemence that could match the worst of war-mongers, was to catch an echo of the intemperance of a younger Despard; even her dark brows and bold features bore a resemblance to Charlotte in her youth. In Molly's company, Charlotte was warmed and found inspiration. She composed poetry, long, optimistic, fiery stanzas dedicated to the workers' revolution which would soon be coming. Molly took down her words in shorthand; a printer was found and eventually, at the age of ninety-one, Charlotte enjoyed the satisfaction of publishing a slim volume of verse. It was entitled *In the Light of the Red Dawn*.

For forty-five years, ever since she was widowed, Charlotte Despard had been in strife with society. Even when she began her public career she had seemed, from the dignity of her bearing and the silver of her hair, to be already old; but wherever the wave of social reform broke most fiercely against the excesses of Victorian materialism, she was to be found there – in the campaign for the abolition of the workhouse, in the fight for women's suffrage, in the resistance to conscription and the crusade for a negotiated peace in the First World War, and in the battle for Irish independence. When she was almost eighty she moved to Dublin, and with the same fury laboured for the release of Sinn Fein prisoners, led demonstrations of the unemployed, and sowed the seeds of Marxism there against the narrow materialism of de Valera's government. Frequently absurd and mostly right, she had seen one after another of her causes derided and opposed and sometimes triumph, but at the moment of success she would already be engaged in another conflict.

Like a twentieth-century Don Quixote she readily discovered monsters and false knights where others knew there to be only institutions and politicians; and, like the old hero, she owed her vision to much reading and a simple unqualified determination to bring justice into the world. Her indignation made her seem ageless, and her voice was as insistent as time. Through the babble of events she made it heard in the Cabinets of Balfour, Asquith, Lloyd George, Cosgrave and de Valera.

At the top of the hill stood Stormont Castle, symbol of a government as unyielding as any. At the foot lived Charlotte Despard, devoted as ever to the idea of sweeping it out of existence. The contest was unequal – hard, practical men of affairs, backed by the panoply of State, against the utopian dreams of an old widow. Yet, if Westminster and Dublin had moved – not much, but a little – why then Stormont itself might one day crumble away. Her whole life suggested it would.

2

There was much to be expected, albeit little that was good, from a young girl whose dream hero was Milton's Satan. The Prince of Darkness, the first rebel in creation, was not an example to be followed by a child, still less a child of the Victorian era; but for any who did a notable future might be predicted, in this world or the next. 'So long as I live,' Charlotte Despard wrote in her old age:

I shall vividly recall the fearful joy and admiration with which I used to stand up and throw out Satan's address to the Sun:

> As thou that with surpassing glory crowned
> Lookst from the sole Dominion like the God
> Of this new world, at whose sight all the stars
> Hide their diminished heads, to thee I call,
> But with no friendly voice, and add thy name
> O Sun, to tell thee now I *hate* thy beams.

The emphasis on 'hate' was her own. The daylight world of Charlotte's childhood was an affair of rules and prohibitions from which she turned away to the shadowy regions that exist inside every child's head, and there she meditated rebellion against authority's loathsome law. Unlike other children she was never tempted out into the open by the affection or understanding of an adult, for her upbringing was left in the hands of a succession of strangers.

Her father, Captain William French, had retired from the Royal Navy in 1836 to his family estate at Ripple in Kent. His naval career, passed during the doldrums of peace and financial stringency that followed the Napoleonic War, had given little scope to his natural bent for action. He had taken part in the battle of Navarino, in which he had lost an eye; and later, still thirsting for active service, he had joined Sir Charles Napier's naval contingent in Portugal, fighting on behalf of Dom Pedro. At the age of thirty-two, this energetic, forceful man had married Margaret Eccles, an exceptionally wealthy heiress who was fourteen years younger than himself. Her family had the good and growing fortune to own property on the banks of the Clyde and around the outskirts of Glasgow, a city that was welling over with people drawn there by its infant shipbuilding industry. Together with a handsome dowry, Margaret Eccles brought to the Frenchs' home of Ripplevale a puritanical sense of piety and an unstable temperament, all of which left their mark on her seven surviving children.

The conjunction of Scots and Irish blood is often explosive, and the mixture may be partly responsible for the extravagant quality of Charlotte's life, for although the French family had been settled in Kent for half a century, they were of impeccably Irish descent. The first of the family, a Norman knight, had arrived in Wexford, and his descendants, moving westward, had won for themselves, by the strength of their arms and the cunning of their marriages, a vast demesne in Galway which they ruled as petty kings. Like the Celtic aristocracy into which they merged, their claim to innumerable acres of moorland, mountain and pasture was based on their own vaunting power and little else. When English law arrived with Strafford in 1635, the Frenchs, and many others who failed to show proper title to their lands, were dispossessed, and their last pretensions to independence were soon afterwards laid waste along with their lands in Oliver Cromwell's brutal pilgrimage through Ireland. Within two generations the old nation was destroyed, and the new one was riven by the countervailing religious and nationalist sentiments which sprang from the plantation of Ulster and the destruction of James II's kingship by William of Orange in 1690.

John French, Tierna Mor, sided with William and, in the benign climate created by backing the victorious cause, managed to restore the family fortunes to such an extent that when he died £1000 was spent on his funeral and the tenants of his 47,000 acres did not draw a sober breath during the three days of his wake. Secured by the Crown in possession of their estates, the Frenchs of French Park in County Roscommon proved themselves the Crown's good servants by sitting in its Parliaments at Dublin and Westminster, and by holding commissions in its Army. When Charlotte's great-grandfather settled in Kent he already had one foot in English society, but at the same time he was also the grandson of Tierna Mor, descendant of the greatest chieftains in western Ireland.

Something of his ancestors' restless vitality apparently infused the character of Captain William French, who ran his small estate of Ripplevale with fanatical concern for efficiency. 'He was', wrote his son, 'a man of great strength of character, firm will and self-reliance, and these personal qualities were hardened and developed by eighteen or nineteen years of strenuous service.' Every detail of organization in the house and on the estate came under his narrow gaze, to be reviewed and inspected as though only his unwearying alertness ensured the obedience of his retainers. He was a magistrate and Deputy-Lieutenant of the county, and the same remorseless attention given to the misdoings of offenders made him an object of fear on the Bench. The one surprising exception from his vigilance was the upbringing of his children, and the reason, it must be supposed, was that the first five were all daughters; Charlotte was the third to be born, on 15 June 1844, and it was not until 1852, two years before the Captain's death, that his wife produced an heir. His wife was excluded from his preoccupations as completely as his daughters and, while the world about her was being ordered with a naval passion for exactitude, Margaret French was gradually becoming a recluse. Married at eighteen and exiled to the foreign countryside of Kent, she passed most of her adult life either in pregnancy or recovering from seven births and several miscarriages. Exhausted by this physical and emotional battering, she withdrew from William French's clockwork environment to immerse herself in the devotional literature of her Presbyterian forebears, and the children whom she bore with biennial regularity were left to their own devices.

Ignored by both parents, the small clan of girls grew up free from the officious attention of adults, other than the sporadic assaults of a succession of nannies and governesses. In Charlotte's memory, it was at first a benign neglect:

Looking into the dim past I see a little company of girls (there were five of us before any boy was born), in a beautiful old Kent garden. . . . The show garden was kept in trim order. We were not allowed to run about on the lawns. That however was a matter of small moment to us, for we had a wonderful playground of our own – a wild corner, hidden away behind a large and imposing rockery with which the superior and alien race never meddled. . . . Through the summer days we enjoyed ourselves, planning out houses, planting gardens and digging deep holes which served the purpose of robbers and smugglers.

The fragment of autobiography which she wrote in her old age refers to one adult only with any sympathy – a teacher she encountered as an adolescent. Her parents are not mentioned and grown-ups in general appear as hostile shadows; the real world is her garden and the only real people are the five sisters playing there. It was a self-constituted republic, without rules, but with intricate rituals; their games were serious, their private jokes irrepressibly funny, and among them Charlotte was happy with the unfettered and seemingly endless joy of a child who is out of range of adult eye and ear. Those earth-stained, secretive and ill-disciplined girls fiercely resented any attempt to teach them the merits of manners and cleanliness, and, trapped between the children's savagery and the parents' indifference, few nurses or tutors survived for long. Each departure must have seemed like another victory to the citizens of the hidden garden; certainly the alliance forged there survived until they themselves had been absorbed into the adult world.

When Charlotte was ten years old, the paradise was abruptly destroyed:

Some interfering superior person reported that we were entering into friendly relations, by means of holes in a tall hedge, with some village children outside. We were then given prim, box-hedged gardens in full view of the library and morning-room windows, and told to cultivate them. I never cared for my new garden and deeply envied the happy village children who could run about as they liked and did not seem to be troubled by those superior persons, nurses and governesses.

This rude intrusion was the result of Captain French's death. Since his widow was quite unfit to assume the strange responsibilities suddenly thrust upon her, the guardianship of the family was taken on by a Captain Smith, a friend of her late husband; and it was he who had decided that the children should be more strictly supervised. The new regime was obnoxious to Charlotte, and at the first touch of its reins she bolted. Having gathered together all the money acquired through tips from generous relatives, she ran the three miles to the nearest station and tried to buy a ticket to London, where she intended to earn her living as a servant:

Needless to say, I was stopped, but I had gone so far that I could not return that night, and I spent it alone in a little awe and some importance at a station inn. After that, lest I should infect my sisters with my spirit of insubordination, I was kept in solitary confinement for three or four days, and then sent away to school.

Confronted by those muddy, untamed children, their guardian had decided on stern action. The long succession of governesses testified to their impossible behaviour and, now that a scapegoat had been found, the severity of her punishment was intended as a warning to the others. School was a hated imprisonment for Charlotte, and of the year she spent there, she would only say: 'That is a hideous time which I never like to remember.' Subjected to a close discipline for the first time in her life, she worked herself into a succession of illnesses and for the sake of her health was at length sent home.

The experience had not curbed her spirit or made the work of her governess any easier. In the conventionally strict Victorian household, the rebellious child soon came up against the Fifth Commandment, 'Honour thy Father and Mother', and learned that behind adult supremacy lurked a Divine Power. It is surmise, but a fair surmise, that in the face of her insubordination one of Charlotte's hard-put-upon governesses exclaimed, 'God punishes little girls like you', and thereby made the idolization of Satan a little easier. Charlotte's revolt against the unctuous tyranny of the nursery was typified by an incident which she still quoted eighty years after it occurred:

One day I was taught to sing a little hymn by my governess. It went like this:

> 'I thank the Goodness and the Grace
> That on my birth hath smiled,
> And made me in these happy days
> A happy English child.
>
> I was not born a little slave
> To labour in the sun
> And wish I was but in the grave
> And all my labour done.'

That hymn was the turning-point. I demanded why God had made slaves, and I was promptly sent to bed. Oh, how I hated the nurses and governesses, and I stood at the gates of my home and envied the little village children. They were free. They had liberty.

On the one hand, God and the governesses, on the other poverty and freedom – and those, broadly speaking, remained the battle lines throughout her life.

The idyll of the garden was fading rapidly. It was not only starched aprons and schoolrooms that interfered, but the passage of time. As Charlotte grew older, reading, rather than digging holes, became a more attractive form of escape from adult attention. Poetry formed her staple diet. Besides her precocious taste for *Paradise Lost*, she discovered in the romantic verse of Wordsworth and Keats licence to dream of a life remote from the saw-toothed nagging of her elders, and later, when she began to write novels, her heroes migrated with the instinct of ring-ouzels to the wild freedom of mountainsides, clifftops and windswept moors.

As the children grew older, John French became the spoiled pet and master of his sisters. His favourite game was to wear one of their nightdresses as a surplice, and then preach a sermon to his admiring congregation. It was an apt conceit, for by his mere maleness he was set far above the girls, both spiritually and socially. Eight years older than he, Charlotte became his willing slave, pandering to his smallest needs and whims, and in so doing she set herself a pattern of behaviour towards him that never materially altered; whatever he might do, she adored and forgave him; but never, not even when he was a full-blown Field-Marshal commanding the British Expeditionary Force in the greatest war in the nation's history, could she quite see him as anything but the baby brother.

This childish world was not entirely closed against news from outside. As a precocious campaigner herself, Charlotte passionately supported the Italians in their struggle for independence. She joined the cheering crowd at Dover which welcomed Garibaldi to England, and when she came to read Mazzini's political essays, she at once adopted their author as 'my master and my mentor'. The *risorgimento* coincided with her adolescence, and at that impressionable age she was stamped with an enthusiasm for political rebellion and democracy which could never be erased.

Lucifer and Italy focused her discontent, but there had to be other, more deep-seated irritations to give rise to such a persistent rage against authority. From a psychological aspect, Charlotte's revolt may reasonably be seen as an attempt to extract the love and affection which her parents failed to give. Her mother was by now perpetually secluded and gradually losing her mind, and beyond the hierarchy of nannies and governesses was only the stern and well-nigh anonymous figure of her guardian. The close companionship of her sisters compensated in part, even if it did not wholly assuage her hunger for affection; but neither her siblings nor a succession of instructors, short-sighted and short-tempered, could answer the need for a sense of certainty. It is notable that her five sisters all married hard-minded husbands whose autocratic habits provided the guidance they had lacked as children. Her brother John found something of that missing assurance in military discipline; but, as he confessed in an account of his boyhood, 'I think the absence of a powerful, directing mind brought to bear on my childhood has had a certain influence on my life.' Whether he was alluding to the unbuttoned extravagance with which in adult life he overstepped the bounds of sexual and financial propriety, or to the restless ingenuity of mind he brought to cavalry tactics, must remain uncertain, but beyond doubt the deep want of a father-figure was accompanied by a striking disregard for convention. His life in that respect was cut from the same pattern as that of his sister Charlotte.

In 1860 Margaret French's feeble hold on reality finally gave way, and she was committed to a lunatic asylum. Since harmless lunacy in a wealthy widow could easily have been treated at home without incurring the disgrace of certification, it is possible that some streak of violence, long suppressed by the weight of scripture and catechism, finally broke loose, requiring her to be forcibly restrained. If this was the reason, it may well have been from her that her children inherited the choleric temper which friends and enemies alike learned to fear. Her insanity did not reappear either amongst her children or in later generations, but the obsessive streak, which in her was so destructive, showed up in Charlotte and John to healthy advantage, as single-minded devotion to their chosen goals. For bequeathing that gift, Margaret French, who died after five years' confinement, deserves not to be entirely forgotten.

Even before their mother was committed to the asylum, the French children had effectively been orphaned, and in 1857 it was decided by the family trustees to send them to live with relatives of their mother in Edinburgh. The Eccles family were strict

Presbyterians, and with a grim sense of duty they endeavoured to educate the high-spirited children who had been wished upon them with the values of their faith. 'Unless we were converted there was no hope of safety in the future, and converted people kept themselves apart from the world', Charlotte remembered being told. 'Operas, theatres and dances were sinful. Light literature, everything indeed that was interesting and human, must be accepted with great reserve. It was sinful to sew or knit or open a book of fiction on a Sunday, and anything like pride in dress or appearance was treated with suspicion.' From the Eccleses she learned to recite, and hate, another hymn, which, for full effect, should properly be read in the miminy-mouthed Edinburgh accent of her foster-parents:

> Why should our garments, made to hide
> Our parents' shame, provoke our pride?
> The art of dress did ne'er begin
> Till Eve our mother learned to sin.

As she was now too old for governesses, Charlotte was sent to a school for young ladies in Atholl Crescent, where an old Scotch dominie inspired her to memorize stirring passages of prose and poetry, and commended her for preferring Satan's lines in *Paradise Lost* above those of the good angel. ('I'm sorry to say, I found the latter as dull as the trim garden of my childhood', she remembered.) Under his benign guidance she began to develop what eventually proved to be an excellent memory and the only real weapon in her intellectual armoury. This was the one happy experience she retained from that period, but hateful though she found 'the Scotch puritanism' of her foster-parents, the years in Edinburgh left an ineradicable imprint. It could be detected in her speech, where for example, she talked of the 'forenoon' rather than the morning and of a 'haar' rather than a sea-mist; but its most obvious result was a ferocious sense of duty and an unwavering belief in self-improvement, which were for ever in conflict with her undisciplined mind. As she later confessed, 'I had not been taught to do any one thing thoroughly [and] I may say that throughout my life this has been my great drawback. I have indeed taught and drilled myself and I think I have succeeded in partially overcoming the disadvantages of an inferior, slipshod education.'

The Eccles family would surely have approved had they but known, but in 1863 all links between them and their foster-children were broken. In that year Mary French became twenty-one and legally independent, and it was perfectly apparent that the Eccleses had by then lost all patience with the brood, for they wasted no time in transferring to her the responsibility for bringing up her brother and sisters.

To the satisfaction of both sides, the French children shook the dust of Edinburgh from their feet and moved into a large house on the outskirts of York, where Mary presided over the family of five girls, aged from ten to twenty, and one twelve-year-old boy. For some time after the move, Charlotte still went to school, but at eighteen she left to help her two older sisters in running the house, and for the first time in her life found no superior authority against which to kick. Instead it was slowly borne in on her that the harried child, the butt of ill-tempered governesses and minatory Presbyterians, had been replaced by a young heiress as privileged and independent as the prospect of an income of £2000 a year on marriage could make her. William French had not been poor, but it was the magnificence of Margaret Eccles' marriage portion which had enabled him to endow his son and each of his daughters so handsomely.

The discovery of her new status was not altogether welcome to Charlotte French. Delightful as it was to live in the reconstituted republic of her sisters, this later version did not possess the charm of the original, for the alliance which had once been formed in self-defence against their superiors was now based upon possessions and a social standing which set them above most of the people around them. A visit which she paid to a rope-making factory soon after she arrived in York gave her a glimpse of a world outside her experience, whose inhabitants were immeasurably more oppressed than she had ever been. Seated before vast piles of rags, women and young children, no more than eight or ten years old, were laboriously picking the cloth in order to make rope from the threads; it was sweated labour and their wages were calculated according to the weight of rope produced. That such misery could exist was as mystifying as it was shocking, for Charlotte could not understand why her fierce resentment of its injustice could not have the same alleviating effect in this case as it had in hers. The passage of time had changed the game and,

27

emerging from childhood almost uneducated except in her instinct to rebel, she was less prepared than most of her contemporaries for the harshness of the rules which governed adulthood. When the children moved to London in 1865, she learned that the same inflexible rules must govern her own conduct, and the conflict between her private ambitions and the expectations of society left her angry and confused.

That was a strange time, unsatisfactory, full of ungratified aspirations. I longed ardently to be of some use in the world, but as we were girls with a little money and born into a particular social position, it was not thought necessary that we should do anything but amuse ourselves until the time and the opportunity of marriage came along. 'Better any marriage at all than none', a foolish old aunt used to say.

Foolish or not, the old aunt was merely expressing an opinion which was held to be a truth almost universally throughout the nineteenth century. To be born a girl of 'a particular social standing' was to be born with a vocation for marriage; as for a novitiate, the whole purpose of Charlotte's training lay in the vows she would eventually take. Her education had been typical. 'We were taught a little music, a little drawing, no science or mathematics, but a little literature, geography and history. Manners of course!' she wrote. 'The impression left on my mind is of incompetent teachers and indifferent learners – nothing thorough.'

It was the education of a geisha girl, having as its end the amusement and entertainment of a man within rigid conventions, of which the most important was to conceal any hint of genuine feeling. In her aunt's youth, the crime of giving way to emotion, or 'sensibility' as it was known, exercised not only the popular novelists like Fanny Burney and Maria Edgeworth, but the compilers of manuals of behaviour, or 'courtesy books'. Their advice was simply to offer young men what they wanted – 'soft features and a flowing voice, a form not robust and demeanour delicate and gentle', according to James Fordyce, the author of *An Enquiry into the Duties of the Female Sex*. From this it followed that energy, intelligence and opinions should be camouflaged. In his book, *A Father's Legacy to his Daughters*, Dr Gregory warned against frankness of any kind: 'On some occasions', he wrote, 'it might render you more agreeable as companions, but it would make you less amiable as women: an important distinction.' This was Macchiavellian, but it fitted the facts.

Even Mary Wollstonecraft, in her pioneering work, *A Vindication of the Rights of Women*, accepted without question the central importance of marriage. Indeed, the gravamen of her charge was that Gregory and Fordyce had 'encouraged the arts of the mistress rather than those of the wife and mother'. Although she advocated greater independence for women, it was not for their benefit but their children's. 'So forcibly does this truth strike me', she wrote, 'that I would rest the whole tendency of my reasoning upon it, for whatever tends to incapacitate the maternal character takes woman out of her sphere.' Yet even the most independent mother had first to find a husband, and, as the novelists of the mid-century suggest, the golden rule was still self-restraint. In *Shirley*, Charlotte Brontë gave the recipe in all its bleakness: 'A lover masculine so disappointed can speak and urge explanation; a lover feminine can say nothing: if she did, the result would be shame and anguish, inward remorse for self-treachery. . . . Take the matter as you find it: ask no questions; utter no remonstrance; it is your best wisdom.' The full force of that stoic philosophy pervaded George Eliot's work, but the tone was at its most resigned when considering her own sex: 'We women', she once wrote, 'must stay where we grow or where the gardeners like to transplant us.'

Meekness was not more congenial to Charlotte French than self-control. She had survived almost unscathed every attempt to discipline her temper or mould her emotions, but now she felt the great weight of social pressure forcing her towards her proper destiny. Her recollection of this time is bitter:

The woman of the well-to-do classes was made to understand early that the only door open to a life at once easy and respectable was that of marriage. Therefore she had to depend upon her good looks, according to the ideals of the men of her day, her charm, her little drawing-room arts, and the frills and furbelows with which fashion decreed she should disguise herself. MAN would have it so.

In London she went to a school in Maida Vale to be 'finished' as a young lady, although by most standards she had barely been started. Her education completed, she at once flouted the best advice of finishing schools and novelists by falling hopelessly in love with a young man, and learned all too soon what Maria

Edgeworth described as 'the misery of an ill-placed attachment'. The brief affair left one enduring monument. In an inspired moment, the young man, perhaps a little overwhelmed by the un-concealed fierceness of her emotions, recommended her to read Shelley. 'He would just suit you', he said, and thereby united her with the real and lasting love of her life.

It is important to emphasize that although she was almost nineteen, Charlotte had preserved intact an innocence of ideas which was child-like. Her mind was still a *tabula rasa* when 'there came to me, like a shining light from worlds invisible, the glory of womanhood as seen by Shelley'. In place of the father she had scarcely known, the teacher she had never respected and the lover she had just lost, Shelley became her guide, instructor and passion. She had read his Odes, but not the longer poems, *Queen Mab*, *The Revolt of Islam* and *Prometheus Unbound*, which were deemed un-suitable for the young. 'Vividly I remember the joy over Cythna in *The Revolt of Islam* – she pleaded with her poet-lover to let her bear her part in the revolution of the future. "Can man be free," she said, "and woman still a slave?" A thousand times No! was Shelley's teaching.' The loneliness and confusion that had been caused by society's demands upon her as a young woman gave way before the warming discovery that her rebellious instincts were not only shared but publicly proclaimed to be morally correct. 'I can only compare its effect upon me', she wrote, 'to the lighting of a fire in a room that had been dark and cold.'

She was still alight with the joy of Shelley's message when she saw for the first time the poverty and squalor of London's East End. 'I longed to speak to these people in their misery, to say, "Why do you bear it? Rise as the men of Argolis did under Laon and Cythna. Smite your oppressors. Be true and strong." ' Some safer instinct intervened before the assorted street-arabs, mud larks, sewer-rats and sweatshop slaves could be startled from their supine state, but her impulse was a true reflection of Shelley's spirit, which made rebellion a philosophy for all of society's constituent parts.

The aspect of Shelley at which Charlotte French first caught was his glorification of the independent woman, but his ideas were remarkably homogeneous and by the time she had absorbed all his poems and the commentaries on them she was in possession of what almost amounted to an ideology. From Plato he took the theory that each idea and physical entity was only the shadow of an ideal form, but as a child of the French Revolution he believed that man could by his own untiring efforts bring those ideal forms into reality, making himself absolutely free and absolutely equal with his brother man. In political terms his ideas, lifted largely from William Godwin, advanced a form of socialism of which Marx approved and from which the Chartists drew inspiration. It was grounded solidly in the Romantics' hatred of the Industrial Revolution's factories, which dehumanized their workers so that they became

> Scarce living pulleys of a dead machine,
> Mere wheels of work, and articles of trade
> That grace the proud and noisy pomp of wealth.

Government, religion and force of habit sustained this intolerably wicked system, and against all three Shelley wrote in praise of revolution, violently in the *Mask of Anarchy*, confusedly in *The Revolt of Islam* and cosmically in *Prometheus Unbound*. The targets presented by politicians – 'I met Murder on the way, He had a mask like Castlereagh', and by the Church 'the very light of Heaven is venal' – were easy enough to hit, but insidious custom 'whose path is paved with human hearts' could not be overcome by direct rebellion; a moral force was required to break its ivy stranglehold.

It was in *The Revolt of Islam* – a rambling parable 'illustrating', Shelley wrote, 'the growth and progress of the individual mind aspiring after excellence' – that he hacked most vigorously at the ubiquitous tendrils of custom, and plucked up its languishing prisoner, woman:

> Can they whose mates are beasts condemned to bear
> Scorn, heavier far than toil or anguish, dare
> To trample their oppressors?

For all its violence of language and imagery, the poem's theme was metaphysical and, as Shelley carefully commented, 'Love is celebrated everywhere as the sole law which should govern the moral world.'

The picture of love militant triumphing over the forces which disguised man's perfection received its most brilliant treatment in *Prometheus Unbound*:

31

The loathsome mask has fallen, the man remains,
Sceptreless, free, uncircumscribed, but man
Equal, unclassed, tribeless and nationless,
Exempt from awe, worship, degree – the king
Over himself, just, gentle and wise.

Even in her nineties, Charlotte Despard never lost sight of that
utopian vision. By then it had a communist hue, just as earlier it
had borne the colours of Sinn Fein, pacifism and socialism, but
for her its special poignancy was the description it contained of
woman set free:

And woman too, frank, beautiful and kind
As the free heaven which rains fresh light and dew
On the wide earth past; gentle, radiant forms
From custom's evil taint exempt and pure;
Speaking the wisdom once they could not think,
Looking emotions once they dared not feel,
And changed to all which once they dared not be.

Where men were imprisoned by factories, women were the prisoners of marriage, in Shelley's opinion. 'How long ought the sexual
connection to last?' he asked baldly in the notes to *Queen Mab*, and
provided the answer: 'A husband and wife ought to continue so
long united as they love each other: any law which would bind
them to cohabitation for one moment after the decay of their
affection would be a most intolerable tyranny.' Because the law
did so bind them, social hypocrisy flourished and its victim was
woman. 'Prostitution is the legitimate offspring of marriage and
its accompanying errors. Women for no other reason than having
followed the dictates of a natural appetite are driven with fury
from the comforts and sympathies of society.'

When Charlotte first discovered Shelley, forty years after his
death, his political extremism could be viewed with equanimity,
for all but the most pessimistic Victorians believed that the world,
despite its imperfections, was inevitably improving, and each new
advance in technology, however alarming, seemed to prove it
further. On the other hand the attack on marriage was, if anything, more scandalous than when it was first made, because it
threatened the spiritual, sexual and legal nexus that sustained
society.

By the mid-century the last remants of eighteenth-century

rationalism had given way to that evangelical Protestantism whose tone and practice had been set by John Wesley. 'I want to know one thing,' he had written in the introduction to his sermons; 'the way to heaven, how to land safe on that happy shore. God himself has condescended to teach the way. . . . He hath written it in a book. O give me that book. . . . Let me be *homo unius libri*!' Quite pragmatically, therefore, the Bible had been taken as an instruction manual for religious, business and family life alike, and it left no room for doubt concerning the proper relationship of man and woman. It had been determined by St Paul, who said, 'But I would have you know that the head of every man is Christ, and the head of every woman is the man'; but its roots lay in the very origins of Judaeo-Christian mythology. When Adam and Eve were expelled from the Garden of Eden, the punishment for Eve's complicity with the serpent was specific: 'In sorrow thou shalt bring forth children, and thy desire shall be [subject] to thy husband, and he shall rule over thee.' It was woman's moral weakness which justified man's dominion, and it must continue to do so since her original sin could never be expiated. As an old Celtic psaltery put it:

> I am Eve, great Adam's wife,
> 'Twas my guilt took Jesus' life.
> Since of Heaven I robbed my race,
> On His Cross was my true place.

Soft and dangerous, a paragon liable to turn prostitute, woman needed the strictest supervision, and Shelley's suggestion that it was no crime for her to have sexual appetites independent of her husband's desires touched upon the Achilles' heel of the patriarchal society.

In 1857, William Acton, a gynaecological authority, wrote judiciously, 'I should say that the majority of women (happily for society) are not very much troubled by sexual feelings of any kind.' His opinion was echoed a generation later by the author of *Psychopathia Sexualis*, Krafft-Ebbing, who added significantly, 'If it were otherwise, marriage and family life would be empty words.' Since the stability of society depended on the denial of woman's independence, even in her most basic instincts, the law, not surprisingly, sustained such an arrangement. A legal authority in the late eighteenth century had placed in the category of those who 'live under natural incapacities, and therefore cannot exercise a sound discretion, or so much under the influence of others they cannot have a will of their own . . . women, idiots, lunatics and infants'. When a man married, he possessed the self-same rights and responsibilities over his wife that he held over his child: that is to say, he was to feed, house and protect her, and pay her debts and damages, and in return he had full control over her property and activities. The arrangement aroused Charles Dickens to ridicule in *Oliver Twist*: ' "The law supposes that your wife acts under your discretion", said the magistrate. "If the law supposes that", said Mr Bumble, "the law is an ass – an idiot. If that's the eye of the law, the law is a bachelor." ' Nevertheless the law was quite consistent with its purpose, which was to buttress a patriarchal society.

To question woman's place was, therefore, subversive of society as a whole, a fact which Karl Marx soon made obvious in his notes on the work of two anthropologists, Jacob Bachofen and Lewis Morgan. These two had suggested that, in its primitive state, society was matriarchal, with property held in common; and Marx commented that the first development of private property occurred when patriarchy supplanted the original system. It followed that the destruction of capitalism would be linked with women's independence and the overthrow of the patriarchal society. Thus to supporters and opponents alike of the Victorian society, women's subservient place was, if not the key, at least the symbol of its continuance.

'I remember how, even in those days', Charlotte wrote, 'I felt with hot indignation the disabilities of women':

In the midst of a conventional circle I was continually seeking to find expression for the force that was in me, trying to learn, asking to serve with my life in my hand ready to offer, and no one wanting it. I must not, I was told, pursue certain studies – they were for boys – I must not be so downright, it was unladylike. Heaven had decreed that I should be a woman and (it would sometimes be added) a privileged woman. I must prove my gratitude by gentleness, obedience, and submission.

Her dilemma was pitifully apparent. She was nineteen, impulsive and eager for affection, and at the same time jealous of her long held freedom and informed by Shelley that 'A system could not well have been devised more studiously hostile to human happiness than marriage.' Her first hesitant attempts to explain her Shelleyan reservations were roundly slapped down. 'You will get yourself talked about', she was warned. 'Girls cannot be too particular. Remember what's expected of you.' The iron laws of courtesy books told her to be pleasant and charming, and above all discreet, while Shelley berated:

> . . . that common, false, cold, hollow talk,
> Which makes the heart deny the *yes* it breathes.

The ordeal of being in the marriage market was not made easier by the egotism and pomposity of young men showing off for her benefit, as they supposed. 'Very young men are not as a rule passionate admirers of the fair sex', she wrote in one of her novels. 'They like to be admired and caressed by women, they delight in imaginary conquests, but their chief cultus is the ego . . .' A photograph of her at the time shows a spirited, challenging face, not one to allow the posturings of over-sized boys to pass unpunctured. In classical terms she was not quite beautiful, the nose rather too prominent and the stubborn jaw a little too heavy, but there could have been no doubt about the appeal of her blue eyes, striking beneath dark brows, and the heavy waves of chestnut-coloured hair brushed back from her forehead. There must have been many young men who were tempted to reach past her prickly manner; but all were doomed to failure, for there can be little question that she was looking for a father-figure. Besides the obvious lack of paternal affection in her childhood, the evidence of the novels and stories written after her marriage points to that conclusion; there is scarcely one piece of her fiction, published or unpublished, which does not portray a leading character is search of his or her father – it was more than a theme, it almost amounted to an obsession. Pulled as she was between the need for guidance and the instinct of rebellion, between the wish to love and the fear of marriage, it was hardly surprising that none of the half-grown men she met succeeded in breaking through the barrier of contradictory expectations.

Two of her sisters were more fortunate and soon found clever, inflexible husbands who filled the paternalistic role nicely. The more impressive was Gavin Jones, who married her younger sister Margaret in 1865. An engineer, he had escaped from Cawnpore during the Indian Mutiny owning nothing more than a pair of red flannel drawers, but from that thin foundation eventually built up a cotton industry in the town which transformed its economy and made him an exceedingly wealthy magnate. Equally stubborn, though less ambitious, was John Lydall, the husband of Mary. In the words of his grandson, he was 'a man of narrow and puritanical opinions . . . a replica of Mr Barrett of Wimpole Street'. For the good of his soul he became a Plymouth Brother, and for the good of his health he kept his two daughters unmarried to care for him after his wife's death.

With these two marriages the family began to break up. In 1866 John, whose first ambition was to join the Navy, went to a crammer's to prepare for the exam, and Kate, the youngest of the family, was sent to a school in Brighton. Freed of responsibility, the remaining sisters, Caroline, Charlotte and Nellie, engaged a chaperon, gave up their London home and escaped from the tedium of parties and polite conversation with dull young men to the romance of travel on the Continent. For three years they wandered through Switzerland, Bavaria and the Tyrol, on a curious route which avoided any centres of culture and stuck to mountain, lake and forest. It was a fair reflection of Charlotte's obstinately romantic preference for the works of nature over those of man; but, beyond the comment, 'We had some rather curious adventures in the course of our wandering', she made no reference to those years in her short autobiography. The novels provide scarcely any further clue. In the last two months before they returned to London, they stayed in Venice, and in one of Charlotte's books the young heroine has a passionate romance with a middle-aged adventurer in that city; but if it had a model in her own life, the experience would seem to have left no other mark. More probably, the pattern of those years was contained in the comment of another of her characters, who remarked of her travels: 'Young English ladies are thought much of abroad. And very innocently we enjoyed the attention we excited.' Well chaperoned, and ignorant of any foreign language beyond a smattering of French, it would appear likely that most of their abundant energy was expended on mountains and rivers

On their return Nellie was married to John Lydall's brother, Wykeham, but the two older sisters found London no more attractive then before, and decided to continue their travels. On this occasion they went alone, for at twenty-eight and twenty-six they were of an age to chaperon themselves. Caroline French, her elder sister, was also Charlotte's favourite. They resembled each other in character, extreme and fierce in their opinions, and in their preference for wandering abroad together there was a suggestion that they might eventually become a couple of self-sufficient old ladies whose asperity made all other company but their own intolerable. The first objective on their journey was Paris, and that accident of choice diverted Charlotte from the possibility of spinsterhood.

Soon after their arrival in the city, France became the latest victim of Bismarck's grand design for inflating the new German Empire. Having manufactured war, Germany's armies proceeded to destroy the French at Metz and Sedan, then began to close in on Paris. Charmed by the gallant patriotism that exuded from the Parisians in their hour of defeat, the two sisters delayed their journey until it was impossible to go on and they were forced to travel back to England. As her tour had now to be postponed Charlotte went to stay with friends in Sussex, and there encountered a quiet young man named Maximilian Despard, who had just returned from the Far East. There was only a few years' difference in their ages, but in his calm self-assurance he had the authority of an older man. He had a house in North London, close enough to where she was staying for them to meet frequently and for her to discover that he was amusing, Irish and as radical in his opinions about the world as she was. One after the other her romantic expectations appeared to be answered, and when he asked her to marry him she gladly accepted. The courting had been swift. They met in the late summer, and on 20 December 1870 they were married. The life of Charlotte French had been filled with violent emotion, vague aspiration and aimless travel; it remained to be seen whether she was fitted for her life as Mrs Despard.

3

In Ireland the name of Despard was resonant with rebellion. Generations of the family had devoted themselves to the service of the British Crown, maintaining its power, practising its religion and enforcing its law, but their staunch loyalty paled to insignificance beside the flamboyant revolt and remarkable end of one black sheep. The founder of the family, Philippe d'Espard, was a Huguenot refugee sent by Queen Elizabeth to Ireland as a land commissioner. From him his descendants inherited an estate in Queen's County and a Protestant faith, which flourished symbiotically; a seventeenth-century Despard fought profitably for King William 'of glorious, pious and immortal memory, who delivered us from popery, slavery, brass money and wooden shoes', and his son came into an estate worth about £20,000 a year. Of that Despard his grandchildren ruefully remarked that 'he loved a law wrangle, and was on the right side in every case but his own'. In the comparative penury brought about by his litigiousness, the grandsons took to soldiering; one became a general and another, Edward Marcus, became a traitor and a patriotic hero.

After a distinguished career as soldier and administrator in Central America, Colonel Marcus Despard was removed in 1792 from his post as governor of a British settlement on the Yucatan following complaints by some of the colonists. He lobbied, petitioned and appealed against the injustice of his dismissal, and when the constitutional forms of protest produced no result he began to employ others. In a letter written in the spring of 1796, his brother John noted:

I have had no account of Marcus since last July when the Newspaper mentioned his being taken up and carried before a Magistrate for being amongst the Mob that was breaking Mr Pitt's windows. I should not be surprised to hear of his having gone to France, as his political sentiments seem to agree perfectly with those of that country.

Although his whereabouts were a mystery, it is probable that he spent part of the time with the Irish revolutionary Wolfe Tone, who shared his enthusiasm for the French Revolution. By 1796, they were in close correspondence about the prospects for revolution in Ireland.

The name and principles of Wolfe Tone still remain sacred to Irish Republicans for he united, under the banner of Liberty, Equality and Fraternity, both Presbyterians smarting under the discrimination of the Dissenting Laws, and Catholic peasants resentful of their landlords. In 1798 the United Irishmen launched three uprisings in Ulster, Wexford and the West of Ireland, while Marcus Despard was appointed to rouse the mob in London. With little difficulty the government put down the insurrection, and aborted Despard's part in it by suspending habeas corpus and detaining him without trial. By the time he was released in 1801, Tone was dead and Ireland had been incorporated as part of the United Kingdom. Unrepentant, Despard declared publicly that rank must be abolished and that every citizen was entitled to 'recover those rights which the Supreme Being has conferred upon his creatures'. His efforts towards this end led to his being charged, in November 1802, with conspiracy 'to commence a cruel and bloody rebellion', in order to procure the independence of Ireland and the overthrow of the government. Specifically, the Tower of London, the Bank of England and the Houses of Parliament were to have been seized, and the King assassinated. 'I have weighed the matter well,' Despard had told his fellow-conspirators, 'and my heart is callous.' With five companions he was found guilty of treason, and for the last time in British history men were sentenced 'to be hanged by the neck, but not till you are quite dead; then to be cut down, your bowels taken out and cast into the fire before your faces, your heads to be taken off and your bodies quartered'. In the spirit of the nineteenth century, which was just struggling into existence, the drawing and quartering were omitted, but the remaining ritual produced a macabre scene, recorded by half a dozen pamphleteers on the spot. After he had been hanged, the Colonel's body was taken down to be beheaded:

A Surgeon, in attempting to sever the head from the body by a common dissecting knife, missed the particular joint aimed at; he kept haggling at it, till the Executioner was obliged to take the head in his hands and to twist it several times round, when it with difficulty severed from the body. It was then held up by the Executioner who exclaimed, 'Behold the head of Marcus Despard, a Traitor!'

With that gory scene, there disappeared the last Despard who had claim to history's attention and, apart from her husband, to Charlotte's sympathy. His unyielding adherence to democratic ideals and his commitment to the cause of Irish independence offered a beguiling foretaste of her own career.

The remaining Despards led lives of some profligacy and little industry. Their general outlook on the purpose of life might have been summed up in a reply given by Marcus's brother, Frank, when it was suggested that he should put a certain legacy in bank. 'No,' he said, 'it was a Godsend and I'll pitch it to the Devil.' They were extravagant, litigious and obsessive in their eccentricities. One spent a lifetime breeding miniature and quite useless foxhounds, the size of Pekinese, and another spent his Army pay, while stationed at Gibraltar, buying rotten eggs to throw at the Jews. Most confined their enthusiasms to hunting and claret, and their lives within the limits of the family estates at Mountrath in the centre of Ireland. They married Wellesleys, Pakenhams and each other with monotonous regularity, and three successive generations of George Despards married three successive Gertrude Cardens, the last of whom produced Maximilian Despard. The Cardens introduced a strain of chronic ill-health which afflicted that branch of the family, and the marriage of Maximilian's parents was considered extremely unwise since the Carden and Despard lines were by then so interwoven as to raise anxieties about inbreeding.

Born in 1839, the seventh of eight children, Maximilian did not escape the inheritance of the Cardens. He was from the start a delicate boy, and at an early age caught scarlet fever from which he failed to make a full recovery. As in many such cases, the fever developed into nephritis, or chronic kidney disease, an ailment from which he was to suffer all his life, and which eventually killed him.

His father was a stipendiary magistrate in Queen's County, and a notoriously hard man, whose life had frequently been threatened by the Whiteboys and other secret societies of the peasants. His unpopularity among local people must have intensified the loneliness of his son for, while his brothers escaped to school and university in Dublin, Maximilian was kept at home with only tutors and his two elder sisters for company. In that closely circumscribed world, he was thrown back on his own resources, and grew up quiet and self-absorbed. In 1846 his father died, and by then Ireland was withering in the potato blight, which had returned for the second year. With most peasants reduced to grubbing up the rotten growths for nourishment, others taking to the boats for the United States, and the least fortunate lying light in a coffin, the landlords dependent on their rents were left without income, and many sold out to newly prosperous merchants from Dublin and Liverpool. An interest in a large iron foundry at Mountrath saved the Despards from this recourse, but the prosperous state of the eighteenth century had passed for good.

The first Despard had been a surveyor and engineer, and many of his descendants, including Marcus, had inherited his gift for figures. Few of them could have put it to more effective use than Maximilian. Following his older brothers to England, he joined a shipping firm in London, and was sent out to Hong Kong as their agent in the early 1860s. For anyone with a calm heart and a calculating mind, there was money to be made in Hong Kong, and it was apparent that Maximilian Despard possessed the necessary qualities. The British tenancy of Hong Kong was barely twenty years old, and its purpose was to trade in two drugs, tea and opium; indeed, it may be suggested that the British addiction to tea grew out of the Chinese addiction to opium. Since the Treaty of Nanking in 1842, opium, grown in India, had been marketed in China under British protection. It was paid for in silver, and the problem of disposing of an ever-increasing flow of bullion was solved by using it to buy tea. The trade might have been designed for gamblers; selling one commodity for another commodity with which to purchase a third, while the money value of all three was in a state of continual fluctuation, was an exercise which could and did break the biggest firms or make a young man's fortune. It was not in Maximilian's character to be reckless, but he made money quickly, trading on his own account in tea and precious stones. He had need of fine judgement in nose and eye, and the courage to back it, but the rewards were in due proportion, and in 1865, when a group of business men proposed to found a bank, named the Hong Kong and Shanghai Bank, he had

£6000 to put into the venture. Of all his transactions, that showed the soundest judgement, for the bank flourished beyond expectation, and by the time of his death his original investment was worth about £30,000.

Money and marriage went together, and the possession of one made the arrangement of the other much less painful. His brother Richard, negotiating for the hand of his future wife, was too poor to ignore the size of her dowry, and thus had to swallow with a good grace homilies from his prospective father-in-law which could have been uttered by Mr Micawber: 'One thing only I will caution you against', wrote his father-in-law, 'and that is the fatal argument (alas all too often urged), "We cannot do with less than so-and-so", my good friend, we *can* do with less than so-and-so, and let me tell you more, we can, if we are wise, do with even less than that.' Maximilian was exempt from the humiliating need to accept penny-pinching advice of this sort; besides, he had developed a taste for luxury which was incompatible with 'making do'. When he came to England in 1870, he had money enough to marry whom he chose.

He was thirty-one when he met Charlotte French, and the contrast in their characters could hardly have been more emphatic – she reckless and emotional, he shrewd and self-disciplined. Yet the charm each had for the other was undeniable. Neither of them lacked courage, but in Charlotte it had a blazing quality and Maximilian, delicate in health, must have felt himself warmed by her energy, while his gambling instinct could only have been challenged by her sharp, unbroken spirit. On her side, the price of her independence was willingly paid for the shelter of his decisiveness and clarity of mind; but these father-like qualities were made still more attractive by a feminine sensitivity which was the result of his frail state. 'I have never really cared for a man who was not in part a woman', she once said, and in the complex nature of her new husband there clearly was such a part.

His character was the reverse of the Irish stereotype, but she was delighted that he was Irish – and by Ireland itself when she saw it for the first time on their honeymoon. Westfield House, where they stayed, was a fine eighteenth-century building, near Castletown on the river Nore, with an enormous, old-fashioned walled garden below it, and a spreading view south to the Kilkenny hills. To Charlotte it epitomized the beauty of what she now claimed as her native country, and the happiness she felt there invested it with the power of a talisman so that she felt refreshed each time she returned to it. Her Irishness was at first a myth, an impulsive, exuberant personality which could be assumed whenever she wished to apologize for a burst of temper or an unusually reckless act. Equally, her Ireland was an ideal of a nation, warm, friendly and beautiful, tarnished only where English industrialism had taken hold. When she wished to criticize the hypocrisy of English manners, or condemn the tyranny of English factories, she could do so from an apparently concrete standpoint which conveniently matched the cast of her own mind. The development of her Irish nationalism from fantasy to actuality imitated the growth of the movement itself, and it is hardly too much to say that to be Irish at all after the suppression of the Fenians in the 1860s was an act of imagination.

Although she and Max (as she called him) frequently returned to Ireland, the greater part of their early marriage was spent in London, broken by extended visits to their home in Sussex. The details of their relationship remain obscure, for her comments on it were guarded, even by the standards of the age; but from them, and from her activities during and after her marriage, the broad outlines emerge. 'I married happily', she once wrote, 'in the sense that my freedom in that relation, often so difficult, was always respected.' Compared to the tyranny her husband was entitled to exercise, that was no small thing but, as a tribute, it lacks the passionate affirmation she otherwise gave to people and causes which engaged her heart. Although this was never spelled out, her references to him give the impression that she was disappointed in her first high hopes. It seems all too probable that where she expected love, she found a well-judged affection beyond which Max was both physically and temperamentally incapable of going. The powerful mind which compensated for his congenital ill health had developed, in the chaos of Hong Kong's commodity trade, an edge as cool and precise as a lawyer's; indeed, he had, in his wife's opinion, 'a much better head for law than many a trained lawyer', and it left little room for passion. If her freedom was simply due to an absence of real emotion, it was a chilly liberty. While he did not impose his views on his wife, her naive ideas were no match for his lucid rationalism, and it was evident that she was persuaded to adopt attitudes and habits with which she was at heart uncomfortable. Throughout their married life she took his political, spiritual and social principles for her own, but within a couple of years of his death she had divested herself of them all.

Max's politics were those of John Bright, and despite wealth and possessions he supported the case for fundamental reforms in society, from a wider franchise to safety regulations in factories and ships. As Radicals, the Despards lived in continual expectation that the logic of their position would prevail, and recurrent frustration that it did not. 'Like many another woman', Charlotte wrote, 'I soothed my disappointment and expended my superfluous energies in taking up all sorts of causes – sweated women workers, crèches in poor districts, inspection of factories, temperance.' Typical of her causes was the Nine Elms Flower Mission. The missionaries were kindly ladies with country gardens, who undertook to distribute flowers in London's slums, so that their inhabitants should have a touch of colour to brighten their dark homes. It was a thoughtful, if not especially demanding, act of charity; it showed concern, while avoiding the pitfalls of giving money – which, it was held, only made matters worse by encouraging a feckless attitude. In short, it was the kind of work which the most respectable lady could perform with the utmost propriety. There was nothing of social rebellion in it.

Nine Elms, the slum which Charlotte visited, was an island of shabby streets in Battersea, surrounded by railway lines and bordered to the north by the Thames. Its population was largely Irish, drawn there first by the railways and reinforced by refugees from famine and coercion, and it was from a sense of kinship that Charlotte Despard decided to work in the area. Over the years she developed a friendly acquaintanceship with many of the women, and endeavoured, within limits, to help them with their crushing problems of drunken husbands and consumptive children. Max was willing to offer advice, but it was not in his nature to become more deeply involved, and Charlotte followed his example, although, as she later showed, 'getting involved' was her deepest instinct.

Before she married, she had longed 'to be of some use', 'to serve', 'to have a career', and it was clear that the thin activity of the Flower Mission did not fulfil that longing. There were few careers that a married woman could follow without causing comment, but for a century, novel-writing had been regarded as a suitable, even praiseworthy, occupation for ladies. Under Max's guidance, Charlotte directed her unconsumed vitality towards literature.

The circulating libraries, of which Mudie's was the biggest, preferred novels to come in three volumes so that their subscribers had to pay thrice over to read a single work. To fill the necessary 700–800 pages, authors resorted to ingenious sub-plotting, long flights of moralizing, and the creation of a multiplicity of characters. Having chosen the format, Charlotte Despard was obliged to follow the pattern, and her novels are none the better for it. The plots of the seven published and three unpublished stories defy summary. Wildly romantic, they twist from ruined Scottish castle to elegant West End drawing-room by way of Siberian forest and Swiss Alp. Stereotypes populate them: the fishermen are gnarled, the servants are faithful and the foreigners sinister; the heroine of *A Modern Iago* is a prototype for most of the others, with her 'Golden hair, large melancholy eyes, like as the summer sky at noon, and her cheek . . . in colour like the seashell's delicate pink lining'; for the heroes, Erick Graeme of *Wandering Fires* could serve as model, being, in the words of one reviewer, 'Aesthetic, poetic, egotistic, ravishingly handsome, and fabulously rich'. Years later, after Charlotte Despard had turned her attention to suffrage work, one of her admirers described her literary career as 'brilliant', and suggested that, had she continued, she would have become 'one of the foremost literary figures of our time'. This was, at the least, hyperbole.

Her strength as a political leader was an unfailing certainty that situations and people could be improved, but the same certainty in her novels became a handicap. In her desire to show that suffering and searching brought out the best in people, she never allowed her characters more than a cardboard existence, but pushed them relentlessly through a sequence of unlikely mis-adventures to a happy ending, where lovers were reunited, fathers rediscovered, and the survivors could congratulate themselves on being better now than when they started. 'Above all, he had through much tribulation entered into the higher – the spiritual sphere, which I think is never closed to the honest seeker.' That conclusion (to an unpublished novel) epitomized her purpose.

In her own words, she was consumed by 'a literary interest in great ideas', and her moralizing was shaped by the momentous flux that uprooted the Victorians' spiritual certainty in the last quarter of the century. Evangelical Protestantism, the faith of those devout achievers of the mid-century, had already come under fire for its sanctification of worldly success when its authority received a more fundamental blow. The literal interpretation of the Gospels had in fact been undermined in 1835 by the textual analysis of David Strauss, but it was not until the publication of Ernest Renan's *Vie de Jésus* in 1863 (translated in the same year), that a wide public realized that the dating, authorship and context of the Gospels were under question. As the old confidence slowly ebbed, the search began for alternative faiths and ideologies.

Well-schooled by Shelley, Charlotte Despard had no great regard for organized religion, and under the influence of Max, the arch-rationalist, she adopted an agnostic view as the proper solution. But the ferocity of those childhood battles with God argued a strong spiritual sense, and her unease about doubting God's existence can be found in her books. On the one hand, her heroine in *A Modern Iago* reads Renan, and concludes: 'The end of humanity is to produce great men, only through them can our salvation come.' But on the other, the author herself meditates on the possibility of life after death, and comments: 'Yes, old and fond these paradoxes may be, but they have power, for it is at life's dark moments they assert themselves.' Almost all her leading characters try to suggest some solution to the uncertainty: for one, it is 'to forget ourselves as individuals, to learn our relation to humanity, and to keep our eyes fixed on the coming perfection'; for another, it is 'the laying-down of self-will altogether, the recognition through sorrows and contradictions manifold of a Divine love'; and another simply declares that 'a God is made with . . . tears'.

In her own life the search for spiritual certainty persisted almost to her death, and it is an interesting reflection of her psychological state that, in her books, that search frequently becomes blurred with the hunt for lost parents. Unfortunately, so far as the novels were concerned, her doubts were smothered by the same moralizing blanket that took the life out of her plots and characters. There was some compensation in the exuberance of her catastrophes – epidemics, storms, bankruptcies and sudden death occurred in profusion – but the overall result was best described by a review in *The Athenaeum* of her first novel, *Chaste as Ice, Pure as Snow*: 'it occasionally nearly rises to tragedy, but is never pathetic [i.e., moving], and is seldom either humorous or absolutely dull'.

There is something badly out of place in these elaborate fables. With one exception, they bear no direct relation either to the outside world or to the causes which interested the author both before and after her marriage. The exception was *A Voice from the Dim Millions*, a short, 25,000-word story of a factory-girl, in which the descriptions of urban squalor and the degradation of sweated labour were clearly based on Charlotte Despard's observation of scenes and people in Nine Elms. Even here, the formerly characteristic note of rebellion is lacking, and instead something nearer resignation prevails. It is possible that, having made a success of her first book, which was taken up by Mudie's and was sufficiently popular to require a second edition, she simply stuck to a proven formula; but, with the powerful and recent example of Mrs Gaskell before her, she could well have given expression to her social concern within the framework of a romantic 'three-decker' novel. It almost seemed as if she were censoring her strongest passions.

The clue to the mystery may be suggested by her recurrent theme, that the abnegation of the will was necessary to achieve happiness, that selfishness tended to misery, that self-sacrifice was a cosmic law, and so on, stoical sentiments common enough in much women's writing, for obvious reasons, but quite uncharacteristic in the life of Charlotte Despard.

Her undisciplined self periodically caused her grief, but it is fair to assume that the disciplined Max found it intolerable. Having set his wife to control her impulses, having substituted his own well-thought ideas for her emotional decisions, having discouraged her impractical ambitions and diverted her energy into writing, Max may, with the best motives, have gone a little further and persuaded her that she would avoid the flashes of irritation, and much distress for both of them, if she moulded herself in his image: that is, rational, thorough and, the invalid's virtue, fatalist. To achieve these admirable qualities required a ferocious struggle with her rebellious self. All the old enthusiasms had to be dismissed, and the theme of suffering to gain wisdom was taken as a sacred text. A bullying husband could not have brought Charlotte to this point, but the very freedom which Max allowed, together with the shining example of his own character, convinced her. It was, in a way, the education she had missed. Charlotte learned to approve of Bright's Radicalism rather than rail wildly against injustice; instead of her furious, Luciferian hostility to an authoritarian God, she adopted what she called 'the modern sceptical spirit' and simply abandoned the battleground and became an agnostic; and her adolescent identification with the poor became a more mature pity for their state. None of this was completely bad, and from much of it she derived great benefit; but all of it was alien.

In 1880 Gladstone was returned to power with the old hero Bright in his government, and the Despards looked forward to far-reaching reforms that would curb the evils of sweated labour and slum housing, and extend the franchise to male rural householders on the same basis as it was exercised in parliamentary boroughs. The movement to include women amongst the new voters did not interest them. Like most Radicals, they saw it as a manoeuvre to strengthen the Conservatives by enfranchising wealthy, middle-class women, and it seemed irrelevant compared to the necessity of helping agricultural labourers to gain a voice in Parliament.

The great hopes of 1880 rapidly turned to disappointment. With a handsome majority the Liberal government appeared incapable of passing any genuinely radical measure until, nearing the end of its life, the great Reform Act of 1884 became law. Ireland dominated affairs and Charlotte, extravagantly claiming that she had been 'a Home Ruler all her life', gave ardent support to Parnell who seemed on the verge of achieving that goal. Despite the attention paid to Ireland, the Liberals did succeed in passing one Act of which the Despards approved. In Nine Elms, Charlotte had been deeply upset by the tale of a working woman whose drunken husband, long separated from her, had twice burst into her house and stolen her savings. As Charlotte Despard discovered when she went to the police about the case, 'stolen' was hardly correct, for in the eyes of the law the husband had a better right to his wife's money than she did. In 1882 the Married Woman's Property Act was passed, allowing wives to own property independently of their husbands, and Max informed his wife, 'Tell your friend that from today she is free to make her own life.'

No other aspect of the women's movement deeply engaged her. She was aware of the expansion of higher education for girls, through the opening of Oxford and Cambridge colleges to women and the granting of degrees to them by St Andrews, and she knew of the determined efforts by a few women, like Dr Garrett Anderson, to gain their medical qualifications; but, as she said herself, she merely 'watched with interest'. If the opinions she expressed in her novels were a true reflection of her feelings about the relationship of the sexes, she had come to accept a 'realistic' opinion on this matter too. Women were different from men because the purpose of their life was different – to raise a family demanded qualities other than those necessary to earn a living. But only the most immature men treated women as inferior. They were emotional and vulnerable, but that did not preclude their having brains. It was the most despicable of her male villains who said to a woman, 'We reason, you are guided by your instincts', and he was neatly put down with the reply: 'If we were birds or insects that would be an appropriate speech.' But the question of woman's independence, like her vote, did not arise. She was made for marriage and motherhood and, if she incurred hardship, that was the fate of her sex.

In 1879 the Despards moved to a new home, quite incongruous with their political sympathies but in keeping with Max's oriental taste for magnificence. 'Courtlands' stood in fifteen acres of park and garden on a low hill overlooking the Mole valley, a few miles outside Esher in Surrey. It was an imposing house, built early in the century, but its chief attraction for Charlotte was a large and ornate garden, the source of many hampers of flowers for Nine Elms. Below the formal garden was a small wilderness, carefully untended, which sloped down to a small stream; and here she liked to sit alone and dream. The surrounding countryside was well wooded, but beyond the leaves were other parks and expansive gardens leading up to large houses with too many wings. To one side lived Lady Emma Talbot; to another Sir Robert Collins KCB; and next door, utterly obscured by a mile of trees and rolling ground, lived Her Royal Highness the Duchess of Albany in the most magnificent building of them all – Claremont, which had been built by Clive and which had, in its time, sheltered Prince Leopold of the Belgians, Queen Victoria and Louis Philippe. To be a Radical in such surroundings, one would have

49

to dream, and with a dozen indoor servants there was little else to occupy the hours away from writing.

In his quiet, intelligent way, Max had done well. He continued to trade in tea and gems and, as the stones never lost their value and tea now poured down the nation's throat like a brown Niagara, he continued to grow richer. His friends were largely his colleagues: in tea, the Ridgeways; in diamonds, the Hirschels and Geilers. He liked Pre-Raphaelite art, and the painter Felix Moschelle was a close companion. But most of all he prized the friendship of those few men who, like himself, had made a success out of nothing. One such was Joseph Lucas, founder of a Birmingham engineering firm, and another was Gavin Jones, Charlotte's brother-in-law, whose textile mills were transforming Cawnpore. The large confidence which came from having risked and succeeded created a bond between them, but it was not necessarily shared by Charlotte. With the Jewish diamond merchants she had an affinity, but otherwise her preferred companions were children: the children of friends, of relatives and of neighbours, for she had none of her own.

Some of the disappointment in her marriage certainly sprang from her childless state. She was twenty-six when she married, and it must have been apparent before long that there would be no children. Since all her sisters, except Carrie who married late, were burdened with clusters of offspring, the cause presumably was the inbreeding in Max's parentage. She later wrote with feeling of 'the thousands of women [who] . . . have passionately craved for the sweetness of motherhood of which an inexorable fate has betrayed them', but otherwise she never gave voice to her own disappointment. Yet it was evident enough in the hungry way in which she took all children for her own. At Courtlands she organized such massive picnics for them that they nicknamed her 'the Quartermaster-General'; later, her social work began with an attempt to feed and nurse slum children; and finally, when she became a suffragette, some of her most powerful arguments concerned the need to improve the condition of mothers for the sake of their children. If her activities were the measure of her loss, the loss was large indeed; but she did not allow regret to devour her, and as a suffragette she was at pains to emphasize that motherhood was only one option of many open to a woman.

Like many of their elders, some children felt overwhelmed by her, but she had an appealing habit of behaving as though they were sensible people who could be entrusted with responsibilities, and with whom she could discuss some of the social problems of the day. Not every child was enthralled, but half a century later her favourite Despard nephew still fondly remembered the serious conversations they had had when he was ten about the wretched wages paid to road-menders.

Lacking children of her own, Charlotte Despard's true family remained her brother and sisters. Mary, the eldest, had died, but the others remained united by deep affection and the exclusive, aristocratic wilfulness which marked them all. In Charlotte it was presently under a tight rein; but in Caroline it showed up in the offensive candour with which she delivered her opinions, and Margaret's haughtiness was so evident that she was known in Cawnpore as 'la Reine', a gibe which Gavin Jones was turning into fact. But the trait reached its full flower in John French, who had left the Navy to become a soldier. The devotion which his sisters lavished upon him was not shared by their husbands; in fact, they considered their brother-in-law at best an embarrassment, and at worst a scoundrel. In 1884 he was thirty-two years old, a major in the 19th Hussars, and on the verge of bankruptcy. With magnificent prodigality he had, in slightly more than a decade, managed to dispose of everything he had inherited: income, capital, and property. Even the Eccles family silver had gone into pawn. In the eighteenth century, a cavalryman who loved long-legged horses and women might have been forgiven for spending everything on them, but Victorian propriety was less charitable. 'Sorry fellow, French', John Lydall used to mutter, and he stuck to his opinion long after the ne'er-do-well had become a Field-Marshal and a peer of the realm.

Less obvious to the Plymouth Brother was French's capacity for work, which was as prodigious as his appetite for pleasure. While on the one hand he had spent on women and other necessities the modern equivalent of about half a million pounds before he was fifty, he had in the same time read extensively, written the definitive manual on cavalry training, exercised his mounted troops to a high state of efficiency, and led them to three famous victories over the Boers. As a result, in his sixties he owned half a dozen mistresses, no home, and a military reputation second to none in the British Army. His sisters lent him the money to pay his debts, until their husbands realized that the loans would never be repaid and put a stop to it; but Charlotte chafed under the restraint, and later, when a widow with control over her own money, she continued to finance him whenever it proved necessary. 'A *beau sabreur*' to Colonel Repington, the military historian, and 'a sorry fellow' to his brother-in-law, he was to his sister never more than 'a naughty boy'.

The vigour of John French stood in marked contrast to Max's failing health. Soon after coming to live at Courtlands, he was found to have Bright's Disease, a progressive deterioration of the kidneys. The winter cold of England became intolerable, and for the rest of his short life the Despards travelled abroad from autumn until early summer. Apart from one visit to the Mediterranean, they always sailed to India; from there sometimes on to Ceylon, to Australia, and once, by way of Hong Kong and the United States, around the world. Caught by repeated, nagging pain, Max gradually retreated into himself and was content to stay in the heat of the Indian plains while his wife went up into the hills to explore the Buddhist temples in the caves of Karli and Bhaja. He was still first of all a shrewd business man and after a visit to the Muir Mills at Cawnpore he could not resist investing £3000 in Gavin Jones' enterprise, even though he himself would be unlikely to reap the benefit. The consequences of his wife's explorations were equally long term.

In Charlotte Despard's last novel, *The Rajah's Heir*, which was written at this time, the plot is based on the Buddhist theory of the transmigration of souls. On the death of the old Rajah, his soul inhabits the body of a young English boy who goes to claim his inheritance in India, and in so doing grows to understand the inner nature of Buddhist teaching. This theme is developed against the bloodthirsty background of the Indian Mutiny, whose timbre may be gathered from the description of a sepoy's murder by the hero's girlfriend:

His long knife was beside him. She drew it out of its sheath, and – and – .

'She killed him!' hissed Tom from between his closed teeth. 'My brave little girl! my heroine!'

'She killed him!' echoed Lady Elten. 'Think of it, with those little slender hands.'

In the face of so much slaughter the Europeans turn to the teachings of Buddha for enlightenment. Significantly the heroine, like the author, has stopped believing in God because 'wherever I looked there was pain and misery', but to her joy she is brought to understand that these are the karmas incurred by past acts of selfishness, and with almost fierce pleasure she anticipates the Buddhist state of desirelessness: 'the self must be slain – will – desire – love of the things which are not He'.

The heroine's spiritual odyssey bore a strong resemblance to the author's, and it was evident that in the last years of her husband's life, Charlotte Despard was searching for a more satisfying, if less 'realistic', creed than agnosticism. The concepts of karma and the transmigration of souls offered her the chance to believe in an after-life without the encumbrance of a churchly God, and it was also reassuring that Buddhism should endorse such Shelleyan tenets as the inner perfection of man and the importance of a vegetarian diet. While Max still lived there was no opportunity of exploring further, but a seed had been planted which eventually grew and blossomed lavishly. In England, Charlotte began to attend seances, and learned to use both the planchette and automatic writing to communicate with 'the other side'. Initially she tried to reach her dead sister, Mary; but easily the most successful communicant proved to be Mazzini, with whom she established close relations and whose political advice she became accustomed to seek after she had been widowed. The books of Morag MacLeod and Edward Carpenter, celebrations of Celtic and socialist mysticism respectively, gave her an inkling of the heterodox currents now moving in religious and political life. 'Too long have women acted the part of mere appendages to the male . . . ,' Edward Carpenter wrote in Love's Coming of Age. 'In order to have souls of their own they must free themselves and greatly by their own efforts.' Quite abruptly, Charlotte was made aware of the great changes that had taken place since her marriage.

She must have understood that Max's approaching death would remove the one authoritative figure from her life, but her personal search for some new assurance, greater than the old, was in itself an echo of the spiritual and political ferment within Victorian society. A revolution had transformed its accustomed values, and she had now to catch up on the developments of more than a quarter of a century.

When *On the Origin of Species* was published in 1859, the old perspective of mankind as a timeless, unchanging creation was altered beyond recognition. Although Darwin's ideas took time to work into the common consciousness, it is not too much to say that, before him, mankind seemed static in an improving world, and thereafter appeared to be as ductile as plasticine in an invariably challenging environment. As Galileo had set the world revolving, so Darwin released man from stasis: he was no longer a being created once and for all, but the most adaptable survivor of endless propagation and massacre. Although the mechanism of evolution, natural selection, is purposeless and purely nihilist, evolution itself, as it settled into people's minds and coloured their thoughts, became a supremely optimistic and purposeful idea. It was incorporated into political and spiritual concepts, and everywhere its vocabulary became that of progress. The contradiction is explicit in Tennyson's *In Memoriam*, that poem which better than any other expressed the Victorian mood, its evangelical purposefulness and its morbid doubts. Written in 1850, it anticipated both the quandary set by natural selection and the optimism derived from evolution. Examining Nature's methods, 'red in tooth and claw', Tennyson posed the bleak question:

> Are God and Nature then at strife
> That Nature lends such evil dreams?
> So careful of the type she seems,
> So careless of the single life.

Recoiling from the dismal prospect that the individual's existence was without importance, the poet found comfort in a more distant perspective:

> . . . A soul shall draw from out the vast
> And strike his being into bounds,
>
> And moved thro' life of lower phase
> Result in man, be born and think
> And act and love, a closer link
> Between us and the crowning race
>
> Of those that, eye to eye, shall look
> On knowledge; under whose command
> Is Earth and Earth's, and in their hand
> Is Nature like an open book;

No longer half akin to brute,
For all we thought and loved and did
And hoped and suffered, is but seed
Of what in them is flower and fruit . . .

Where its laureate led, the nation followed. The gore and waste could be set aside for higher intelligence to comprehend, but in man's superiority to his ancestors the Victorians found both confirmation of their faith in progress and the promise of an awe-inspiring goal: if improved ape became man, might not improved man become something close to the angelic? Imperceptibly, the end of material improvement was taken to be a spiritual trans-formation – in Tennyson's words 'that one far-off divine event,/ To which the whole creation moves'.

Material teleology became the spirit of the last quarter of the century. The conservative Basil Ransom, in Henry James's *The Bostonians*, published in 1886, described it as 'a feminine, a nervous, hysterical, chattering, canting age', and he longed to recover the old ability 'to look the world in the face and take it for what it is – a very queer and partly very base mixture'. But that 'realistic' attitude could no longer be defended once it was understood that a changed world could change man. There were socialists, imperialists, philanthropists, and feminists, all vociferous that their '-ism' was the true path of evolution; but all agreed that the shortcomings of society were responsible for the disparity between what man could be and what he was. It was the very condemna-tion that Shelley had uttered when the century was young, but now evolution had provided the key to his utopia. Nowhere was this more obvious than in the different strands of socialism that flourished in the last two decades of the nineteenth century. Municipal socialists held that mankind might be transformed by the provision of gas, electricity and sewers; Christian socialists believed that a revival of primitive Christianity would achieve the same end; but the best depiction of the 'far-off, divine event' was provided by Karl Marx, in the withering away of the state after the dictatorship of the proletariat had been established. When that point of evolution was attained, the organs of law and government, which were required to check and order the activities of unregenerate capitalist man, could be dispensed with by the higher order of communist man. As Bertrand Russell observed,

'Marx professed himself an atheist, but retained a cosmic optimism which only theism could justify.'

That brand of utopian socialism, which began with the French Revolution and ended in Stalin's prison camps, was the goal to which Charlotte Despard was now edging. Although Marx had provided a scientific base for his theories, the detail of his work was hardly known to British socialists until the end of the century, when cheap translations became available, and it was his broad conclusions which attracted those appalled by the grossness of capitalism. To them, socialism was as much a spiritual as a political faith, and many of them came to it, like Charlotte Despard, after a flirtation with mysticism.

At times it was almost impossible to disentangle the threads. The Fellowship of the New Life looked for a spiritual revolution to inaugurate the classless society, and eventually spawned the socialist Fabian Society, which had the same goal but believed in more gradual methods; the Theosophist Society, which grafted occult knowledge on to Darwinian theory and the Hindu Vedanta, aimed at establishing 'the Brotherhood of Humanity', and called on society 'to secure to every one of its members the minimum of welfare . . . which will enable each to develop to the full the faculties he brought with him into the world'; while the revolutionary syndicalists incorporated Henri Bergson's quasi-mystical belief in an eternal 'life-force' into their politics. It was quite appropriate that while Charlotte Despard was investigating the mysteries of spiritualism, she should also have taken an interest in the beliefs of the anarchist group led by Prince Kropotkin in London. Although she liked to boast that 'our little society helped quite a few to escape from Siberia', her participation was limited to sympathy and cash; anarchy, like the planchette, was foreign to Max's rational world. Following, for the first time, her own line, she had automatically been tempted beyond the frontier of moderation. As her widowhood was to show, she hungered for absolutes in politics and religion alike, and it was a measure of her husband's strength of mind that she did not feel that hunger until his life was almost over.

The disease did not follow a steady course. Months of despair were followed by the occasional shining week of hope as Max seemed to improve, but each renewal of strength was a little shorter than before. Much of the time he remained sunk in silence, and Charlotte distracted her mind by writing. In the winter of 1889 they went to India once more, but on the return voyage Max suddenly weakened. The ship put into Tenerife, and he was taken ashore, accompanied by Charlotte and his younger brother, Fitzherbert. This time there was no new surge of strength and, knowing that little time was left, they took him aboard the next homeward-bound ship that called at the island, so that he could die in his own country. As the SS *Coptic* entered the Bay of Biscay, he fell into a coma, and on Good Friday, 4 April 1890, Maximilian Despard died.

4

The death of Max, so long expected, arrived all the same as a prostrating blow to Charlotte. He had been buried at sea, so there was no body to mourn over, no detail of funeral and interment to demand her attention or assuage her grief. She came home to the house at Esher and found it as it had been, unchanged but for the absence of Max. His possessions, his plate, linen and carriages were there, but of him there was nothing. It was too big a space to leave unfilled.

For the only time in her life, Charlotte suffered a spiritual collapse – the entire determined and optimistic cast of her thought crumbled away before the fact of Max's death. She shut herself up in Courtlands, refusing to accept visitors, and immersed herself in misery. Her only interest was the planchette, by means of which she attempted to communicate with him beyond the grave.

Max had given her a framework around which her own attitudes and manner of living could grow and develop. Deliberately she had tried to take on the colour of his thinking, to form assumptions corresponding to his and to lead a career of which he approved. When the framework was withdrawn the edifice collapsed. It was as though the shape that she had given to her life was flawed by the instincts which had been repressed, so that it could not sustain itself. Without Max she was a void, and in the extremity of her despair there was a haunting echo of her mother's collapse and eventual loss of sanity.

Rescue came from an unexpected quarter. Hearing that her neighbour had become a recluse, the Duchess of Albany sent her an invitation to Claremont, a summons which Charlotte later admitted had 'at that time the power of a Royal Command'. In the course of the visit, the Duchess gently suggested that she might take up again her work for the Nine Elms Flower Mission. It was the sort of 'good work' to which Victorian widows often turned for consolation, and it was especially attractive in this case as an activity of which Max had approved. In the late summer of 1890 she began again to cram her carriage with baskets of flowers for the mean houses of Nine Elms, and in so doing she took the first faltering step from her stricken state.

In Nine Elms death was a commonplace, a rich lode of emotional turbulence which was mined and stored and exhibited. All shared in it, all were familiar with it. For the many Irish, it was an occasion to let their sorrow flow until they were sated with its drawing, retching absence of reason, and when they returned to the casual smallness of life, they brought back the satisfaction of a great experience. It was something to be talked of, compared and passed around. And it was a subject, especially, of women's lot: they were the mourners and wailers, they sat over the sickening baby while the man was at work, they washed and laid out the body, and they returned to the empty house without occupation to distract them. This was the time when women friends dropped in to condole and comfort, and share their memories. Death had made them good consolers.

'It was,' as Charlotte Despard later said, 'my friends of Battersea who best helped me bear my desolation.' Bereavement transcended the barriers of class and upbringing and where earlier she had been a nervous stranger bottling up her desire to incite the poor to riot by quoting Shelley at them, she now found common ground with them as a widow. In the process she encountered an instinctive warmth of emotion which she had never known, either among the chilly Presbyterian relatives of her mother, or in the carefully weighed enthusiasms of her husband. The bond that it created bound her to them and, as her visits continued, it coalesced into a determination to be with them and to do what she could to identify herself with the generosity of their nature. At first her actions were confused, for in spirit she was still moved to act in a way of which Max might have approved.

Late in 1890 she bought a house near Nine Elms, at 95 Wandsworth Road; but, for the time being, she continued to live at Courtlands. In his compendious survey, *Life and Labour in London*, Charles Booth described the area of her new house as being 'as low and degraded as any part of London'. The buildings had been designed around enclosed squares or 'courts', small, cramped spaces where piles of refuse and stinking bones piled up. These attracted beggars and tramps, who roamed about the courts picking through the rubbish for anything salvageable as food or clothing. Since these scavengers were not above supplementing their basic living with robbery, Booth's investigators required a policeman to accompany them on their visit and, when he heard that they intended to publish a description of the place, the constable told them, 'You cannot make it too bad.' The local authority, the Lambeth Vestry, aggravated the squalor by refusing to spend money cleaning the streets, and as a result the roads, like the courts, were overflowing with garbage from the crowded houses on either side. The windows were usually broken or roughly patched so that the shouts and sudden screams of drunken arguments inside could be clearly heard above the yells of children playing out in the streets. As an initiation into life among the poor, Charlotte Despard could hardly have chosen a rougher spot.

It was common enough for a Victorian widow to sublimate her grief in work among the poor. The energy which had been devoted to the service of a husband was well-honed for such a purpose, and there were scores of charitable organizations to channel it in that direction. The churches, belatedly discovering their social conscience in the last quarter of the century, encouraged it, and the widow's own piety might demand it. If there was a touch of officiousness about her charitable activities, it might be said in mitigation that she was a creature of hierarchy, cold-moulded by duty and obligation.

The extravagant choice of Wandsworth as a prospective home entirely lacked that chilly touch. It was an extreme, almost wild, step which was only brought into proportion by similarly impulsive actions later in Charlotte Despard's career. She once confessed: 'There is scarcely anything I have done in my life of any importance into which I have not been pushed. I have never felt it was from my own initiative.' She acted intuitively, rather than deliberately, responding to the warm sympathy she had received in Battersea and finding herself impelled to escape the smart society of Esher, as she had once wanted to break past the gates of Ripplevale. It was not work among the poor that she wanted, but life with them.

Yet she would hardly have been human had she not felt some apprehension. She was not prepared in any way for the environment of Wandsworth. Flower missions, visits to factory crèches, an interest in sweated labour were the tiniest details compared to the sweeping luxury in which she had lived. Her social concern had been felt in large rooms, broad acres and clear air; it was another matter to be confined in the smoke-blackened squalor itself.

A reluctance to abandon altogether the habit of life she had established with Max may be deduced from an unpublished novel which she wrote early in 1891 while living in Wandsworth Road. In the midst of the desolate, broken-windowed grime, and distracted by roaming beggars, uproarious fights and howling children with scabbed knees and congested lungs, she composed a two-volume romance entitled *Spiridion*, which is almost indistinguishable from her earlier three-deckers. Its eponymous hero is, like so many other Despard characters, in search of his father, and the trail leads from Sicily through high and incredible adventure to a ruined castle in Scotland and a beautiful French girl. He returns to Sicily in time to join Garibaldi's invasion and discovers his father to be a wicked anti-democrat whom the Great Liberator is about to string up. Redeemed by the son's prowess in the invasion, the father is set free, and a thoroughly happy ending is ensured by the beautiful French girl's reappearance in Sicily in the last chapter. The remoteness of this rather absurd tale from the grim reality of Wandsworth Road is a measure of the adjustment which Charlotte Despard was required to make.

In 1891 John French was posted to India in command of the 19th Hussars. He was now the father of two young children, whom he preferred to leave at home rather than expose to the uncertainties of the Indian climate, but even on a Lieutenant-Colonel's pay he could not afford to maintain a separate house in England. His difficulty precipitated Charlotte from her comfortable present into the uninviting future, since the obvious solution was for his family to move into Courtlands, which was in any case too large for a solitary, middle-aged widow, while she made her permanent home in London. Although she retained a small cottage on the estate and, in 1892, even returned for a few months to serve on the Poor Law Board at Kingston, the dingy back streets of South London now became her permanent home, and one strong link that chained her to the memory of Maximilian was broken.

In Wandsworth, her activities and her surroundings served to pull aside the wraps that had shrouded her personality. It was not a steady, continuous process, but a series of small, often unrelated, adjustments to new surroundings or assertions of old enthusiasms. She had begun to read Thoreau and Walt Whitman, the prophets of simplicity and naturalism, and under their influence her preference for the uncomplicated way of life she had enjoyed as a girl quickly revived. Living alone, she was able to follow Shelley's advice and become a vegetarian, and in the poverty of Wandsworth she could adopt a plainer form of clothing than a more formal class of society would have approved. A simple, habit-like black dress without ornamentation became her invariable garb, set off by the eccentricity of a black lace mantilla. In that bustled, stayed and busty age her refusal to lace her spare figure into corsets, or to cover her head with an extravagant hat, rendered her distinctive to the point of oddness. By the time she began to wear open sandals instead of narrow shoes, it seemed quite in keeping with the rest. The bizarre person who attracted stares in the street was far removed from the respectable character whom Max had moulded. Yet the change was not quite unexpected.

There had been something excessive about the violence of her reaction to his death, a racked quality, which was closer to remorse than sorrow. It might have been for the long absences from his side, culminating in his last solitary voyage, but perhaps also it came from her very failure to find more deeply sympathetic a clever, self-contained man made distant by illness. Wherever she lived thereafter, Max's bust occupied a prominent place, and her badge of mourning, the black mantilla, was worn to the end of her life; but, significantly, one emblem which might have been expected of a grieving widow was missing – neither in writing nor in speech did she ever quote his opinions. Without being aware of it, he had shackled her. 'It was only after my husband's death,' she once said, 'that I was able to give full expression to my ideals.'

Her emergence from his shadow was not impeded by lack of money. As a bride she had been well off, as a widow she was extremely wealthy. Her husband's shrewd investment in the Hong Kong and Shanghai Bank had increased in value some six times and now brought in an income of approximately £3000 a year In Cawnpore, Gavin Jones' Muir Mills had flourished under conservative management and, although the book value of the company had been reduced by a third owing to a policy of over-cautious depreciation, Charlotte's income from the shares still came to £500 annually. Her marriage settlement produced a further £2000 a year, even after her brother's depredations; and in addition to Courtlands and its surrounding acres, she owned houses in Sussex and Croydon.

Financially, then, she was independent. But, in a way that was purely Victorian, she was socially independent also. A widow had fulfilled the function required of a woman. She was entitled to sympathy for her lonely state, but no domestic duty was expected of her. She was more than a spinster; and, though considerably less than a bachelor, she was, so far as a woman could be, a free agent.

In an important way, Charlotte Despard still had not exorcized the grief of her husband's death: without a religious faith, she had no certainty of the survival of his soul. The misty suggestions of table-rapping via the planchette provided only the frailest support for her desperate need to believe, and the probabilities of agnosticism, which answered well enough in life, crumbled before the last question of all. She needed authority, and since it could no longer be found in Anglicanism, she turned to the Catholic Church. Ever since her stay in Paris before her marriage, the pageantry of the Catholic rite had made a powerful appeal to her imagination and to her sense of mysticism, and now, from the Irishwomen in Nine Elms, she discovered the spiritual consolation of those rituals, of masses sung and candles burned for the soul of the dead. The road to Catholicism originated with Max's death, but her conversion less than a year later represented a betrayal of his rationalist way of thought.

Without questioning the sincerity of her faith, one may still feel some doubts about its orthodoxy, for she returned to Christianity still firmly clinging to her faith in Shelley and the transmigration of souls.

She was not satisfied by a doctrine which suggested that suffering in the world resulted from the imperfection that had existed since man's Fall. To accept that meant accepting that man was not perfectible in this world, and everything in Charlotte Despard revolted against such a passive dogma. Intuitively she preferred the wisdom that underlay Shelley's assertion that 'mankind had only to will that there should be no evil and there would be none'. By that same intuition she rejected the doctrine of Hell. The Athanasian Creed enjoins a belief in the Last Judgement, when 'all men shall rise again with their bodies and shall give account of their works. And they that have done good shall go into life everlasting, and they that have done evil into everlasting fire.' As a statement, that is unequivocal – can any other have provoked a quarter as much terror in fearful minds? Charlotte Despard preferred the Buddhist concept that the soul is purified in the course of several lives. This was not a rational decision, but an intuitive insight. Hell did not fit in – since the whole living spirit of Christianity was love, there was no place left for vindictive torture.

Perhaps she should not have become a Catholic. She had, after all, been instructed to have no secret doubts or mental reservations. But she was not dishonest, for in her own way she had neither. Intuitively she knew that Catholicism was right and that Hell was wrong.

It is a hard matter to deal with intuition, but it must be done, since it guided Charlotte Despard in this matter and through all her work – a source of continual strength to her, and of recurrent aggravation to her colleagues. It was not a faculty that could co-exist with logic: it acted as a reflex, overriding rational thought as a physical reflex overrides controlled physical movement. She often associated it with children, and in her books she made much play of the little girl lisping her dislike of a spuriously genial friend, or the little boy trustfully clasping the hand of a ferocious beggar, later to be revealed as his long-lost father. Intuition was innocent – it could neither deceive nor be deceived. Logic, by contrast, was both deceptive and servile, a tool used by clever men to defend themselves or attack their enemies. It must be admitted that in Charlotte Despard logic was a primitive faculty; neither in her education nor in her marriage had she the opportunity to exercise it independently, and now that she was a widow it was an attenuated appendage to her robustly developed emotions. She used it to infer, but not to reason; to justify her actions, but not to analyse them.

Her understanding dealt in absolutes – moral questions which demanded an unequivocal response – and it set little store by the scepticism and relative values of reason. To Charlotte Despard, a course of action was right or wrong, not preferable or impracticable. She lacked perspective and a sense of context; instead, she saw each individual aspect of her world sharply coloured and well defined, as in a painting by 'Le douanier' Rousseau, and its very distinctness invited her to respond immediately. It was the focus of a child, to whom every object appeals as a thing by itself, having no relation to anything else, but so intense and so fresh that it must be sucked and tasted. Intuition was more than a perception – it was an impulse to act.

In almost every description of Victorian streets, children abound: Fagins, Pips, Olivers, urchins, guttersnipes, shavers, whipper-snappers, limbs of mischief, ready to hurl a half-brick at a toff in a top hat or snivellingly beg a penny for a crust of bread. All the energy now channelled into classroom and playground went teeming into the streets. The intricacy of their street games suggests how much they had to offer by way of entertainment, but when these palled there were only the more adult pursuits of begging and breaking windows. (One commentator reckoned that in poor areas, the number of smashed panes was a good indication of the health of the children: unbroken windows were a symptom of listlessness and malnutrition.) When they could earn some money, they took to the pubs and betting. 'See the sudden life in the street after a great race has been run and the newspaper is out,' wrote a clergyman in the 1890s:

Boys on bicycles with reams of pink papers in a cloth bag on their backs come scorching through the streets, tossing minor bundles to smaller boys who wait for them at street corners. Off rush the little boys shouting at the top of their voices; doors open, factory gates part, men and boys tumble out in their eagerness to read, and it is the betting news alone that they are eager about.

Since 1870 there had been elementary schooling available to all children, but until 1880 it was voluntary, and only in 1891 did the elementary schools cease to charge fees. For the poorest families, education was a dispensable luxury even when it was free, and if a daughter was required at home to care for the younger children, or a father wanted his son with him on a rag-and-bone round, schooling was dropped. Their childhood was short in any case. By eight or ten they might be working a seventy-hour week behind the counter of a shop or following a costermonger's barrow through the streets, crying up business with an infantile intensity that was good for trade. The lucky ones who were going to learn a craft were apprenticed to their masters at thirteen or fourteen.

It was these children, untended or hurried into premature adulthood, who aroused Charlotte Despard's fiercest pity. In Wandsworth, where families were living in one or two rooms, children were pushed out into the streets as soon as they could walk, in order to leave more room for the others. Poor feeding made them susceptible to illness and infection, which took long to heal – needlessly long in many cases, because the parents were ignorant or distracted and the doctor an unacceptable expense. Quite practically, therefore, Charlotte Despard hired a nurse to come regularly to her house, and then scooped up from the streets those who looked most in need of treatment. Soon there were queues of parents and children at the surgery, but the presence of so many patients waiting restlessly for attention was a fresh problem. Again taking the most direct course, Charlotte Despard opened up the entire ground floor to give them a place to occupy themselves. The toys that richer children had – tops, hoops, tin soldiers and skipping ropes – were provided, and soon newspapers also, for it was impossible to separate 'children' from 'young adults' of the same age who had earned a penny or two for betting. Inevitably, there were wounds that took time to heal, earaches, stomach-aches and headaches that recurred, and poisoned hands and feet that needed a second visit. The children became accustomed to playing there; compared to the bleak streets and their overcrowded rooms, a visit to the nurse was a visit to the playground, and to be cured was an unforeseen punishment. Guilefully they invented fresh illnesses, and the owner of 95 Wandsworth Road was only too delighted to be taken in. 'Soon', she wrote, 'even the youngest realised that the slightest ailment was a chit which allowed them to enter the club.' A second woman was engaged to supervise the children, other activities were introduced, and as the children grew older the fiction of being patients was dropped. A small hall at the back of the house was commandeered, gymnasium equipment was installed and the first fully-fledged Despard Club was in operation.

There was no strategy behind its growth, but the pattern of all Charlotte Despard's future work was there – the immediacy of response to a problem, the willingness to accept the consequences and to build larger to accommodate them, and above all the instinct of compassion. Considerations of personal comfort and convenience, which might have guided someone more practical, were swept aside by that humanitarian impulse.

Knowing how much the children needed fresh air, she organized, in the summer of 1891, a trip to the country for them and their parents. In horse-drawn charabancs they trundled down to Esher and unloaded themselves on to the well-trimmed lawns and clipped respectability of Courtlands. Some hint of the exuberance of the occasion is conveyed in a thin-smiled description by Gerald French, Charlotte's nephew:

It certainly was amusing to some extent, but it had its trying side. For instance, they came equipped with several barrel organs, which of course they never ceased playing from the time of their arrival until their departure. Their women-folk accompanied them, and dancing went on during the greater part of the day on the lawns and on the drive. My father [John French], if I remember rightly, threw himself nobly into the breech and helped to organise sports for the men. He possessed a most acute sense of humour and I think he was more amused than anyone at the extraordinary antics of the invaders of our peace and quietness. They swarmed all over the place, and when evening came and they set on the return journey to London, we at any rate were not sorry that the entertainment had at last come to an end.

It was perhaps as well that Charlotte Despard rarely doubted the rightness of her actions, for the irritation they provoked among her relatives would certainly have reined in the ambitions of anyone more faltering. As it was, the visit to Courtlands raised merely the first note of a crescendo of discordance. Charlotte was not indifferent to it, but, loving her relations devotedly, she was prepared to overlook their weaknesses.

In 1891 a house fell vacant in Nine Elms, and, obeying the dictates of her heart, Charlotte Despard took the opportunity of buying a home among her friends. In some ways the problems of Wandsworth were too diffuse to focus her energies – the area was so large, the Vestry so indifferent and the needs so various that the efforts of any single person were swallowed up. By contrast, Nine Elms was a clearly defined enclave of such acute distress that it was marked out from the other areas of poverty along the south bank of the river. The experienced investigators who worked on

Booth's survey of London remarked that it showed 'the usual signs of squalor in an exaggerated form: broken windows, filthy cracked plaster, dirty, ragged children and drink-sodden women'.

Nine Elms, which is now the site of London's fruit and vegetable market, was then an area shaped like a narrow triangle lying on its side, bounded on the north by the Thames and on the other two sides by railway lines. Its apex, to the east, was a jumble of streets known as 'the Island', caught in the narrow angle between the river and the marshalling yards of the London and South-Western Railway. It was there, at 2 Currie Street, that Charlotte Despard chose to live, in the heart of the poorest bit of an excessively deprived area. In the centre of the triangle, dominating Nine Elms, were the gasometers, retorts and purifiers of the London Gas Light Company. Nearby there were limeworks, flour mills, breweries and an iron foundry. A little further west was the better part of Nine Elms, older houses on one side of Battersea Park Road, and on the other five parallel streets built thirty years earlier for railway-company employees. The base of the triangle was a railway spur which ran north to the river and cut Nine Elms off from the open spaces of Battersea Park. There were only two exits from the area, both to the south, and the result was, as Charles Booth described it in 1898, 'one of the best object lessons in "poverty traps" in London'.

The human body was the analogy Booth used to express his idea of town planning. Streets were arteries, and a free circulation of people and traffic to and from the city's heart was essential for the health of the organism – where circulation was impeded, the area putrefied. People could not get out to find jobs and were reduced to costermongering, one step above begging. Those who did find jobs moved out to a more convenient place, with the result that the area they had left became exclusively populated by the very poorest of the community.

Since Charlotte Despard's first visits in the 1870s, Battersea as a whole had changed enormously. The population had doubled to 258,000 in 1891 and was still growing by about 5000 a year: Booth estimated that 58 per cent of the heads of families had been born outside London, a very large proportion of them coming from Ireland. In southern Battersea, near the open country, the houses were substantial and their owners prosperous business men. A particularly well-planned development, called the Shaftesbury

Park Estate, had been built nearer the centre of the borough for the salaried employees of the railway companies and other concerns. It was only in the north, near the Thames, that there was wild overcrowding of the poor and unemployed, living four or five to a room.

The cause of this massive surge of population was the dramatic fall in wheat prices, as cheap grain came into the country from across the Atlantic. At fifty shillings a bushel, a wheat farmer could make a living; but by 1884 the price had fallen to forty shillings, and ten years later it slumped to twenty-two. During the same period, the conditions and slave-wages paid to agricultural labourers had improved, as Joseph Arch's Labourers' Union made use of the voting power they had acquired in 1884. Caught between upper and nether millstones, cereal farmers fought off bankruptcy by wholesale sackings; in village after village those concerned in the long cycle of plough, harrow, sow, reap, stook and winnow were forced from the land. The slump spread further, catching up grain merchants, millers, blacksmiths, carters and many small farmers themselves. Those who had money laid by emigrated, the rest came to join the reserve of labour in the towns. Field skills were irrelevant in the factory, and so by necessity they were dependent on casual or unskilled employment. It was this great influx of workers without industrial skills which gave the distress at the end of the nineteenth century a particularly fierce edge. Casual work depended on the season and the volume of trade and in winter, when all activity slowed, thousands of men and women were, as a matter of course, dismissed.

Almost one in three jobs in London was casual – that is, by the day, week or season. In Nine Elms the gasworks was the biggest employer of labour, and it provided a dramatic example of the system. It was exceptional in requiring most labour during the winter months, but at all times the day began at first light when a crowd collected round the gaswork gates. The foreman brought out a list of the numbers wanted that day for work in shovelling coal, or hauling out clinker and ashes. Generally it was first come, first taken, but as the waiting men pushed forward, the foreman often selected friends or those who had greased his palm. If there was work enough, everyone might be taken; but when the demand for gas was low, or during a trade slump, when there was no other work available, the gates would close on up to two hundred disappointed men. There would be some who had walked four or five miles to be there at dawn, and some who had come day after day without success. By the time that they knew there was no work at the gasworks it was too late to try anywhere else, for each place took on its men at the start of the day.

In this seasonality of labour, there was a rural quality; during the summer a man expected to earn enough money to keep him through the fallowness of winter unemployment, but the margin of error was small and a trade slump or spell of bad weather could send thousands to the workhouse. Against such a threatening background, every stroke of good fortune was accepted with spontaneous joy, and spent with openhanded pleasure. When the man was in work, the wife and kids lived on luxuries, simply because it was certain that when he was out of work they would live on crusts, and because regular periods of unemployment were a fact of life.

Such was the world in which Charlotte Despard now lived. It was not a missionary expedition from which she could return to a comfortable house in the country. It was not even a missionary settlement, such as Canon Barnett had established in the East End where young men from the university might spend a few dedicated years before turning to some more amenable public service. By religion, nationality and domicile, she was a citizen of Nine Elms. It was the start of a new life and the realization of an old ideal.

There were aspects of that life to which she could never become accustomed, and the worst was the coal dust. The demand for coal was so enormous that a special wharf had been built at Nine Elms for the collier-boats which brought it in from South Wales. Apart from the requirements of the railway, Price's candleworks needed it as the raw material of their night-lights, the Wellington Soap Works made soap from it, the limeworks burnt lime with it, and above all the London Gas Light Company needed it, by the thousands of tons, to produce 'town gas'. It stood in long, gleaming black banks, wafting a gritty dust over the district so that it often resembled a mining village. Each summer when the windows had to be left open, Charlotte Despard remarked on its pervasive presence, and when she returned from a trip out of town, she was struck again by its taste in the air.

Chemical and gaseous smells mingled with the sweet, glutinous scent of two breweries. Noises erupted night and day, from the factory hooter in the early morning, and the rhythmic throb of the gasworks purifiers, to the endless shriek and slam-bang of shunted goods wagons in the marshalling yards long after dark. To all these she soon became immune, bothering only to record in her diary the occasions when they ceased. But the sound to which she never became used, and of which she never tired was the sound of children playing in the street. When she wanted to express the frustration of her own childhood, the memory to which she constantly returned was that of peering enviously through the barred gate at the village children outside. Now she was among them, like them free from supervision, free from responsibility, and free at last to do what she wanted.

As she had done in the Wandsworth Road, she opened a surgery for the children. It was a small sign of the enclosed, Irish nature of the place that they were shyer here, and more reluctant to trust the stranger who had come to live among them. Gradually the older children were persuaded to bring their younger brothers and sisters to see the nurse when they were sick or injured. Again she noticed the ill effects of a poor and scanty diet of bread and lard, bloaters and tea, but here it was very marked. They lacked vitality and their pale faces were listless and empty, their legs were rickety and their bodies unnaturally small.

Sticking-plaster and medicine were no cure for starvation, so Charlotte Despard produced milk puddings and vegetable broths as well, then set out to teach their parents about proper nutrition and health care. To her bewilderment, good advice was met with indifference and even resentment. Bloaters and tea continued to be the staple diet, and mothers who had, in their own words, 'borne twelve and buried seven', were not inclined to believe that the trained nurse could each them anything about baby care. The appallingly high rate of infant mortality had created an attitude of superstitious fatalism.

For the time being, Charlotte Despard was baffled, but not defeated. She fed and nursed them as best she could, but it was not enough. As unemployment rose in the middle 1890s, the children suffered earliest and most severely, and the efforts of one person could not alleviate more than a fraction of the distress. It was this experience that led her to socialism, and an attempt to reform the working of the Poor Law relief system. Once she understood the helplessness of being unenfranchised, she was precipitated from Poor Law reform into the campaign for the vote; but the insight, energy and obstinacy which she brought to all her subsequent activities were practised first in what she called 'the child-movement'.

In 1895 she bought the corner shop in Everett Street, which backed on to her house, and by knocking away the intervening walls, she created an enormous room on the ground floor. She herself lived in a flat above, while the large space below, lit on one side by the old shop window, became the headquarters of the second Despard Club. It was evidently flourishing when Charles Booth's investigators reported on it in 1898, and they were struck by the mixture of discipline and freedom which prevailed. 'The boys' club she has made her home, or perhaps one might better say, her home is their club. She does not find them unmanageable. They submit readily to her gentle force. "You hurt me," cried a big, strong fellow, but he did not resist when she took him by the arm in the course of order.' Others with far more self-assurance than a Battersea teenager found themselves dominated by her presence. Age was beginning to temper her explosive anger to a steely moral authority, which was reinforced by her appearance. Her hair had turned grey, and the soft contours of middle age were giving way to the fine-boned look of an ascetic, but above her blue eys the heavy eyebrows remained black and expressive.

She had need of authority, for there was no question about the Nine Elms boys' toughness. The youths at the Wandsworth club, who had been reared in a hard school themselves, refused to have anything to do with them, and all attempts to integrate the two clubs failed because, the report revealed, 'she finds the difference in class too great. Her rough boys may go there for gymnasium practice . . . but that is all.' Nevertheless, she rode them on an easy rein. The boys were allowed to smoke in the Club, although, as the investigators noted, 'she laments the stunted growth of the lads and the early age at which they become their own masters'. When the Boer War broke out she took them to hear her speak at an anti-war meeting at the Battersea Town Hall, and shared their wicked glee when the hostile crowd shouted at her, 'Get back to your children!' And, at a time when evangelism was popular, she refused to press her religious beliefs upon them: a

Sunday bible class she took was described as 'more social than religious in character, for though herself a recent convert, Mrs Despard never proselytizes, and the Church of England representative himself says that if some do adopt her religion it is from admiration of her character'.

The glowing reports of Charlotte Despard's work published in Booth's volumes made her name familiar to his thousands of readers, but she had already set out to attract notice more forcefully to the conditions in which she lived. Before she came to Wandsworth she had felt unqualified to give public voice to her feelings, but now, living amongst the poor, seeing the squalor all around her, she was no longer a concerned witness but a participant. A furious indignation forced her to speak out.

Her first nerve-racked speech in public was made at the Wandsworth Town Hall at the end of 1891. It was an ordeal which she could only undergo when her brother accompanied her to the steps of the hall and encouraged her like an old soldier comforting a raw recruit under fire: 'Remember, it's only the nervous who are of any real use,' he said. Once initiated, she drove herself to overcome the terror of the platform and, in response to a growing number of invitations, spoke to a variety of charitable and philanthropic societies in church halls and drawing-rooms. Throughout the next forty years the pattern scarcely altered. She could not eat for hours beforehand; while speaking she was unconscious of anything but the audience's mood; and when she had finished, her listeners' enthusiasm, or lack of it, determined whether she felt herself alive with energy or prostrated with exhaustion. She lacked artifice as a speaker, but the driving need to 'get my message through' gave her speeches a dramatic force to which few audiences were immune.

At first her subject was simply the children, whose suffering was a torture she could hardly bear. Much of it was due to the ignorance of their parents, and her talks dwelled on the importance of education in diet and clothing. As her knowledge of people in Nine Elms grew, it was not the failings of the parents which occupied her but the cruelty of a system in which whole families depended on piecework, and wages were scarcely enough to keep them from starvation. Gradually her speeches became dominated by a theme which she had first put into the mouth of her narrator in *A Voice from the Dim Millions*:

They call our deaths by many names – it is said to be consumption or heart-complaint or low-fever that is responsible . . . and people make it their boast that no one need die of starvation in England. But I should like to ask the doctors what is the cause of the consumption, the low-fever? In nine cases out of ten it is want – want that presses upon us day after day, year after year. . . . Two meals a day – sometimes only one – dry bread and tea, tea and dry bread – eaten with work in the hand and needle flying between the mouthfuls; a straw mattress and bare boards at night with a thin sheet for covering. Stitch, stitch, for thirteen, four-teen, sixteen hours out of the twenty-four. Headache, heartache, sick-ness, rheumatism, but no rest, for a day without earnings means the rent unpaid and the children crying for food. Is it a wonder that it kills?

The anger which then had been aroused by an occasional summer visit was now fuelled daily, and inexorably she was driven on to more direct action than mere speech.

In April 1892 she was elected to the Kingston Poor Law Board as the Guardian for Esher, a post which required her to supervise the running of the workhouse. The prospect of helping the poor in their worst extremity was obviously attractive; it was also one of the few elective posts open to women, and her colleagues – retired generals and comfortable vicars – were quite as respectable as her neighbours at Courtlands. On the other hand, the area had little real poverty; it required no more than £800 a year to finance the Poor Law generously and, compared to the scenes which she saw every day in South London, its problems were insignificant. Her attendance soon became sporadic, and at the end of one year she resigned. It had been a false move; the real misery was in the cities, and her ambition to be 'of some use in the world' could not be reconciled with rural comfort.

As it happened, 95 Wandsworth Road lay within the boundaries of Lambeth, which was the biggest Poor Law Union in London, and had one of the worst reputations for harshness and corruption. The area contained some 300,000 people, of whom three-quarters were crammed in the northern half around Brixton, Kennington and Lambeth, and the size of its pauper population was daunting. There were two workhouses designed to hold more than 1800 people, with another 600 in hospital; while a further 4000 received relief outside the workhouse, and the annual cost of its operation amounted to almost £200,000. In an era when £50,000 was the turnover of a large factory, the Lambeth Poor Law Union represented a massive undertaking. Its affairs were controlled by thirty unpaid Guardians who met for three hours a week, and even if they personally were as pure as Caesar's wife, there was still plenty of scope for mischief.

The rumours abounded, and one, which escaped into the open in 1892, suggested that the Guardians themselves were corruptly assuring jobs and contracts for their relatives. The accusation came from an Anglican curate, and was published in local papers, but under threat of legal action he was forced to retract. People continued to repeat privately what they could not say publicly, that the Relieving Officers, who were in charge of outside relief, fiddled their accounts, that the workhouse Master gave the inmates inadequate rations and sold the surplus food for his own profit, and that the Taskmaster had inmates making furniture for his own house. Although she heard these stories of corruption, from neightbours and the parents of the children at the Despard Club, Charlotte minded less about them than about the numerous tales of inefficiency and ill-treatment. A typical example of which she had first-hand knowledge came to her attention when one of her children came to her for help: because his father was sick and his mother, nursing a week-old baby, could not go out to work, the whole family was in danger of starving. The Relieving Officer had refused to help and, when Charlotte Despard went to him to remonstrate, he ordered her out of his office. Almost four weeks elapsed before he decided to give any relief. During this time she kept the family alive herself, and with some justification she sent off an angry letter to the Guardians complaining about his behaviour. After making enquiries, the Guardians censured him severely, but it surprised no one in Wandsworth that the punishment was for fiddling his expenses, not for inefficiency. As her name became known, similar incidents were brought to her attention and she became familiar with the brusque, contemptuous attitude adopted by most Relieving Officers towards the poor. It infuriated her more than the worst corruption, for it demeaned a person at the very moment when he most needed his self-respect. But to the poor themselves, the cruellest bullying from a Relieving Officer was preferable to the horror of the workhouse.

From its earliest origins, the Poor Law had mingled charity with punishment. The Act of 1598, which first levied a poor rate on householders for the maintenance of the poor in each parish, had specified that able-bodied paupers were to be made to work for their relief, under penalty of whipping or prison if they refused. That system of relief – outdoor by a weekly pension, or indoor in the workhouse – continued substantially in force until 1834, when the poor rate rose to an intolerable level in southern England because outdoor relief was being systematically used to subsidize the low wages paid to farm labourers. Under the new Act passed in that year, the able-bodied might only receive relief inside the workhouse, and there the conditions were to be made 'less eligible' (that is, less desirable) than the worst employment outside. To deter them further, paupers lost all right to personal possessions, and if they had the vote they were disenfranchised. Husbands and wives were separated so that they should not burden the parish further by breeding.

In the course of Victoria's reign, the punitive intention of the 1834 Act gathered force. What had started as a decision to make pauperism less appealing than the most menial job became a policy to encourage a superstitious dread of parish charity. The nightmare of the workhouse which haunted the poor was deliberately fostered in order to exorcize a nightmare in the minds of the Victorian middle classes. They dreaded pauperism as a disease which threatened to become an epidemic unless the greatest vigilance was maintained. Every act of charity had to be strictly controlled if it was not to encourage a feckless attitude in which the germs of pauperism could thrive and multiply. Thus the 'deserving' poor – those who lost their jobs through no fault of their own – were only to be helped with the utmost suspicion, while the 'undeserving' poor, even if they could not be allowed to starve, were to be punished severely for their lack of thrift and their want of social responsibility.

In May 1893, immediately after her resignation from the Kingston Poor Law Board, Charlotte Despard joined a rota of ladies who visited the women's wards in the workhouse to read to the inmates. It was a common enough humanitarian act, which many ladies performed to the mutual benefit and pleasure of readers and listeners; but, in a way that was typical of the widowed, as opposed to the married, Mrs Despard, the small gesture led on without heed to large commitment. In conversation with the women, she learned that many of the elderly had simply been abandoned there, and had never received a visit from friend or relative, nor stirred outside the workhouse gates. Initially she reacted by taking them out in relays to have tea, but once beyond the workhouse walls their tongues were loosened and a flood of complaints emerged about the conditions inside.

Item by item they were merely dreadful – a diet of stringy, half-cooked meat, thin gruel and black rotted potatoes; one towel provided for two dozen women; coarse ill-fitting clothes and heavy boots as their only wear; lack of ventilation, so that the wards were evil-smelling and stuffy; the pervasive, daily, dehumanizing rudeness of everyone in authority – but, taken together, they painted a picture of calculated, institutionalized degradation. When Charlotte Despard asked the old women why they did not complain to the Guardians, she was told that the Guardians ignored complaints and that the Master put the complainers on a diet of bread and water; it was better, they said, to remain silent, because they were too old to survive for long on that fare. Once she had been alerted to the discontent, she began to listen for confirmation during her visits to the workhouse, and from everyone she heard the same story. With measured restraint she wrote to the Guardians, listing the grievances and ending: 'I have had occasion several times lately to think that the present management of the workhouse is deficient, and that the aged inmates are given neither the comfort nor the respect that is the due of misfortune.' The Guardians were unmoved, and replied that in their opinion her allegations were groundless; the food was excellent and the workhouse well managed. There was no way past that impenetrable barrier. As a last resort, she took in three or four of the old women who felt most bullied; but there were hundreds who still had to exist under the harsh regime, and when one of her friends inside was brave enough to protest about the conditions, she was transferred to another workhouse as a troublemaker.

Convinced that no changes could be made from outside, Charlotte Despard felt compelled to work from within, and in December 1894 she presented herself for election as Guardian for Vauxhall. Her work and name were already well recognized and the result was a foregone conclusion. Her first Board meeting in January 1895 marked the beginning of nine years' vigorous reform in Lambeth, and, at the age of fifty, the start of her public career.

The Lambeth Board was not exceptional in its amateur, rather careless approach to its duties. The Guardians drifted calmly through their weekly business, approving without discussion reports from the workhouse, infirmary and schools committees, worrying a little over the financial report, and finally dealing swiftly with individual cases. Even there, they were hardly required to do more than ratify decisions already made by the Secretary: the payment of apprentices' fees, the assessment of a relative's contribution to the upkeep of a patient in a lunatic asylum, the transfer of a girl to the Metropolitan Association for Befriending Young Servants, and a warrant for the arrest of a father for failing to maintain his family. Their policy on relief was determined for them by the Charity Organisation Society, which suggested that applicants should be dealt with in three categories:

The loafers, drunkards, and men of that type should be relieved in the workhouse only. Married men, but thriftless, should be relieved with discretion, but subject to a labour test under strict supervision. Provident men of character with homes worth preserving, should be referred to the District Committee of the Society.

Since private charities like the Society dispensed about one third of all the money spent on the relief of the poor, only the most progressive Guardians ever risked their wrath by ignoring their recommendations, and in 1895 the Lambeth Board was anything but progressive.

It was not likely that Charlotte Despard would fit in easily with such a group, and she wasted no time on tact. She was in a minority of one in opposing the re-election of their long-serving chairman, a Mr Howlett, who owned slum property in Nine Elms. Nor were the twenty-four men flattered by her suggestion that the six women Guardians should constitute the Domestic Committee to supervise expenditure within the workhouse and infirmary. But these were ranging shots. The pressing need was to alleviate the inhumanity of the workhouse.

Her attack focused on Samuel Ayles, the Master of the Renfrew Road workhouse, which held some 1250 people. She already knew that he punished elderly inmates by putting them on a bread and water diet, and at the earliest opportunity she had him examined on the question. Ayles admitted the charge, but said he always consulted the Medical Officer first, to see whether their health could stand it. The Guardians were prepared to accept his explanation, until Mrs Despard persuaded them to find out what the practice was in other workhouses. The enquiry revealed that such punishment was hardly ever used for the old, but the Guardians took no further action against Ayles. Accordingly, Mrs Despard appealed over their heads in a letter to the Local Government Board, broadcasting the information that they permitted the bread and water diet to be

inflicted on persons (aged and weak women, the last about whom I enquired is 74) who are wholly unfit to bear it, and in fact would not bear it did not others supply them with part of their own food. I cannot, moreover, feel comfortable in leaving this matter in the hands of the Master, Mr Ayles, a man not at all gifted as an administrator, and to my mind too young for the important and onerous post.

The Local Government Board asked the Guardians to comment and they, infuriated by her breach of confidence, not only repudiated Mrs Despard's allegations in their entirety but specifically informed Ayles that they were satisfied with his conduct. That the Board of Local Government was not wholly content with this intemperate reaction may be guessed from their stern reply enquiring whether the appropriate regulations had been complied with, in particular that which required the Medical Officer's permission to be obtained in writing. Under Mrs Despard's prodding the requisite certificates were duly presented for her inspection and, although she was thus denied the triumph of exposing an irregularity in Ayles' conduct, she had in fact won the war, for with suspicious abruptness the bread-and-water punishment ceased being applied to elderly inmates.

There were two marked qualities in the widowed Charlotte Despard's character: an aptitude for direct action and a capacity for sustained and almost ruthless indignation. Once she had summed up Ayles as unsuitable for his post, she hunted him remorselessly until the day he left the job. When she noticed a pile of stale, but edible, loaves, about to be removed from the workhouse yard, she told the Guardians, 'I am compelled to believe that someone connected with the workhouse obtains payment for this valuable property.' Ayles denied the imputation, but Charlotte Despard returned to the subject in the summer, when she discovered that more bread was apparently being consumed than the year before, although the number of inmates was lower. Waste was a subject close to the Guardians' hearts, and they adopted a more reserved tone with Ayles. They reprimanded him when Mrs Despard revealed irregularities in his distribution of tea; they severely censured him when Mrs Despard discovered that prayers were not said at breakfast in his workhouse; and they were deeply shocked when Mrs Despard provided circumstantial evidence of his immorality. He had employed, as a servant, a good-looking girl with lax morals, who had once been an inmate of his workhouse, and when she became pregnant (apparently by the bath-house attendant, though other rumours abounded) he had allowed her to take chairs and a table from the workhouse to furnish her flat. It was not enough to convict, but the Guardians had their own opinions. They hedged him round with committees to investigate his every move, and when he retired soon afterwards, many of them openly said that he had been 'a profligate . . . unfit to be in charge of a workhouse'.

Ayles was not the only official to suffer for failing to accord inmates 'the respect that is the due of misfortune'. When a former policeman was brought to the infirmary suffering from an epileptic fit, an attendant flippantly remarked: 'All policemen go up the pole when they get their pension.' For this harmless joke Charlotte Despard persuaded the Board to censure him, and at her instigation a nurse who put a group of inmates to some menial work was dismissed. Ruthless as she was with officials, however, the main thrust of her efforts was directed at bigger game. It was the Guardians who set the tone of the Poor Law in their area. In 1870 Poplar, for instance, had the toughest workhouse in London, with a harsh regime deliberately intended to weed out the workshy from the able-bodied claimants for relief, but when a group of ILP reformers under George Lansbury and Will Crooks won control of the Guardians in 1895, it became one of the most liberal Boards in the country. By changing the Lambeth Guardians' habits, Charlotte Despard hoped to reform the system, and during the course of nine years on the Board she set herself to transform the outlook of her colleagues. She forced them to treat the cases before them as individuals rather than items, she persuaded them to keep a closer eye on the running of the workhouse and schools, she doubled the length of time they spent at Board meetings and she trebled the number of committees on which they sat.

The very indolence of the old Guardians was their undoing. They had long left the running of affairs to the paid officials and possessed little idea of what happened to people in the workhouse, and none at all of what happened to them outside it. Six months after she was elected, Charlotte Despard proposed that four 'call-over' committees should be set up to discover the circumstances of everyone under the Guardians' jurisdiction. Initially there was little enthusiasm for disturbing a smooth-running institution but, by a stroke of good fortune, the Ratepayers' Association had decided that the Lambeth workhouses contained more than their share of paupers from outside the parish; in the call-over committees they saw a chance of discovering the foreigners and sending them back to their original parish. With the unexpected, but powerful, backing of the ratepayers, the committees were established.

The information which they drew up week by week provided Charlotte Despard with the evidence she needed to educate the Board. It was true that the ratepayers also had their way, and some ten families a week were returned to their parishes; but the humanitarian gain was incalculable, as the Guardians were brought to understand that many of those who had been forced into the workhouse under the Charity Organisation Society's formula could be much better and more cheaply relieved outside.

It was an indication of the change that had taken place when, two years later, Charles Booth's reporter heard complaints that the Board had become 'too tender with out-relief'. In 1900 a clergyman in Northampton, to whom the Board had sent money for the relief of a Lambeth woman living there, wrote back: 'Your ratepayers should compel their paupers to reside within the limits of their Union where your Relieving Officers can keep an eye on them. Your ratepayers seem to have more money than sense.' But he was out of date, not only in attitude but in vocabulary, for by then the Board no longer referred to someone receiving out-relief as a 'pauper' but as a 'person'. It was a notable advance.

Even those who remained in the workhouse derived a benefit, since the knowledge of them as individuals made it impossible any longer for the Guardians to imagine them vaguely as a mass of loafers and layabouts; month by month, the minutes of the Board showed the provision of small, humanizing touches – personal combs and brushes, flower stands, bedside lockers, strawberries in season, individual packets of tea. The elderly ladies who were allowed to go out of the workhouse were given decent black dresses instead of the workhouse rags which disgraced them. The women were put to sewing and dress-making rather than the coarse labour of picking oakum, and some of the men to painting, gardening, milling flour and baking. There were bizarre discoveries, mostly owing to Charlotte Despard's vigilance, which underlined how little the Guardians had known of what went on in their two workhouses. Blind people had been left unattended in their darkness without occupation or entertainment. Inmates were exchanged back and forth, in batches as large as seventy, at the whim of a Master, sometimes as a punishment or as a reward, sometimes merely to coincide with his holidays; such was the uncertainty that no one knew how long he or she might remain among friends. On Sundays, missionaries and preachers descended on the workhouse like locusts; as many as three brazen-voiced ministers might be heard thundering out different sermons at the same time in a single ward, and when their discordant amens had died away, ladies from the Norwood Flower Mission would sing hymns, while others read homilies from uplifting tracts and passages from favourite sermons. The place was a bedlam of religion, where the poor were in danger of suffering the dismal fate, conjured up by Sydney Smith, of being preached to death by wild curates.

Committees were formed to regulate these and other malpractices within the institution, and women were brought in to teach the blind to knit; but Charlotte Despard was not satisfied. Hundreds of young people passed through the Guardians' hands each year to be apprenticed, boarded out or sent to charitable institutions, and though they remained the Guardians' responsibility nothing was known of the conditions in which they lived. More committees were formed, and the Guardians' meetings dragged on a little longer; when those comfortable old nodders-through saw the need for action they did not shirk their duty, and Charlotte Despard set them a fast pace, producing voluminous reports on apprentices and boarded-out children, and pushing forward new ideas for employing the workless.

The two favourite solutions were labour colonies and emigration. The Poplar Guardians had bought land in Essex and were beginning a farm there, but they had the backing of a friendly millionaire. The Lambeth Guardians turned down a similar plan for lack of money, but emigration seemed to offer a very satisfactory alternative, particularly for orphan boys. Several hundred were sent out to Canada under the auspices of Dr Barnardo's, who undertook to place them with selected farmers for agricultural training. Deciding that the Board's responsibility for them had not ended there, Charlotte Despard set off in 1902 to visit them. Her journey took her from Quebec to Calgary, travelling by train, stagecoach and horse-buggy, and in the course of it she investigated the Barnardo's organization in Quebec, Ottawa and Toronto, and inspected farms from New Brunswick to Manitoba. She was deeply disturbed by what she found:

When I heard of the large parties continually going out, of the thousands of applications sent in by the farmers, and of the system of supplying the demand, it struck me that, in the nature of things, it was impossible for adequate inquiry to be made as to the fitness of the farmers to train the children sent to them; and if they are not trained – not rendered capable of doing good work in the future – we are simply cheapening labour and pouring a helot class into Canada.

Yet another committee was formed to act on this report. In place of Dr Barnardo's, a new arrangement was made with the smaller Waifs and Strays Society, which undertook to give the Lambeth boys the personal attention which the Board demanded for their charges.

In the years since she had been elected, Charlotte Despard had come close to educating the Guardians to her way of thinking. Remembering the universal hostility with which she had been faced originally, a colleague of hers remarked that she had shown 'the supreme form of courage – never to falter when faced with overwhelming opposition'.

Later she was accustomed to say that 'the Poor Law was my apprenticeship'. It had taught her that idealism could be a practical policy, and it had shown her the merits of direct action; but its most important lesson was one of failure. She had altered the mood in Lambeth, but not the system. The Poor Law, designed to goad the lowest section of society, continued to trap the least fortunate – the old, sick and unemployed – but even these were not the worst casualties of the system. Of every hundred paupers, seventy-two were women and children, and to help them the reformation of a Board of Guardians was not enough; the entire patriarchal and capitalist edifice of society needed to be transformed.

5

'But for the Poor Law,' Charlotte Despard declared, 'I might have remained an omnivorous reader with a literary interest in great ideas.' Those impractical notions of liberty, justice, and the dignity of man, which Max had taught her to regard as remote philosophical concepts, reappeared in all their childhood urgency as practical necessities when seen against the bureaucratic 'realism' and institutional brutality of the Poor Law. When she first plunged into the work, she had instinctively assumed that errors had only to be pointed out to be put right, but it quickly became apparent that all the committees in the world could not make just an unjust system.

Each winter, as casual employment fell off, hundreds of families were forced to apply for relief, and the Poor Law duly inflicted upon them the penalty of being humiliated by its regime, either inside or outside the workhouse, as though their poverty were self-induced. At her first full Board meeting, Charlotte Despard was present when a deputation of unemployed workers begged for employment painting and repairing the infirmary rather than be sent to the workhouse, whose wards were already filled beyond capacity. 'You have no room for us,' one man pointed out; but his argument cut no ice, for the situation recurred annually and the solution was simply to cram in more people in ever-growing squalor until spring brought back the jobs.

Protest though she might, Charlotte Despard could not avoid seeing that it was the unrestricted forces of supply and demand that had created the situation in the first place. 'The hopelessness of the whole business, and the ocean of misery through which I was compelled to wade', she wrote, 'made me search for some remedy.' As it happened, the unemployed men came from the Social Democratic Federation, a Marxist organization, and were able to buttress their case for employment with the convincing argument that municipal welfare projects were in fact cheaper than relief in the workhouse, as well as more humane. Their exposition of socialist economics opened Charlotte Despard's eyes and, as the workhouse population mounted to record levels in the following months, she eagerly explored the alternative solutions which socialism offered.

In 1895 almost any organization opposed to unrestricted capitalism called itself socialist. There were socialist clubs with Liberal or Radical backgrounds, and socialist clubs with religious backgrounds. The Battersea Labour League believed in municipal socialism, and had persuaded the borough council to build public libraries and baths. The Independent Labour Party, founded in 1893, called for 'collective ownership and control of the means of production, distribution and exchange', while the Social Democratic Federation wished to abolish all private property, and the Socialist League advocated pure anarchy. So all-embracing was the term 'socialist' that even Sir William Harcourt, a genuinely old-fashioned Whig, could in a genial moment tell the House of Commons that 'we are all Socialists now'.

It was not easy to decide which was the most promising strand to follow, and Charlotte Despard found herself handicapped further by her past. 'I had been brought up,' she explained, 'in the dear old superstition of my fathers that English men and women are free, and there is no need for revolution. . . . I had thought for a time to find the change I wanted in Liberalism.' Bright was dead, but the heir to his mantle, Joseph Chamberlain, had captured her interest in 1891 with a programme for still more radical reform. In practice it had little effect upon Liberal policy, and when he continued to mouth the same opinions in the General Election of 1895 Charlotte Despard discarded Radicalism as she had the rest of her late husband's principles.

'Party politics held out no hope', she wrote angrily:

I saw the terrible problem of the people's necessities played with. I heard promises made to them which I knew would not be fulfilled. Hot with helpless indignation I beheld their urgent needs turned into party cries for election purposes. At last I determined to study for myself the great problems of society. My study landed me in uncompromising socialism.

The emphasis lay on 'uncompromising'. She adopted the avowedly Marxist teachings of the Social Democratic Federation with the enthusiasm of a convert, and indeed her well-to-do friends soon became accustomed to her repeated assertion that 'Socialism is to me a religion'.

To its followers in Britain, Marxism was the romantic idealism of the *Communist Manifesto* rather than the scientific method embodied in *Capital*, which few had read and fewer still had understood. 'I do not know what Marx's theory of value is,' William Morris once said, 'and I'm damned if I want to know. . . . It is enough political economy for me to know that the idle class is rich and the working class is poor, and that the rich are rich because they rob the poor.' Many found it easy to enlist under that banner and, like Morris himself, equally easy to leave: in 1894 Engels remarked caustically, 'In the fourteen years of its existence the SDF has seen a million people pass through its ranks. . . . Out of one million 995,500 have hopped it – but 4500 have stayed.'

The cause of most people's waning enthusiasm was H. M. Hyndman, the Federation's founder and president, 'a petty and hard-faced John Bull' in Engels' opinion, 'possessing a vanity considerably in excess of his talent'. His despotic control of the Federation drove out the more gifted while the rank and file soon lost interest in his philosophy of pure revolution without any palliative measures for immediate hardships. The heyday of the Federation had been the 1880s, when John Burns and Hyndman had led marches of the unemployed through the streets of London, but by the end of the decade continual in-fighting had destroyed its chance of building a mass movement from the army of unskilled and casual workers who were beginning to join the trade union movement. Instead, their organizers came from the young ILP and other socialist clubs who were prepared to work for more limited goals on the way to socialism.

Nevertheless, shortly before Charlotte Despard joined the Federation its fortunes improved with the return of three important defectors: William Morris, Edward Aveling and his common-law wife, Eleanor Marx, Karl's daughter. In 1893 Morris and Hyndman produced a united declaration of policy entitled *The English Socialists*, which advocated the nationalization of all land, industry and private property in order to destroy the class system and the wage economy which supported it. When London played host to an international conference of socialists and trade unionists in 1896, the Federation's credentials were in good order, and among its delegates was Charlotte Despard.

From the start she had proved herself a useful recruit by organizing meetings, contributing money and speaking wherever she could. The Despard Club's hall at 95 Wandsworth Road had been put at the disposal of the socialist movement in the area and, christened the Social Hall, it became a centre for all forms of working-class politics and entertainment. Lectures and concerts were organized, and the Despard Club extended its activities to include adults. To all who came, Mrs Despard explained as well as she could the economic reasons that lay behind their poverty.

In earlier times, she held, men had worked at home or locally with a few comrades, and all industry was cottage industry. When the articles which they had made began to be mass-produced by machines, they lost their jobs; in effect, the nineteenth-century industrialist had stolen man's work from his cottage and had obliged him to follow it to the factory. There he was stripped of his independence, his skill and his dignity and became no more than a mere appendage of a machine – a Prometheus, bound to his rock and daily gnawed by the vulture of industry. Yet, Mrs Despard insisted, his bonds were imaginary: to be free he had only to realize that everything was his. The land was his and all its ores and coal; he had made the machines, baked the bricks, constructed the buildings, but he had been cheated of it all by the industrialist, who paid him a derisory sum for his labour and claimed the whole value of the result for his own. When the workers understood how they had been robbed, they would rise up and take back what was rightfully theirs, and the whole edifice of capitalism with its hated class structure would collapse, leaving a communist society without rank or exploitation.

The 'impossibilist' philosophy of the Federation, the belief in instantaneous enlightenment and revolt, left its mark on Charlotte Despard's political thought in the form of an unwavering faith that the people had only to be awakened for the country to be transformed. Thus, while she always abhorred any thought of violence, going so far as to insist that 'there must not be any class bitterness', she never attached great importance to the actual process by which the ownership of property was to be wrested from individuals and restored to the community. Yet soon even she found the Federation's lack of interest in short-term measures to improve the condition of the working-class a grave drawback, and, as for others before her, political disenchantment was reinforced by personal disapproval.

In January 1897 Edward Aveling organized a concert at Social Hall, and fell in love with a young actress called Eva Frye as she sang 'Love's Old Sweet Song' to the mellifluous accompaniment of the Social Democratic String Band. Aveling and Eleanor Marx were particular favourites of Charlotte Despard's for they shared her enthusiasm for Shelley and had published a paper demonstrating the consistency of his ideas with socialist theory. She was, therefore, deeply shocked when Eleanor Marx killed herself in 1898 after learning of Aveling's secret marriage to Eva Frye, and the ugly circumstances of the suicide, with prussic acid apparently provided by Aveling, destroyed her romantic belief that members of the Federation must be of a higher order since they had consecrated their lives to the pursuit of a great truth. There was a rumour that Aveling had rushed to Charlotte Despard for comfort after discovering the suicide, but on that matter she was silent and restricted herself to the all-embracing remark that 'The Federation had some pretty strange elements in it in those days.' Once the scales had dropped from her eyes, the deficiencies were very obvious in men like the dictatorial Hyndman, his rabidly misogynist lieutenant Belfort Bax, and above all Aveling, of whom it was said (wrongly as it proved), 'nobody can be as bad as Aveling looks'. Her growing disenchantment was, however, founded on more than personal grounds. The Poor Law had presented her with a problem for which the Federation had no solution.

Sooner or later, every working woman was in danger of having to turn for help to the penal regime of parish relief. When a worker lost his job, fell sick or grew too old to earn a living, his wife went with him to the Relieving Officer; but there were other women who went alone. 'My sister women', Charlotte Despard called them:

those struggling with social problems, and those who slave all their lives long for the community – shop, factory and domestic slaves, earning barely a subsistence, and thrown aside to death or the parish when they are no longer profitable – mothers, bearing and rearing children, seeing them go forth . . . and spending their own last years, lonely and unconsidered in the cheerless wards of the workhouse.

The poor might be the victims of society, but their wives and daughters were victims of the victims.

The discrepancies of morality, of law and of wages, which were aggravating to the better-off woman, condemned the poorer to degradation. The Common Law recognized wives only as the creatures of their husbands – 'something akin to his pet monkey', according to Selden's commentary – but equated his absolute power with his absolute responsibility for her maintenance. Despite the law, husbands deserted their responsibilities with astonishing frequency. Their reasons were often selfish, but often perfectly sound: it was cheaper than divorce, a wife was not responsible for the debts her husband left behind, and there was no work to be found close to home. The flaw in the equation was that a husband had only to be present to exercise power, while a wife could not enforce responsibility except through the courts.

A deserted wife who could not afford a solicitor had no other recourse but to turn to the parish so that the Poor Law Board could sue for maintenance on her behalf. Even then, the sheer number of cases made it almost impossible to track down the missing husband, and, by a wicked irony, the very working of the Poor Law helped to swell the throng of men who deserted their families. When a man was forced into the workhouse he could not leave again, even to look for employment, without taking his family with him, and in consequence they were all forced to stay there until certain that there was work immediately available. In such circumstances it was far more sensible for a husband to abandon his family to the workhouse while he looked for a job that would enable them to live together again. For the best, as well as the worst, of husbands, desertion was a counsel of prudence, and it was hardly surprising that, in every big city where a man could disappear, the noticeboards in police stations were festooned with long lists of names of those who had deserted wives and families.

Almost all single mothers, whether deserted, unmarried or widowed, had to turn to the parish for relief. If they had a job in a shop or factory, the ten- or twelve-hour day made a child-minder essential, and the wages of ten to fifteen shillings a week were hardly sufficient to cover that and all the other household expenses as well. Their ordeal, whether employed or not, was what might have been expected of a system mingling charity with punishment.

Over the single mother the Poor Law exercised a harsh moral supervision. The Relieving Officer would come round to make sure that she had no valuables left (even wedding-rings had to be pawned before the parish would give relief) and to decide whether she had 'a home worth preserving'. By that vague formula, implying clean children, swept floors and, most importantly, no co-habitation, it would be determined whether she should receive out-relief or be sent to the workhouse. In the workhouse, her children were removed (a humanitarian impulse, since it was no place for a child), and she was not permitted to visit them until Charlotte Despard won single mothers that right in 1898. Even then, the mere suspicion of immorality might be enough to debar her, as a report to the Board shows:

We have interviewed June Haughton, a widow with four children at the [workhouse] schools, who applied to visit them. Her application has hitherto been refused as, in the opinion of the officers, she is not a proper person to have communication with the children. As however there appears to be no proof of this, we have, with some hesitancy, authorised her being allowed to visit her children.

If she received out-relief, cohabitation with a man not her husband was sufficient reason to withdraw relief, and from 1889, when the Boards were given the power to take children into care, it was increasingly used as justification for removing their children:

Caroline Collins applied to us to have her daughter Louisa from the schools. The girl was adopted by order of the Board in consequence of the immoral life the mother was leading. She is still cohabiting with a man called Harry Holmwood, and we do not consider it desirable that the child should be sent home to her.

Since the cost of it made divorce* almost impossible for the poor, a deserted wife had to choose between a life of chastity and the risk of losing her children, and every common-law marriage faced the threat of dissolution if the family ever had to turn to the parish

* The Royal Commission of 1912 found that the expense ranged from £70 to £500, and *in forma pauperis*, for those earning less than £2 a week, between £15 and £20. Since the wife had also to prove both desertion and adultery, most simply dispensed with formalities and took a common-law husband.

for relief. It was a vivid example of Shelley's assertion that 'Society avenges herself on the criminals of her own creation'.

With passionate energy and little effect, Charlotte Despard sought to right the imbalance in the moral code. One of her committees goaded the police to greater efforts in tracking down putative fathers and runaway husbands, while the Board, a little reluctantly, agreed to hire detectives and offer rewards, but the size of the problem swamped all solutions. Nor could she mitigate the difficulties faced by the single mother in the workhouse, who needed to find both job and child-minder before she could leave; for the Board categorically refused to care for the children while the mother went out to look for a job, unless she met the Charity Organisation Society's exacting standard of reliability. Mrs Despard's few successes at alleviating the burden on single mothers occurred when she was able to persuade the Board to take in two or three children from a large fatherless family until the eldest could start earning a living. The frustration of her efforts opened her eyes and might by itself have made her a feminist, but instead, and quite typically, a single moment of insight decided her.

She had been attending a Guardians' meeting to hear applications for relief. One of the applicants was a widow with six children, aged from two to eleven years old. Her husband had died a fortnight before, and the Board was prepared to be sympathetic, until the chairman discovered that the husband's life insurance had paid the widow £15 – sufficient to live on for almost two months. Under questioning, the widow claimed that the money had gone to pay off old debts, but when the chairman pressed further, she finally admitted that she had spent more than half of it on the funeral alone. There had been a good oak coffin, a proper hearse and an undertaker's mute in top hat, and there had been black for the entire family, including the youngest. To the chairman it was the maddest extravagance, and he delivered a severe lecture on the folly of dissipating in an afternoon sufficient money to keep her and her family for six weeks.

What was irrational to the chairman made complete sense to Charlotte Despard. The widow's splendid funeral was simply an expression of the extravagant spirit which had sustained her through her marriage. To be a working wife, preparing meals early in the morning before the man left, and again late at night when he came home, and filling the day in between with washing, darning, housework and shopping was a labour in itself, but to bear and bring up six children as well was enough to break the will. 'I would rather be anything than a working-man's wife', Charlotte often declared, but at that moment she understood the prodigality which hallowed the incessant, frenzied struggle. By giving everything, both as wife and widow, the woman before her had given her life dignity, and had affirmed its individual importance.

Against that affirmation was set the whole purse-lipped, disapproving, minatory, penny-pinching, fearful apparatus of the Poor Law, with Guardians, Relieving Officers, Masters, Matrons, and Taskmasters egged on by the shrivel-hearted accountants of the Charity Organisation Society. It was part of the battle which Shelley recognized as materialism against humanity, which Marx recognized as capitalism against the worker, and which Charlotte Despard now recognized as male society against the self-respect of women.

Society had framed its laws around the assumption that women were simply adjuncts of men and, although the intention was not malicious, the effect undoubtedly was. Common Law, which treated woman as little better than a pet monkey, left her defenceless against her owner, and the Poor Law Act of 1834, designed to goad the lowest class of society, punished best those who were lower than the lowest. Against their insistent injustice, the most vigorous of social reformers was helpless. 'I tried to help,' Charlotte wrote, 'tried all I knew, but alas! how futile were my efforts. Turn which way I would, I knocked my head against a law to which neither my sisters nor I had consented. The thought of all this nearly made me wild.'

Then and always, she assumed that the natural ally of woman would be socialism. Shelley had, after all, bracketed them in revolt against authority; the utopian socialist, Fourier, had proposed that '[the] degree of emancipation is the natural measure of general emancipation'; and Engels, using the notes of Karl Marx, had written that '. . . the first, class oppression coincided with that of the female sex by the male'. For all the benevolence of its theorists, the socialist movement only paid lip service to the cause of women's equality.

Most working-men saw women as conservative, naturally

servile, and suspiciously ready to act as cheap labour, breaking strikes and cutting wages, and thus drew the conclusion that they would use their votes to sustain the status quo in politics. Despite the formal adoption of equal rights for men and women as part of the Second International's policy in 1891, the European Social Democratic parties honoured the principle more in the breach than the observance. They demanded 'adult suffrage', but between 1902 and 1905 the Belgian, Austrian and Swedish parties each abandoned the women's vote in order to gain a wider male franchise, while the French and Germans scarcely pretended that it was a serious demand. As Charlotte Despard discovered, the Social Democratic Federation differed only in being honest enough to state frankly its hostility to the enfranchisement of any woman until every man had the vote.

In her fury she precipitately threw in her lot with some kindred souls in the Women's Liberal Federation, and in 1901 formed a women's suffrage group whose purpose, she said, 'was to make the vote the first plank in the women's movement'. The experiment was not a success, for she soon discovered that 'they were Liberals first and suffragists second'. This was insupportable, not only because she had forsworn the politics of capitalism, but because her opposition to the Boer War was far more extreme than the Liberal Party's. The breaking-point came when the group decided to affiliate to the National Union of Women's Suffrage Societies, whose policy was to secure the vote 'on the same terms as it is, or may be held by men'. Since this implied the enfranchisement of ratepayers only, it was unacceptable to Charlotte Despard, for whom the whole purpose of the vote was to protect the interests of the sort of women who filled the workhouse wards and the rolls of the Relieving Officers. Within a few months she had resigned from the suffrage group, and was once more in search of a solution to the double slavery of workers and women.

In 1901 the Labour Representation Council was formed by the trade unions and such socialist groups as were prepared to work for the return of workers' representatives to Parliament. The Federation, still clinging to its 'impossibilist' beliefs, refused to affiliate, unlike its rival the ILP which was ready to use existing institutions, such as the unions and Parliament, to achieve socialism. Charlotte Despard's mind was cast in too romantic a mould to give up an old love easily, but the misogyny and lack of reality in the Federation finally persuaded her that the policies of the ILP were the right ones. 'I believed,' she said, explaining her new attitude, 'that the transition from capitalism to Socialism must be gradual. Industrialism must capture the government machine.' She never entirely abandoned her hope that some instant revelation would occur in the workers' minds, and hardly a strike took place without her uttering a prayer that 'the people's eyes may be opened'.

Her choice of spiritual language sprang from her conviction that socialism, which alone still seemed to remember that the poor were the blessed, was the purest form of Christianity. 'I felt and saw', she had once written, 'how the poor and afflicted – those who were being trampled by the great rush of men – were, in a sense of which the happy cannot know, the true children of the Saviour of men.' The further she escaped from the rationalism which had been her husband's faith, the more clearly she saw that the degradation in the alleys of Nine Elms was not a problem but a sin. 'The most fundamental of divisions,' W. B. Yeats suggested, 'is that between the intellect, which can only do its work by saying continually "Thou fool", and the religious genius which makes all things equal.' His remark can well be applied to Charlotte Despard, who perceived each shoeless child, each peeling wall and each drunken prostitute to be a blasphemy committed by the devil of nineteenth-century capitalism.

By the beginning of the new century an air of spiritual authority, which later dominated her character, had begun to impress those who knew her. Margaret Bondfield, later the first woman Cabinet Minister but then a trade-union organizer, vividly recalled staying with her in 1898 at her cottage in Surrey:

I woke very early and saw her already at work outside. On her knees, weeding her garden at sunrise, she seemed to me like a saint at prayer, and later at breakfast her face shone with the peace and strength she drew from nature. It was these communings in the garden with God that gave her her unique steadfastness.

In a sense, she had rediscovered her childhood, with its singleness of purpose, its rebellion against authority and its garden at the heart of all.

From those who had shared the first garden, however, she was becoming estranged. Their political differences made it almost impossible for her to talk to her favourite sister, Carrie, without the conversation descending into furious argument: 'It is the usual thing, she *cannot* understand my rebellion,' Charlotte wrote sadly after one of these outbursts. With Nellie, who was more temperate, she could keep away from dangerous topics, although it meant that they did little more than exchange banalities. Maggie was still in India; and Katie, the youngest, whose husband, Colonel Harley, had died in the Boer War, now lived in East Anglia, too much encumbered with her fatherless children and too far from London to see anything of Charlotte. Fortunately for her peace of mind, she and Sir John French, as her brother had become since his exploits in South Africa, profoundly misunderstood each other. He took her opinions to be an eccentricity, forgivable in one who had devoted her life to the poor; while she, deeply though she had disapproved of the Boer War, could never quite believe that his soldiering was anything less innocent than the games of the little boy who had strutted about the Ripplevale lawns. 'The wicked war of this Capitalistic government', which she had denounced from anti-war platforms, had had nothing to do with him, and when his cavalry charge through the Boer lines relieved Kimberley, she had been as ecstatic as the most jingoistic member of the public. Preoccupied though French was as Commander of the Aldershot forces, he and his sister still met occasionally, in benign ignorance of each other's true thoughts – the one engaged in the defence of the constitution, the other battling for its destruction.

There was compensation for Charlotte for the estrangement from her sisters in the new friendships she began to form, particularly within the ILP. As she had found with the Nine Elms women, it was easy to respond to their uncomplicated warmth of emotion, whether sharing with George Lansbury, a Poplar Guardian, his hatred of the Poor Law, or enjoying 'the spirit of comradeship' which Will Crooks created around him. She spoke and canvassed for the latter in his successful campaign at the 1903 Woolwich by-election, and it remained in her memory as a pinnacle of happiness: 'What days they were! How we laughed at one moment and at the next choked down a lump in our throats as he poured out his humorous and pathetic stories.' Closest of all was the deep affection she had for Margaret Bondfield, who for her part confessed in her autobiography, 'I loved her and cherished her friendship till her death.'

They had met in 1898, after a disastrous meeting at Social Hall. It had been held to recruit new members to the Shop Assistants' Union, but despite much advertising, not a single shop assistant appeared. Tired and dispirited, the young organizer had burst into tears, until Charlotte Despard comforted her ('like a mother', Margaret Bondfield remembered) and reminded her not to confuse disappointment with failure – 'it was only the call to that increased effort which gives strength for victory'. It was through her that Charlotte Despard was introduced to the women's trade union movement. It was difficult enough to organize women when their jobs were usually unskilled, often sweated and always insecure, but even if a union was formed, it was almost powerless, without the political muscle of the vote, to gain any of its demands. Taught by bitter experience, Margaret Bondfield had become a committed member of the Adult Suffrage Society, the only suffrage group to advocate the vote for all classes of women, and her example persuaded Charlotte Despard that it was the right road to follow. 'I had seen,' she said, 'that women would never make much progress until they were acknowledged as citizens. Trained in a democratic school, I desired this privilege to be as widely extended as possible.' Accordingly she began to urge the benefits of the vote and of unions on the women in the Nine Elms laundries and sweatshops, and on the jam and fruit bottlers in the Crosse & Blackwell factories nearby.

A steady trickle of converts appeared at Social Hall, tramped up the bare wooden stairs to her little, two-roomed flat above the Despard Club, or travelled down to stay in her Esher cottage, which was, Margaret Bondfield remembered, 'open to all the lame dogs and tired workers needing rest and soul refreshment'. Unconventional though Charlotte Despard's beliefs and appearance were, she retained the manners of a Victorian lady, and for the shop assistants, factory workers and office clerks, it was, as one confessed, 'our first introduction to good taste, culture and the kindness of a gracious hostess'. Paintings and furniture had come from Courtlands to fill her small flat. A bust of her late husband stood just inside the door, where it was dusted each morning with an accompanying murmur of 'Poor, dear Max', and his mahogany tea-taster's chest provided her guests with a choice of any blend they cared to have in their bone-china cups. From a high-backed chair, their hostess would conduct proceedings with scrupulous politeness, ensuring that even the most tongue-tied had a chance to give her opinion about the best means of overthrowing the capitalist system. That she was 'a real lady', none ever denied.

A Welsh mother and daughter named Davis looked after her and cooked her vegetarian meals, but the most important member of her household was Rosalie Mansell, a trained nurse who acted as secretary and took care of the clinic downstairs. She had been a matron in the Lambeth Infirmary, where her remarkable efficiency had brought her to Mrs Despard's notice, and when she came to work for Charlotte Despard in 1898, this talent enabled her employer to carry the battle against darkness into yet another field.

Public education, as instituted by Forster's Act of 1870, acknowledged no responsibility for pupils beyond teaching them in the classroom, but Charlotte Despard, seeing childhood as a whole, could not accept such a rigid limitation. The effects of semi-starvation came before her every day in the clinic in the form of rickets, consumption and chronic ill health, and in a thoroughly practical way she had become convinced that before education could begin, the children had to be properly fed and reasonably healthy – 'nourish the body and the brain will benefit' was her slogan. Since the doubts of intellect did not bind her, she could act where more sensible people had found good reason to do nothing, and so in 1899, having had herself elected a manager of the two Nine Elms elementary schools, she lost no time in putting her ideas into effect.

Until her appearance, the managers had followed the precepts of the Education Act, and their meetings consisted of a monotonous consideration of exam results, blocked lavatories, the Inspector's annual report, and complaints about children throwing stones over the wall on to the Conservative Club's bowling green. At her first meeting the new member put forward her theory about nutrition, and proposed that three unused rooms in one of the schools should be transformed into dining rooms and a kitchen. When the Board decided that money could not legally be spent on such a project, Charlotte Despard suggested that she might provide the saucepans, stove, tables and benches herself.

With an effort still visible in the minutes, the Board stirred itself to the point of refusing either to aid or to obstruct her, but that was encouragement enough. The equipment was brought in, volunteers were rounded up, and early in 1899 Nine Elms had a school-meals service for the poorest children, seven years before the government first authorized education authorities to offer such a service. Finding its hand forced, the School Board eventually set up a Committee for Underfed Children to raise funds and run the scheme officially; and when unemployment soared in the winter of 1904 over one hundred children were being fed daily.

The members of the Board were better prepared to resist when Mrs Despard brought to their notice the lamentable number of barefoot children arriving at school. They assured her that there were very few who could not afford boots, and, when that still did not convince her, they insisted that in any case the problem was of such long standing that it could be regarded as a fact of life. Refusing to be fobbed off, she tried to enlist the support of the Inspector of Education, but her colleagues persuaded him that the matter was too small to merit his attention. Forced once more to act on her own initiative, Charlotte Despard set up a fund, with the help of the Ragged School Union, to buy boots. No fewer than two hundred pairs were distributed in the first year – either free or for a shilling each, depending on the family's circumstances – and the money raised was put aside for future emergencies.

In the same high-handed fashion she forced upon the Board the first school clinic in the country, responding to their protestation that the expense did not justify it, nor the law permit it, by employing Rosalie Mansell to examine and treat the children. The work went ahead with medicine and equipment from her own clinic, and once again the Board was presented with a *fait accompli*. Reluctantly the other members agreed to form a Health Committee, and the medical inspection of the children was put on an official basis. Since almost a quarter of those examined proved to be suffering from various effects of malnutrition, ranging from rotten teeth to rickets, the school clinic could be little more than a palliative; but, by identifying the extent of ill health, it helped to prepare the way for the establishment of such clinics on a national basis six years later.

The obstruction of the law, and the managers' maddening lack of initiative, were further evidence of the inefficiency of mono-sexual government and administration. When children could not learn because of illness or poor nutrition, the refusal to spend a relatively small amount on their health and feeding, compared to the huge cost of buildings and staff, seemed such an obviously false economy that Charlotte Despard was forced to the conclusion that women saw these things more clearly than men. They were, she thought, 'gifted with an intuitive faculty which much exceeds that of men . . . They could place their finger on the political mistake or the economic fallacy which mars the usefulness of well-intentioned laws.'

The argument for enfranchising women had become over-whelming; yet the most optimistic adult suffragist thought it would be twenty years before they achieved their aims. Impatiently, Charlotte Despard chafed at the prospect of so long a delay. She had searched for alternatives, but there appeared to be no way past this administrative barrier to the spiritual revolution. In desperation she turned to 'the other side' for guidance. Mazzini, her old mentor, did not let her down, and in great excitement she took the results to Margaret Bondfield. The latter confessed she found them 'interesting, but not convincing', but Charlotte Despard had no doubts that among the random scrawls of her automatic writing a clear message could be distinguished. 'Great upheavals predicted', she wrote in delight, ' – and a Coming.' Eagerly she scanned the world outside for signs of the prophecy's fulfilment.

6

'The history of the twentieth century', Charlotte Despard once predicted, 'will show the rise of two great movements – women and labour.' As we near the end of the century, there seems little doubt about the accuracy of her forecast. It was based on the premise that the Industrial Revolution had destroyed the independence of both men and women. When mass production replaced cottage industry, the nineteenth-century industrialist, who moulded other men into wage-slaves, simultaneously made of women house-slaves:

Compare our own days . . . with the days when much of the work done in factories was done at home, and done by women under the supervision of women, baking, brewing, curing meats, preserving fruit and vegetables, spinning and weaving. . . . Because industry belongs to man, because in an earlier era, he removed it from the home to the factory he is jealous of her presence there. . . . The soft, fragile girl of the mid-Victorian era, who faded into the pale and submissive housewife, was his creation. She made a fine foil to his strength, and she ministered to his glory.

It followed, therefore, that women seeking to regain their independence should unite with workers in the face of their common enemy, the patriarchal, capitalist system, and all Charlotte Despard's work in the suffrage movement was to be devoted to that end. She was fighting against formidable odds; for, just as socialists betrayed the prejudices of the working class, so the suffragists adopted the outlook of the middle class.

The long battle to enfranchise women had begun in 1867, when John Stuart Mill moved that they be included in the Reform Bill then before the Commons. His amendment was lost amid much jocularity, but in 1872 the National Society for Women's Suffrage could claim that, during the previous session of Parliament, over 350,000 people had signed petitions in its favour. The surging advance since Mill's lone voice had been raised five years earlier, justified the Society's confidence in its strategy. Its pamphlet declared:

Women are not prepared to break any pailing [*sic*], material or meta-physical, albeit that they have been taunted with the indifference they thus betray for their rights. But it is just possible that keeping the peace and signing petitions to Parliament may eventually be thought almost as well to prove their fitness for a voice in the Legislature of this country.

That reasonable tone went well with the simultaneous push to admit women to the universities and medical colleges, and the success of the latter seemed to be matched in the political sphere, for when the last great Reform Bill of the nineteenth century was introduced, in 1884, the Society's strategy had won them the promised support of a majority of private members. In the event, they proved to be fair-weather friends, and in the storm of Gladstone's opposition the majority disappeared. Among those who sided with Gladstone was the homespun figure of Herbert Asquith, and the opposing minority included the elegant Arthur Balfour; their opinions on the subject, like the behaviour of the Commons as a whole, remained consistent for the next thirty years.

The National Society for Women's Suffrage did not long survive its humiliation. Internal dissension split it apart in 1888, and only local groups remained to keep the question alive. In 1897 Mrs Millicent Fawcett, the widow of Gladstone's Postmaster-General, created the National Union of Women's Suffrage Societies to unify the groups scattered across the country. Inheriting the remnants of the old Society, the National Union also inherited its policies and its temperate, rational, middle-class nature, which was congenial to Mrs Fawcett. Plump-faced and friendly though she was, her placid surface was the result of constant self-discip-line, learned through difficult years of caring for her blind husband. She was not of a sort to be shaken from her ideals by the slow progress of her cause.

Such working-class support as the National Union commanded came from Lancashire, where Eva Gore-Booth's North of England Society for Women's Suffrage had achieved some success among the vast army of women in the textile mills. In 1903, a member of the society, Emmeline Pankhurst, widow of a Labour lawyer, broke away to form the Women's Social and Political Union, with the intention of recruiting particularly among working women.

The area chosen by Emmeline Pankhurst's new group brought it into direct conflict with the adult suffragists, and Teresa Billington, one of its leading organizers, bitterly remarked that 'Margaret Bondfield and Mary MacArthur laboured against us and made havoc of the support we had collected.' Superficially there was little difference between claiming the vote for every adult, male and female, and demanding it on the same grounds 'as it is or may be held by men'; but suspicion about each other's motives gave the difference a bitter edge. 'Adult suffragists' were believed to be ready to abandon the women's side of their case, as their colleagues on the Continent had done, thus stamping the vote as the exclusive privilege of men. On the other hand, 'women suffragists' were prepared to accept a franchise limited to rate-paying women, and that would confirm it as a right of property. The rivalry was the more intense because both the adult suffragists and the Pankhursts' WSPU were aiming first at the conversion of the ILP (to which each was affiliated) and eventually of the Labour Party as a whole. Thus, when the WSPU embodied its demands in a model Bill, which would enfranchise those women who met the property qualifications of the 1884 Reform Act, their opponents contemptuously dismissed it as 'a rich woman's charter'.

In 1905, the WSPU seemed to have won the battle, because the ILP proposed to the Labour Party conference that women's suffrage should become the party's policy. But the enemy had outflanked them and, instead, the conference voted in favour of adult suffrage. It was a crucial moment, for the WSPU had either to settle for a gradualist approach – to become, as it were, a Labour equivalent of the National Union – or it had to change its tactics.

There was nothing of the long view in Emmeline Pankhurst's character. An impetuous temperament carried her into the movement and her vitality lent it the excitement of cocaine, but her loyalty was to people rather than ideals. Perhaps as a result of their superior education, her three daughters preferred causes. Christabel, the eldest, had a disciplined intellect which allowed her to win a first-class degree in law amid the distractions of the suffrage campaign, and although there was no doubt that she was intellectually arrogant she had good cause to be so. She was of a different generation to the other suffrage leaders, and it is significant that she had grown up in the era of the popular press when, for the first time, photographs and large type were used to carry the sensation of an event to every literate person in the country.

When the Labour Party's adoption of adult suffrage seemed to condemn the WSPU to share the ineffectuality of Mrs Fawcetts' followers, Christabel was not inclined, either by age or temperament, to accept the verdict meekly. She decided on direct tactics and, through a genius for publicity, made a campaign out of a debate. In October 1905, with the end of ten weary years of Conservative government in sight, two senior members of the Liberal Party, Winston Churchill and Sir Edward Grey, came to speak at the Free Trade Hall in Manchester, and there Christabel Pankhurst and Annie Kenney confronted them with the question, 'Will the Liberal Government give women the vote?' When there was no reply, they heckled and were ejected, and on the steps of the Hall Christabel spat, or pretended to spit, at a policeman. It was a technical assault and, when she refused to pay the fine, the magistrate had no option but to send her to prison for seven days.

'The value of a sentiment', wrote Galsworthy, 'is the amount of sacrifice you are prepared to make for it.' By that estimation, the vote was suddenly seen to be valued very high indeed, as much as liberty itself, and no amount of oratory in chilly halls and comfortable drawing-rooms could have forced women to face the abstract idea in more concrete form. A thousand people came to demonstrate at the prison, two thousand to welcome Annie Kenney on her release, and the Free Trade Hall was filled to the doors to hear Christabel Pankhurst speak. Helena Swanwick, later President of the Women's International League, wrote: '. . . their challenge had this effect on me (as it did on countless other women) that, believing in the enfranchisement of women, I could not keep out of this struggle at this time. It bludgeoned my conscience.' And in Nine Elms, Charlotte Despard discerned the possibility of a new dawn: 'I asked myself, "Can this be the beginning? Is this indeed a part of that revolutionary movement for which all my life long I have been waiting?" '

The question was not easily answered. She was attracted by the WSPU's impetuosity, yet repelled by its advocacy of a partial franchise, and a brief encounter with Emmeline Pankhurst in July 1905 had emphasized the difference in their priorities. As a result of the grave level of unemployment, at its highest since 1894, George Lansbury had organized a deputation of a thousand working women from Poplar to put their case to the Prime Minister, Arthur Balfour, for the passage of an Unemployment Relief Bill. Part of the deputation was led by Mrs Scurr, a brush-maker and later a suffragist of forceful temper, and two woman Guardians, Charlotte Despard and Anne Cobden Sanderson, all three of whom addressed the women at Caxton Hall before their meeting with the Prime Minister. They were joined on the plat-form by Emmeline Pankhurst, and there were considerable mis-givings when she urged the audience to use the opportunity to demand the vote. Since it was thought that few of the women there would have been enfranchised by the WSPU Bill, her attempted takeover left a sour taste.

The short wave of publicity that Christabel earned produced in most Labour circles a rather jaundiced reaction. Having con-trived her own arrest, it was thought somewhat hypocritical that she should then claim to be a martyr. The general mood was expressed by Eva Gore-Booth, who broke with her altogether, saying, 'you can't tell one tale in Manchester and another in Oldham'. But one Labour man did support the Pankhursts whole-heartedly, and they could have had no better advocate.

An old friend of the Pankhursts, Keir Hardie well understood the splendour of Christabel's defiance, since he himself was, in G. D. H. Cole's words, 'Above all else a protestant, happiest when he was flouting authority against some inhumane abuse.' He was a convert to women's suffrage long before Christabel's imprison-ment, and had produced for it a telling defence against the accusa-tion of elitism. At his instigation, the ILP had conducted a poll among women who paid municipal rates* and would thus be eligible to vote under the WSPU Bill. The result, which was hotly disputed, showed that, of 59,000 women interviewed, 83 per cent might be regarded as working-class. Opponents emphasized that the sample was small and the criteria vague, but Hardie remained undeterred.

* A judicial decision, known as the 'latch-key' judgement, defined 'a ratepayer' under the 1884 Act to include anyone who paid rent in a household rated at £10 or more and who possessed his own key.

It was his personal intervention that finally resolved Charlotte Despard's doubts. Keir Hardie represented all the qualities she found admirable in the working-man – his bluntness, his integrity, his ability to rise above circumstance, and his 'feminine' capacity for indignation. For her, as for most of the country, he was the incarnation of the ILP, and when he argued that the WSPU Bill was acceptable as 'a first step' not even Margaret Bondfield could dissuade her from listening. He pointed out to her the results of his poll, and the length of time needed to achieve adult suffrage; and, most tellingly, he stressed that the WSPU Bill enfranchised widows, most of whom were indubitably working class, simply because working-men married earlier and died sooner than any other class. Remembering the widow with six children who had applied for relief, Charlotte Despard abandoned her last reservation. 'There is no class of the community to whom the vote would be more precious,' she wrote in an article after her conversion to the cause, 'no class who deserve it more than these working-widows.'

By the summer of 1906, when her doubts had finally been resolved, she was in a position to give her full energy to the suffrage movement. Two years earlier she had given up 95 Wandsworth Road, and since she no longer had a residence in Lambeth she had resigned from the Board of Guardians. She served a further year on the Wandsworth Poor Law Board, but this was an enlightened Board which did not, she decided, require her presence. Her brief tenure had, however, brought her in touch with the Tammany Hall kingdom of John Burns, which controlled Battersea Council and the Poor Law Board. In Charlotte Despard's eyes, Burns was the great apostate. Since his election to Parliament in 1892, his socialism had deteriorated from revolutionary to municipal, and he had now stepped into the Liberals' camp in hope of a Cabinet post at the next General Election. For his public libraries, baths and housing she had the highest admiration, but of the man she used to quote:

> Just for a handful of silver he left us,
> Just for a medal to hang on his breast.

His defection had split the Labour Party in Battersea, but his political machine, which commanded votes and jobs, made it plain that it had no place for idealists. Denied the scope for local work, Charlotte Despard's mind was further concentrated on the wider issue of the vote.

Once she had made the decision to join, she was seduced, as thousands of others were to be seduced, by the atmosphere of women working for one another:

I had found comradeship of some sort with men. I had marched with great processions of the unemployed, I had stood on platforms with Labour men and Socialists. . . . I had listened with sympathy to furious denunciations of the government and the Capitalistic system to which they belong. Amongst all these experiences, I had not found what I met on the threshold of this young, vigorous union of hearts.

In the springtime of its life, the Women's Social and Political Union showed its most attractive face. The liveliness and fierce energy of its Lancashire origins had been transferred to London after the long-expected victory of the Liberal Party in January 1906, and the capital was now witness to what militancy meant. They took with them high spirits, a certain provincial touchiness, edging into arrogance, and the intoxicating certainty that they had found the key to the suffrage lock. 'Tell the women not to be afraid and to follow us,' Annie Kenney wrote to an organizer in the East End before one demonstration; 'if they say it is too soon, tell them we have thought it out carefully and we know it is the best thing to do.' In February, Teresa Billington and she led a great march of working women from the East End to Westminster to mark the opening of the new Parliament, and the novelty of women demonstrating for the vote was still fresh enough to be front-page news in the popular press. There was less attention paid to the sort of street-corner meeting described by Alice Milne: 'The audience had to be started almost by lassooing individuals – to a crowd of ten Mrs Drummond started, it grew to twenty, Mrs Pankhurst built it up, others followed until there were some hundreds listening, and many sympathetic.' That, and countless similar scenes, passed unnoticed; but the spotlight returned for such an exploit as the April demonstration in the Ladies' Gallery of the House of Commons, when members of the WSPU interrupted the debate with shouts and a shower of leaflets. 'The shrieking sisterhood' was the epithet of the popular press; the more serious referred to 'female hooligans', but soon almost everyone was using the *Daily Mail*'s description, 'suffragettes'.

The difference between the suffragists and the suffragettes was compared by Mrs Fawcett, the doyenne of the former, to the difference between the nineteenth-century leaders of the Irish party, Isaac Butt and Charles Stewart Parnell: 'Mr Butt was a genial gentleman who got nothing. Mr Parnell ... got Land Acts, the three F's, extension of the franchise, and practically anything he wanted short of Home Rule.' By flouting the conventions of the House of Commons so that all other business was prevented, Parnell had focused attention upon a problem to which most MPs had been indifferent or hostile, but for which, out of sheer self-interest, they were forced to produce a solution. The analogy was not lost on the suffragettes, but they overlooked two consequences of Parnellism. In the first place, the rules of the Commons had been reformed so that all its business was strictly controlled by the government of the day; in the second place, the Liberals, who had been split by the Irish question, were left with a deep trauma about any matter which threatened to divide them again. The suffragettes might have 'a conclusive and irrefutable case', as the Prime Minister, Sir Henry Campbell-Bannerman, assured them in May, but while his Cabinet remained divided, he would not allow Parliamentary time for a suffrage Bill: 'educate the country,' he advised, 'agitate and pester the government', and his advice proved a torment to his successor.

Until July, Emmeline and Christabel Pankhurst were detained in Manchester by their respective duties as Registrar of Births and Deaths, and as law student. The motive power in London was supplied by Annie Kenney and Teresa Billington, who directed their energies at the sort of ILP supporter they were accustomed to finding in Lancashire. In April, the first London branch was founded, with women like Anne Cobden Sanderson and Edith How Martyn, well-educated Labour sympathizers, among its members. The most radical of the Pankhursts, Sylvia, was the Union's secretary, and when she resigned in June to continue her art studies it was politically consistent that Charlotte Despard should have been appointed in her stead. (The demands of her Nine Elms work required her to share the post with Edith How Martyn – a shy, clever person, and the first woman to win a Bachelor of Science degree.) Yet it was a straw in the wind that Emmeline Pankhurst should have expressed the fear that Christabel might resent an appointment made without her approval.

On her arrival in London in July, Christabel Pankhurst lodged with Emmeline and Frederick Pethick Lawrence in their flat at Clements Inn. The Lawrences were wealthy socialists, whose flair for administration and finance had transformed the chaos of unpaid bills and overbooked calendars at headquarters into 'a smoothly organised management machine', as Teresa Billington put it. In the interests of efficiency the headquarters had been transferred to offices beneath their flat, an arrangement which proved unexpectedly useful to Christabel Pankhurst's ambitions. Amalgamating the Lawrences' talents with her won political expertise, she soon established a triumvirate to run the Union.

Teresa Billington was despatched to organize branches in Scotland, Annie Kenney on a similar mission to the West Country, and the two secretaries were discreetly bypassed. Quite abruptly the East End work lost much of its impetus, and instead drawing-room meetings in the West End and the suburbs became more common. A weekly 'At Home' was instituted so that interested ladies could meet Christabel Pankhurst at Clements Inn. Alice Milne, a Lancashire textile worker, was slightly shocked by the sort of people she saw there:

We found the place full of fashionable ladies in rustling silks and satins. . . . It struck me then that if any of our Adult Suffrage Socialist friends could have looked into that room, he would have said more than ever that ours was a movement for the middle classes and upper classes. What a fever our Union members in Manchester would have been in, if such ladies made a descent on us in Manchester!

Christabel Pankhurst was neither the first nor the last young provincial to be gulled into thinking that fashionable metropolitans were as influential as they believed themselves to be, and the consequence was to be seen in the rapid metamorphosis of the WSPU from a Labour to an establishment pressure group.

An October by-election at Cockermouth in Cumberland gave Christable Pankhurst her first opportunity to reveal the new political stance. Instead of supporting the Labour candidate, she announced that the WSPU would be independent of all parties which did not advocate women's suffrage. The change in direction caused no disquiet, and even Charlotte Despard, the most left-wing of Labour supporters, favoured political neutrality, on the ground that the women's movement was too idealistic to engage in party politics. But in successive by-elections, a bias towards the Conservative candidate gradually developed as the WSPU's overriding purpose of putting pressure on the Liberal government translated itself into support for the official opposition. In sympathy as well as membership, the WSPU was drifting on to a Conservative course by the spring of 1907.

Charlotte Despard was slow to see the danger. Emotion rather than the detail of policy concerned her and, at the very moment when the first suspicions and jealousies were beginning to split the WSPU apart, she listed among its attractions: 'True love of comrades, strenuous co-operation of those who have realized that union means strength, [and] a firm faith in a fair vision of the future.' Neither then nor later did she ever alter her opinion that the most exciting discovery of the suffrage campaign was the atmosphere of women working together, for themselves and by themselves. No political difference could shake her faith in the essential unity that came from sharing the same sexual fate of enforced passivity, and the same sexual exhilaration in militant action. The thrill of defying convention gave the WSPU élan and driving power, and provided Charlotte Despard with another, more naive, excuse for her failure to question the change of political alignment. The ultimate victory over social convention was to undergo the disgrace of imprisonment, and in her eyes it had conferred on Christabel Pankhurst a moral dominance which those still free had no right to question. Prison was a rite of initiation, and she looked forward to the experience with almost spiritual anticipation.

Her chance seemed to have come when she was invited to take part in a demonstration in the Lobby of the House of Commons, in October 1906, which carried a lively risk of arrest and imprisonment. To her chagrin, she was told on the day before the demonstration that officers of the WSPU were to avoid arrest. She did not observe this ruling too officiously. She was conspicuous among the crowd of women in the Lobby, and when police pulled Mary Gawthorpe, an elfin suffragette, off the bench from which she had tried to address the assembled visitors and MPs, it was Charlotte Despard who sprang up in her place. She too was hauled down, and every woman was cleared from the Lobby, passing an inspector at the door who called out the names of those he wanted arrested: 'Take Kenney, take Billington, take the two little

Pankhursts.' To her intense disappointment Charlotte Despard was hustled out under his eye without being named. Obedient to her instructions, she left the Commons without further protest, but was mortified to learn that Emmeline Pethick Lawrence, the treasurer, and Edith How Martyn, her fellow secretary, had flouted orders and pushed their way back into the Lobby to ensure their arrest.

The publicity gained by the Lobby demonstration was enormous, and it took its tone from the presence, among the ten women sent to prison, of Anne Cobden Sanderson, daughter of Richard Cobden, one of the founding fathers of modern Liberalism. The relationship was an embarrassment to the Liberal government, and her venerable figure made it impossible for the papers to categorize her as a member of the 'shrieking sisterhood'. Overnight they adopted a more sympathetic tone: 'No class ever got the vote except at the risk of something like revolution', declared the Liberal *Daily News*, and the *Daily Mirror* took a similar line, demanding, 'By what means, but by screaming, knocking and rioting did men themselves ever gain what they were pleased to call their rights?' When some of the older suffragists criticized the militants, Mrs Fawcett again defended their actions: '. . . far from having injured the movement', she wrote, 'they have done more during the last twelve months to bring it within the realm of practical politics than we have been able to accomplish in the same number of years.' Each act of militancy brought in a wave of recruits to every suffrage society, Mrs Fawcett's as much as Mrs Pankhurst's; nevertheless, it was a generous endorsement.

Suppressing her disappointment at remaining free, Charlotte Despard dealt as best she could with the mountain of work which the WSPU's popularity had created. Because office-work was never one of her strengths, another secretary, Caroline Hodgson, was appointed to help her, but she continued to feel that she could have served the WSPU better by going to prison.

When the Lobby prisoners were released, she felt that she had fulfilled her obligations, and on 20 November returned to the House of Commons to address an unauthorized meeting from beneath the statue of Richard the Lion-Heart. As she had hoped, the police intervened and took both her and her companion, Alice Milne, down to Cannon Row police station, but only the latter was charged, although she had not spoken a word to the crowd.

Frustrated once again, Charlotte Despard returned to King Richard's statue and made another speech, but by then it was evening and there were few people left to hear the words of an angry old lady spoken in the gathering gloom.

The magistrate before whom Alice Milne appeared remarked that it was clear the police had been acting 'under instructions' in letting her better-known companion go free. Presumably the Home Secretary, Herbert Gladstone, wished to avoid the sort of publicity which Anne Cobden Sanderson's arrest had stirred up, since Charlotte Despard was known to thousands for her work in Nine Elms, and to hundreds of thousands as the sister of the Boer War hero. The suffragettes preferred to believe, more dramatically, that the government feared a riot in Battersea; while the newspapers repeated the rumour that her brother had threatened to resign from the Army if she appeared in court. Rapid promotion since the Boer War had brought Sir John French to within a fingerhold of the Army's most influential post, Inspector-General of the Forces. He was the personal choice of Haldane, the Secretary for War, who considered him the most promising general in the Army, and as such his resignation would be awkward, both militarily and politically. Whatever the reason, it seemed that the stakes were loaded against the arrest of the secretary of the WSPU.

Liberty was irksome. Just as she had felt unqualified to speak for the poor until she lived as they did, so she considered herself an apprentice suffragette until she had undergone the craft's initiation of imprisonment. She had failed twice, but a third opportunity presented itself at the opening of the new session of Parliament in February 1907.

On the day that the male legislators were to hear the King's Speech outlining the government's programme for the coming year, a 'Woman's Parliament' was summoned to meet at Caxton Hall. Some four hundred women assembled to be addressed by the leaders of the WSPU. One after the other, the speakers presented the irrefutable case for women's suffrage, demonstrated the grotesque injustices that stemmed from its denial, and pointed to the stark conclusion – reason was not enough, militancy alone could win them justice. Every speech was punctuated by reports brought in from Parliament, a scant thousand yards away, of the government's latest proposals. Each one – education, licensing, land taxation – affected women as mothers, wives or citizens, yet there came no news of women's enfranchisement. It was like a dark counterpoint to the flaming words delivered from the platform, and the women's fury rose higher until the last message arrived that the King's Speech was ended without mention of the vote.

At once Emmeline Pankhurst moved that a resolution condemning the omission be delivered to the Prime Minister, and there was an angry shout of acclamation. 'Rise up women!' she called, and back came the impatient answer, 'Now, now!' Before anyone else could move, Charlotte Despard, alight with the temper of battle, came down from the platform, and led the surging crowd out into the drizzling February afternoon. As they moved down the narrow street towards Westminster, umbrellas began to mushroom along the line of marching women, and from under their protecting shelter there emerged the familiar strains of 'John Brown's Body' with the unfamiliar words of the Women's Anthem:

'Rise up women for the fight is hard and long,
Rise in thousands singing loud a battle song.
Right is might and in its strength we shall be strong
And the cause goes marching on.'

They emerged into the open space by Westminster Abbey as a column four deep, and the blocks of police stationed there attempted to split them up into small groups. The women eddied round their lines and moved on as a solid phalanx towards the House of Commons. At their head marched Charlotte Despard, by now so determined on arrest that she had taken the precaution of camouflaging her familiar appearance under a thick motor-veil, which streamed out behind her in the breeze.

In front of the Commons was a double line of policemen, and a number on horseback drawn up on one side. Without a plan, but inspired by the prospect, Charlotte Despard flourished her umbrella like a standard and led the singing army into Palace Yard. As though they were not there she walked straight into the police line, and at once her followers pressed in behind and around her. The foot police heaved back and the mounted police began to back their horses into the press, trying to break it up. 'Something like pandemonium ensued,' the *Daily Mirror* reported. 'The women began to fight like tigers and they received and inflicted many bruises. Over the whole extent of Palace Yard a dense mass of people swayed and heaved.' The police had been told to avoid making arrests if possible, and for a time there was a stalemate as they tried to push the women back. In the crush, Charlotte Despard almost had her back broken when the weight of a policeman's horse trapped her against the unyielding line of constables on foot. Then the order was given to make arrests, and one of them seized her, so roughly that the sleeve of her coat was ripped off. She was escorted down to Cannon Row police station, and there, to her unconcealed pleasure, was formally charged and arrested. 'I am heartily glad to have done it at last', she told the reporters afterwards, and waved away any suggestion that the police had been less than kind. In her hour of triumph she could afford to be generous.

Her brother, however, was distinctly testy. He offered brusque sympathy for any hurt she might have suffered, but added, '. . . if she insists on joining in with these people she must expect it. We have tried all we could to keep her from mixing up with these foolish women. . . . They are all vain and some of them are a little mad I think.' When reporters asked him whether the arrest would indeed provoke his resignation, he replied irritably, 'What has it to do with me? I wish she wouldn't do these things, but I can't prevent her.' It was not the last coolness between them, but the warmth always returned. Charlotte was unable to believe very seriously in his public manner – she took it to be a game, her darling Jack being military – and in the end her unfaltering affection succeeded in assuaging his wrath. After her release from prison, she wrote admiringly to congratulate him on his appointment as Inspector-General. They were each getting ahead in their respective careers.

On 14 February, having refused to pay a forty-shilling fine, she was taken with thirty-one others to begin her initiation – twenty-one days in Holloway, in the second division. To modern eyes, the remarkable feature of the prison regime was that, except for half an hour of communal exercise, during which prisoners were forbidden to talk, they were kept in solitary confinement twenty-four hours a day. Her cell was 'dirty, dimly-lit . . . with a strange, sickening smell in it. It was stone-paved, and there was a narrow stone bench in one of the angles. Nothing else except a barred window high up in the wall.' There was a spyhole in the door, which mesmerized her like an eye gazing at her with an unwinking stare. After a week she was unable to sleep, read or concentrate, and one evening in February, when a dull cloud of London fog oozed around the gas jet which lit her cell, she almost collapsed, suffocated by 'all the undeserved, manufactured pain that was living and breathing in the fortress'. Prison was a spiritual wasteland. Locked away, yet always within range of the spyhole, she was alone but had no solitude. The stone cell echoed to the crash of keys, the thud of boots and the shouted commands of wardresses outside. There was neither interest nor kindness shown. Voices snapped out orders, food was slammed down and the cell inspection was a brisk drill ended by the door banging shut again on loneliness. She had taken three books with her, Shelley's *Collected Poems*, Mill's *The Subjection of Women* and Thomas à Kempis' *Imitation of Christ*, and in the last of these she had marked a passage for her own guidance: 'For Thy life is our path, and by Holy Patience we walk unto Thee who art our crown.' In the outside world it was a text which she found useful when her hot temper flared up, but amid the mindless cruelty of prison she found its quiescence irritating. During exercise she saw the effect of the regime on the faces of the women prisoners – prostitutes, petty thieves and drunkards – a worn, stupid look to which she reacted angrily, 'one may have too much patience. *They* have.'

When she emerged in March, prison had lost both its glamour and its terror, and was seen for the sterile and degrading place it was. At the same time, the moral stature she had imputed to those suffragettes who had undergone the experience before her was sharply diminished. When other ILP members began to feel disquiet about the political direction in which the Pankhursts were steering the WSPU, she felt competent to give a lead to their protest. Together with Anne Cobden Sanderson, Edith How Martyn and others, she bound herself not to engage in any activity which might injure Labour's interests, and a message to this effect was sent to the ILP conference in April. In it they pledged their support for the Party, and added that, to avoid any conflict of interest, they would refuse to work in any by-election in which a Labour candidate was standing. As a challenge to Christabel Pankhurst's leadership, it was the essence of moderation, almost dove-like in its innocence; but a challenge of sinister proportions it was taken to be.

When the message was read out at the conference, Emmeline Pankhurst, who was present, understood it to be a pledge never to appear at any by-election *except* to support a Labour candidate. At once she came to her feet, and declared, 'We are not going to wait until the Labour party can give us the vote. It is by putting pressure on the present government that we shall get it.'

For three years the Pankhursts had tried to persuade the ILP to support women's suffrage; they had endured its rule-book prevarication in the obscurity of ILP committee rooms, and its overt hostility in scarcely less obscure ILP halls. Now, at the head of a movement more glamorous, more daring, and more revolutionary than the dim bureaucracy of Labour, they decided to cut loose from the hamper of its indifference. They resigned from the ILP and, soon afterwards, Christabel was in friendly correspondence with Arthur Balfour, the leader of the Conservative Party.

When Charlotte Despard and her friends tried to find a way of putting a brake on this proclivity towards the Tories, they found there was no means of influencing the leaders. While the movement was young, the informality of a small and busy office ensured that everyone's opinion was heard, but the WSPU had grown out of all recognition. In October 1906 there had been no more than half a dozen branches, and the Clements Inn headquarters were run on a financial shoestring. Six months later, there were fifty-eight branches, and income at headquarters had risen to £100 a week, but the executive structure had not altered. Administration and finance were controlled by the Pethick Lawrences, and tactics were the preserve of the organizing secretary, Christabel Pankhurst. The WSPU's president, Emmeline Pankhurst, was by far its most popular figure, but then her character was designed for loyalty; she had devoted herself to her husband in his lifetime, and now she put all her energies at the service of her eldest daughter. Between the leaders and the ordinary members there was an invisible wall, and behind it the triumvirate could afford to ignore opposition, as completely as the Prime Minister ignored them.

Next to Emmeline Pankhurst, the most popular person in the WSPU was probably Teresa Billington Greig,* whose appearances in London aroused scenes of enthusiasm to rival the President's.

---

* She had married in 1906, and added her husband's name to her own.

She was a fine, demagogic speaker, passionate and satirical by turn, and proof of her ability as an organizer could be found in the largest branches – in London and Scotland – both of which she had founded. Before the WSPU had even moved to London, she had suggested that it should adopt a constitution based on the ILP's and, after some inconclusive exchanges, had drawn up a version herself, which was unveiled at the October meeting to finalize plans for the Lobby demonstration. Amid the general euphoria, it had been accepted without question, but its significance, indeed all memory of it, had been swept away in the excitement. For different reasons, Teresa Billington and the ILP members now decided that it should be brought into operation.

Like the ILP, the WSPU consisted of autonomous branches affiliated to a central headquarters, and to this structure the constitution proposed to add an annual conference, to which branches could send delegates in order to approve the broad lines of policy and to elect the officers. That conference was due to take place in October 1907.

A little cautiously, Charlotte Despard and the other ILP members began to put forward their case to the branches. They were reluctant to oppose the Pankhursts openly, but their proposition that policy should be decided democratically appeared so eminently reasonable that it was widely accepted. Meanwhile, in Scotland, Teresa Billington Greig recruited with evangelical zeal, and having set up new branches in almost every major city she instituted in July an elective, semi-autonomous council to regulate suffrage activities there.

The growth of this powerful barony north of the border was a threat which the Pankhursts could not ignore, and Christabel wrote to her mother: 'Teresa Billington is a wrecker . . . we have just to face her and put her in her place. She has gone too far this time.' But the threat was not confined to Scotland. By August it was apparent that the majority of provincial branches intended to send delegates to the conference to question the WSPU's political alignment and, if necessary, to elect new officers.

To the triumvirate the situation seemed to promise catastrophe. 'Newcomers were pouring into the Union', wrote Emmeline Pethick Lawrence:

Many of them were quite ill-informed as far as the realities of the political situation were concerned. Christabel, who possessed in a high degree a flair for the intricacies of a complex political situation, had conceived the militant campaign as a whole. . . . She never doubted that the tactics she had evolved would succeed in winning a cause which, as far as argument or reason were concerned, was intellectually won already . . . she feared the ingrained inferiority complex in the majority of women. Thus she could not trust her mental offspring to the mercies of politically untrained minds.

In order to maintain their control, the triumvirate instituted a counter-plot to suggest that it was the constitutionalists who wished to subvert the WSPU from its political neutrality. They revived the canard that Charlotte Despard and her friends had pledged themselves only to support Labour candidates, and suggested that other, more base, impulses lay behind their enthusiasm for a constitution. This they made clear in a pamphlet published after the rupture:

While we have been occupied with the National Campaign the seventy branches have been used as a happy hunting ground for intriguers, whose device was to get control of the Union, to modify the policy of independence and change the methods of work. . . . Apart from those whose past association and life have been bound up with political causes that are dear to them and which they can hardly be expected at an advanced age to leave, we have against us others whose motives are less pure. . . . Always while we were hard at work they were getting hold of the local union and spreading suspicion and disaffection. . . . We yielded concession after concession in order to satisfy those who wanted to get power within the movement by other means than sheer devotion and hard work, but the power only made them stronger to spread disruption in the ranks. Then at last we saw clearly that nothing would satisfy them until they had the leaders of this movement completely down.

With their backs to the wall, the triumvirate summoned Emmeline Pankhurst back from a speaking tour in the North of England, and she unhesitatingly decided to abrogate the constitution. The Pankhursts *were* the WSPU, and those who would not follow them were seceders and should be shown to be so.

The first step was taken at committee meeting of the WSPU's officers on 10 September where Emmeline Pankhurst announced that the October conference would not take place. The constitution, she said, had been annulled and a new committee would be elected by those present. Apart from herself, they consisted of the treasurer, Emmeline Pethick Lawrence, the two secretaries, Charlotte Despard and Caroline Hodgson, and five paid organizers. The efficiency that made their demonstrations so impressive had thus been applied to the coup d'état, so that its prime beneficiary, Christabel Pankhurst, could be absent, but a majority be guaranteed by the presence of the organizers. Charlotte Despard did not yield without a fight. Angrily she demanded to know on whose authority the changes had been made and, with the amused, self-composed air which was typical of her, Emmeline Pankhurst replied that she alone was responsible. A new organization, the National Women's Social and Political Union, had been formed, and no one could serve on its committee who was not in absolute accord with her. She then read out the names of the new committee, with the pledge each had to sign: 'I endorse the objects and methods of the NWSPU and I hereby undertake not to support the candidate of any political party at Parliamentary elections until women have obtained the Parliamentary vote.'

As they had anticipated, Charlotte Despard refused to sign such a sweeping endorsement – the undertaking of political neutrality being no more than a smokescreen. She declared that she would wait until the pledge had been approved by the conference. But, unexpectedly, Caroline Hodgson did put her name to it, which undermined the fiction that they had both seceded. Undeterred by the detail, the putsch rolled on. That evening a meeting of the London members, those most loyal to the Pankhursts, took place at the Essex Hall. Standing on the platform, Emmeline Pankhurst told them of the plots and stratagems that had been hatched in the dark shadow of the constitution. With a dramatic gesture she held out a copy of the offensive document, and, amid shouts of approval and protest, ripped it in two. With her vicarious ambition, with her haste, her boldness and resolution, there was more than a hint of Lady Macbeth in Emmeline Pankhurst; 'a woman self-inspired,' wrote Teresa Billington Greig, 'possessed with the spirit of hurry and impatience, paying any price her aims demand, but paying every price with a pang.'

Deprived of the great engine-power of the Pankhursts and the unmatched efficiency of the Pethick Lawrences, the constitutionalists might have been expected to wither quietly away. Certainly there was little enough but the sense of rightness to sustain them immediately after the rupture. Seventy of them gathered on 14 September to plan their strategy, and resolved to follow the rejected constitution faithfully in every detail. To strengthen their claim to legitimacy, they elected the secretary of the original WSPU to the chair of a provisional committee instructed to organize the conference, and by that (largely symbolic) move they ensured that their movement was ineradicably stamped by the piercing and idiosyncratic vision of Charlotte Despard.

When the conference met on 12 October, with its legal standing strengthened by the presence of delegates from a majority of the extant and solvent branches, there was an angry demand that the Pankhursts be sued for the return of funds, literature and offices rightfully belonging to the WSPU. For the first time Charlotte Despard made her influence felt when she persuaded the delegates that the larger importance of the women's movement must override the instinct for revenge, and the Pankhursts were accordingly left in undisturbed possession. Even the title, Women's Social and Political Union, was conceded to them some six weeks later, when the members decided to choose a new name to avoid confusion. 'There was little to be expected from a society', Teresa Billington Greig later wrote, 'that commenced its separate existence by making a free gift of the funds, name, prestige and achievements, which had been acquired by the efforts of all combined.' But, under its new banner of the Women's Freedom League, the society defied expectations by outliving, outworking and outfeminizing every other suffrage society. When it finally died away in 1961, it was the last survivor of the suffrage campaign and bore the honourable, but lonely, distinction of linking that early struggle for women's rights with the first stirrings of the women's movement today.

7

The newly hatched Women's Freedom League was a contradiction. Its members had refused the military discipline of the Pankhursts, but claimed to be militants. They declined to belong to Mrs Fawcett's constitutional movement, but devoted much time to the observance of their own constitution. They wished to be criminals and committee-women at once. The uncertainty of their perch required constant self-balancing between the heroics of militancy and the fussy irritations of democracy, and the process began with the selection of a title.

There is much significance in a name. The suggestions had ranged from the Women's Enfranchisement League to the Women Emancipators, and when a poll of the members produced a majority for Women's Freedom League neither the suffragists nor the feminists were satisfied. 'There is no great enthusiasm for the new name,' a member commented, 'but it has yet to gain respect and affection for the work done under it.' From the start, however, it symbolized the infinitely great ambitions of Charlotte Despard. Privately she thought of it as the League of Women for Freedom, and publicly told the League at its first conference, 'Our cause is not only votes for women, but the binding together of all womanhood with human rights.'

Her feminism was sketched in broader terms than that of any other suffrage leader, and its starting point was the importance of self-discovery. In 1910 she wrote:

Hypnotized by a false presentation of morality, religion and duty, we women have been cajoled or forced into a false conception of ourselves. We ask first for enlightenment. We wish using our own capacities, seeing with our own eyes, and not with the eyes of men to understand our true position, to see clearly what are our duties and our rights.

To throw light on that position she ranged far beyond the vote. When sweated women workers, forging iron chain at eight shillings a hundredweight, went on strike in 1910 for higher pay, she urged the League to support them because they were symbolically breaking the chains 'which woman has forged round her own consciousness from the moment she permitted herself to be the instrument of man's pleasure'. After meeting Booker T. Washington, the black advocate of equal racial rights, she used the example of Negro self-help to show that women too must rely on themselves, because the prejudices which enslaved them had also shackled the minds of men, and she used as an illustration the claim of the male worker to be paid more than his female counterpart since he was the breadwinner of a family: 'A shoddy sentimentality. It is worse than stupid, it is dangerous because it fosters the fatal error that women are and ought to be economically dependent on men.'

Finally, and insistently, she used the law's severity in cases of prostitution and infanticide to show the moral discrimination it exercised against the female sex. 'Women are legal slaves', she insisted, and the proof was that no male client ever appeared in the dock with a prostitute, nor the father with a mother accused of murdering her child. These were not popular causes to take up. When Daisy Lord, an unmarried nineteen-year-old, was found guilty of murdering her new-born baby, Charlotte Despard alone dared assert that the father was equally guilty, and that a bewildered homeless girl who had given birth only a few hours before could not possibly be deemed to be in her right mind except by an all-male jury. After attending the trial of another such case, she wrote angrily: 'There was not one incident which did not force upon us the bitter consciousness that under the present law woman is held to be the property of man.'

The goal of 'seeing with our own eyes and not with the eyes of men' was too massive to be reached by any one route. It required the exercise of democracy in the League, since 'women, trained through long ages to subjection, have even to learn to think independently'. It needed a sense of solidarity with all women; whether working, unemployed or criminal, 'the common sisterhood of woman' bound them all. Above anything else it required economic equality because, as she said, 'Fundamentally all social and political questions are economic.' With equal wages, the male worker would no longer fear that his female colleague might put him out of a job, and 'men and women will unite to effect a complete transformation of the industrial environment'. And in the home, a woman needed economic independence to live as an equal with her husband. 'It is indeed deplorable that the work of the wife and mother is not rewarded. I hope that the time will come when it is illegal for this strenuous form of industry to be un-remunerated.'

It was a noble attempt to grapple with a vast problem, but as a plan of campaign it lacked precision. In contrast, the Pankhursts offered a sharply defined goal and strategy, and by suggesting that enfranchisement symbolized emancipation they made the latter concrete and attainable by Act of Parliament.

Between the suffragettes and their goal lay the formidable hurdle of Asquith, Prime Minister since April 1908, who was hostile to the vote, personally and because it seemed that most of the women to be enfranchised would be Tories. With a majority of 84 overall, and the largely reliable support of 83 Irish and 53 Labour MPs, the Liberal government elected in 1906 could afford to ignore any opposition to its policies from outside Parliament, and indeed the subject of women's suffrage was not even raised in Cabinet until June 1910, after the Liberals' dominance had been wiped out. The only effectual opposition to the government came from the House of Lords, which hacked the heart out of Liberal legislation on schools, drink and electoral reform. Regard-less of Asquith's own dislike of women's suffrage, the conflict that developed between government and Lords quickly made the passage of any contentious measure an impossibility.

The political log-jam did not affect the WSPU's plans to win a quick victory. 'We are not a school for teaching women to use the vote,' Christabel Pankhurst told her followers soon after the split. 'We are a militant society, and we have to get the vote next session.' Haste was the keynote of her strategy, which concen-trated the whole brunt of its force on Westminster and Fleet Street. It combined Parnellism and public relations – a threat to the politician and a quote to the journalist – and its best example was the demonstration in Parliament Square in October 1908, when 60,000 women were summoned by poster and hand-bill to 'Rush the House of Commons'. The publicity was enormous, but it had the flavour of a stunt. The newspapers were alerted in ad-vance and, for all the wild rhetoric, the organizers, when charged in court, rested their defence on the very innocuousness of their intentions. Great rallies were held (almost half a million assembled in Hyde Park in June 1908) to show the mass support they commanded, and when the government remained unmoved, more demonstrations took place, and Cabinet Ministers were roughed up and shouted down.

The cause became better known and more women were attracted to it; but it was the same primitive excitement, writ large, as had been aroused when Christabel Pankhurst first went to jail in 1905. The argument was not elaborated – in fact it was simplified, to suit the intelligence of popular papers and young girls – and the vote, which once had been seen as an instrument for improving social conditions, was now demanded by the WSPU's leader for 'its symbolic value'. 'They want a measure of women's suffrage on the statute book', Teresa Billington Greig wrote, 'and they have engineered an advertising campaign to secure this end with the least possible delay.'

In retrospect it was a fatal error to abandon democracy and expel so many women with a wide experience of social reform; but at the time it appeared not to harm the WSPU, which soon became more popular than ever, nor did it seem to do the League much good. Reacting against the despotism of the Pankhursts, the League became determinedly democratic: there was no president, all officers were elected by the annual conference which also had to approve major policy decisions, and an elected executive committee exercised control over tactics. As a result its policy often gave the impression of being vague and inconsistent, and Teresa Billington Greig, the chief organizer, chafed against 'the development of red-tape democracy which caused the concentration of over-much attention upon matters of machinery and management'.

It was in the area of propaganda, which needed no democratic approval, that the League shone, and it pioneered a variety of methods of attracting attention to its demands. In November 1907, League members carrying sandwich-boards to advertise the vote stopped traffic in the streets; when Winston Churchill fought a by-election in Dundee in 1908, 'La Belle' Moloney earned her nickname by following him everywhere with her bell ringing like a bad conscience; and, at the opening of Parliament in 1909, Muriel Matters floated across London in a balloon, scattering leaflets from Hendon to Woolwich. They carried banners designed by Walter Crane; they performed a masque in which Ellen Terry starred; and Ella Wheeler Wilcox, author of *The Battle Hymn of the Republic*, wrote them a special anthem.

By contrast, the League's militancy was sober, being designed to make women conscious of their subjection to law or custom rather than create popular impact. Their first attempt to protest against the sexual inequality of trying prostitutes but not their clients was a failure. In the winter of 1907 they began to interrupt proceedings in such cases with shouts of 'Where's the male criminal?' and 'Equal rights for women' until they were ejected, but the protests were too sporadic to have effect. The instinct to go for the courts was sound, however, and when the League returned to the idea later it caused a dramatic upheaval.

When Parliament opened in February 1908, the same low-keyed approach dictated its tactics. Instead of employing the mass parade, which was thought to be 'self-advertising', small groups of women picketed the houses of Cabinet Ministers to remind them that women's suffrage had been omitted from the King's Speech. Ten were arrested and, for that mild prick to a politician's conscience, were sentenced to six weeks in the Third Division, which was reserved for 'prisoners of undesirable character'. The harshness of the verdict was without precedent. In recognition of the picketers' fate, the League instituted its own Victoria Cross for supreme gallantry, the Holloway Badge, and, at its second conference in February 1908, the delegates stood at Charlotte Despard's suggestion for a minute's silence in their memory.

That note of conscious self-dramatization was characteristic. There was a whiff of the schoolroom about the League in its early days, whether solemnly romanticizing its heroines, or plotting daring japes or enthusiastically rounding up helpers for meetings. High spirits helped to paper over the cracks of appalling poverty. A year's rent and expenses amounting to £100 had been guaranteed by Charlotte Despard for their first headquarters at 18 Buckingham Street, but there were only two guineas in the bank on the first day after the split, and every piece of furniture had to be begged from members. 'We began almost to live in Buckingham Street', Marion Holmes recollected ten years later:

What jolly 'scratch' teas we had on the bare office tables, and what startling plots and plans we hatched round them! Everyone took a willing hand in the cleaning and washing up, and it was no unusual thing to see Mrs Billington-Greig or Miss Irene Miller, or some other favourite orator suddenly down her broom or tea-cloth and rush off with a belated memory of an expectant audience.

The adolescent atmosphere was not deceptive. They were just beginning to find themselves as independent people, and the sensation was that of youth. Even Charlotte Despard, in her seventh decade, confessed, 'I was older at twenty than I am now.' For 150 years women had been taught to efface themselves in public, to grace a conversation with wit but not significance, to serve a machine with labour but not skill, to attract admiration but not attention. Each public action to draw notice to the condition of being a woman was a defiance, and a fair gauge of its impact on observers was the psychological pressure it placed on the participants. Even the relatively undemanding form of exposure required of sandwich-boarders terrified those who did it for the first time, while the much more severe test of militancy and prison demanded a rare degree of courage (hence the Pankhursts' use of large crowds, so that participants could find comfort in numbers). But those who did defy convention experienced the elation of self-discovery, mingled with the excitement of successful graduation. By such intangibles was the League kept alive through the winter of 1907/8.

The publicity surrounding the arrests for picketing aroused interest, the determined efforts of the unpaid officials channelled that interest into membership and, in course of time, the frantic activities of the three professional organizers coalesced those members into branches. The routine required a juggler's skill for, even as new branches were added, old ones tended to wither away if neglected for too long. Members of the executive committee and organizers raced across the country to galvanize local secretaries into action and breathe fresh life into faded enthusiasms, before moving on to unmapped territory where a hall had to be booked, a meeting advertised and someone braced into shouldering the awful responsibility of becoming secretary of a new branch.

The guiding spirit of the League in these early days was Teresa Billington Greig, who had been voted to the chair at its first two conferences and held the post of organizing secretary, or chief strategist. Much of her time, however, was spent in Scotland, and the majority of members were far more accustomed to the face and opinions of Charlotte Despard, who was nominally cast in Emmeline Pankhurst's role as roving firebrand. Her life was a succession of telegrams, railway journeys and speeches. Seemingly tireless, she shuttled across the nation, weaving the cloth of the Freedom League a little more strongly with each traverse. At the beginning of 1908 the League had only twenty branches, but by the spring there were representatives in most of the major towns in England and Wales and in the largest burghs in Scotland's central belt. Accordingly, it was decided to begin carrying the message to more rural areas, starting among the small towns and villages of south-east England, and a horse-drawn caravan was purchased to act as a mobile headquarters and platform for the tour.

In May, Charlotte Despard wrote from Pontypridd to a friend: 'A little note hastily at the end of an exciting day to say that I hope you will come to us on the 16th, when we are sending off the Woman's Suffrage Caravan on its travels . . . as the times have been pretty exciting lately, there will be plenty to talk about.' The excitement was caused by the reception given to her and Mrs Fawcett during a joint tour of Wales. It had been a lively test of courage and lung power, for Wales was Liberal country and had no love for suffrage workers. They were howled down in Cardiff, pelted in Swansea and, at Pontypridd, an angry crowd broke in through the doors of a theatre while their meeting was in progress. Audience and speakers retreated on to the darkened stage and drew the heavy curtains shut behind them. There among the shrouded props, while the mob roamed dangerously through the stalls, Charlotte Despard put the suffrage argument in a hoarse whisper to a small knot of terrified listeners. Danger invigorated her and it was as well that she thrived on it, for the battered caravan was to show that in physical abuse the country had fewer scruples than the town.

'We were greeted in these rural districts with a hostility and violence quite terrifying to the uninitiated,' wrote Margaret Nevinson, who travelled with the caravan; 'yelling, shouting and musical instruments drowned our arguments; rotten eggs, fruit and vegetables ruined our frocks – obscenity unspeakable offended our ears.' For five months Charlotte Despard led the caravan on an uproarious tour of Surrey, Sussex and Kent, which reached its climax one day early in October when she took the vehicle into the market square at Maidstone to hold a meeting. As she addressed the shouting crowd, stones were hurled by youths at the back, and one struck her on the forehead. With the blood running down her face, she got up on to a chair so that her assailants could see and hear her better. There was a fresh shower of stones and granite chips and the crowd surged forward, knocking her to the ground and smashing the chair to kindling. She was helped to her feet and dauntlessly climbed on to the caravan to speak again, but at once her makeshift platform was besieged by jeering people who hammered on its sides and tore off the tailboard. At length she admitted defeat and retreated inside, whereupon the caravan was bombarded with rocks and broken granite.

The astonishing hostility which the caravan touched off in country towns, long before the militants themselves had offered provocation by their own destruction of property, would seem to suggest that in conservative areas the men felt attacked simply by the suggestion of equality for women. Boys and young men were usually the main aggressors – those, in short, who would feel most threatened by sexual equality – but for the most part they had the tacit support of the adults in the crowd. It was an instinctive fury which, when it had subsided, left the participants ashamed. With courage that was not less astonishing, the women in the caravan made a point of returning the next day to any place where they had encountered violence; and they almost always discovered, as Charlotte Despard did in Maidstone, that their audience was subdued and attentive. In Sevenoaks she was pelted with clods of earth and fireworks, but there again the pattern held good, and the following day she was listened to quietly.

Not every town greeted them with violence, and she sent back glowing reports of days spent blissfully rolling down quiet country lanes to some peaceful village, where she and her helpers were heard with interest and sympathy. Revelling in the contrasts between one such evening in an attentive market square, another where the stones and obscenity flew and the caravan was rocked on its wheels, and a third in a quiet morning-room, when the loudest noise was the clink of tea-cup on saucer, she appealed for volunteers to take out another caravan and share in the fun. Although a second was added the following year, it was a measure of the challenge provided by the rural mob that there were never

above: In Belfast with Jack Mulvenna and Molly Fitzgerald
(far right)

left: The young Charlotte Despard

right: Field Marshal Sir John French

above left: Margaret Bondfield

above right: Mrs Solomon with Emmeline Pankhurst

above: Suffragette meeting 1909 (Mrs Drummond, Christabel
Pankhurst, Sylvia Pankhurst, Jessie Kenney, Emmeline
Pankhurst, Charlotte Despard)

top: The Women's Freedom League National Executive Committee
below: The suffrage caravan

above left: Alison Neilans, 1908
above right: Muriel Matters, 1909
above: With Anne Cobden Sanderson, 1909

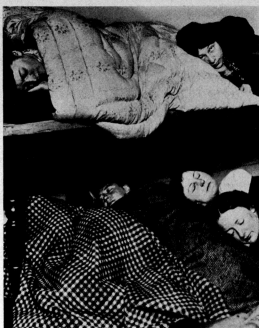

above left: Charlotte Despard
above right: The night of the census, 1911
above: Speaking in Hyde Park, 1 May 1920

THE VOTE.
JULY 13, 1928.

SPECIAL DOUBLE VICTORY NUMBER.

THE VOTE

THE ORGAN OF THE WOMEN'S FREEDOM LEAGUE.

NON-PARTY.

VOL. XXIX. No. 977.   *Registered at the G.P.O.*   TWO PENCE.   FRIDAY, JULY 13, 1928

OBJECTS : To use the power of the Parliamentary vote, now won for Women upon equal terms with men, to elect women to Parliament, and upon other public bodies; to establish equality of rights and opportunities between the sexes ; and to promote the social and industrial well-being of the community.

PRINCIPAL CONTENTS.

MRS. DESPARD'S VICTORY SMILE.

MONDAY, JULY 2. Mrs. Despard leaves the Palace of Westminster after hearing the Royal Assent in the House of Lords to the Representation of the People (Equal Franchise) Act 1928.

above: Irish demonstration
1924, Maud Gonne
carrying placard

right: With Russian
ambassador, June 1933

Anti-fascist rally in Trafalgar Square

enough members to keep it fully staffed through the summer. The sort of bravery Margaret Sibley evinced when she brought it to Bedford in 1909 was not a common quality. Three days running she had to be rescued by the police from a hostile mob, and on each occasion the crowd outside the police station became so large and threatening that, for their own safety, the police rowed her across the river which ran behind the station. Nevertheless, by the end of the week, she was able to set up a platform in the town square and address a throng of people without interruption.

Wherever it went the caravan left the germs of the suffrage fever. In more populous areas there were often enough new members to form fresh branches of the League and, of the twenty-three new branches set up in 1908, almost half were in the south-east. Even that probably does not measure the full effect in rural districts, where scattered members of the League often joined with other suffrage sympathizers to form an independent local group. It was not uncommon for a society which might be affiliated to Mrs Fawcett's NUWSS to have as members both women who had signed the pledge of allegiance to the Pankhursts and others who had paid a subscription to the Women's Freedom League.

Unlike Christabel Pankhurst, who refused to allow the WSPU to join other societies in their activities, Charlotte Despard wanted all the suffrage groups to cooperate as they did in rural areas. Immediately after the split with the Pankhursts, she had chaired a meeting of the NUWSS, the Women's Co-operative Guild, the Adult Suffrage Society and the Men's League for Women's Suffrage, at which those present had agreed to act in unison where they could. In practice, this turned out to be little more than the joint organization of rallies, but Charlotte Despard's tour of Wales with Mrs Fawcett was a sign that it might be taken further. In June 1908 there was a united League-and-NUWSS march to the Royal Albert Hall, where some 10,000 women inside and outside the Hall were addressed by the two leaders. Eight days later the WSPU's monster meeting in Hyde Park swamped all numerical significance, and by late summer the rivalry between local branches to recruit members was leading to charges of poaching, which began to sour the relationship. The final breach came in October 1908, when the 'grille protest' resulted in the destruction of property and Mrs Fawcett felt obliged to sever all links. A little sadly, Charlotte Despard wrote to her in November: 'I feel differently from you about what is necessary for the success of our movement in this strange and critical time, but I shall always have the same admiration and affection for your personality. I hope that when this evil is over we shall be able to meet on a common ground.' Her sentiments were shared by Mrs Fawcett, and it may well be that the friendship of those two contrasting personalities – the one massively self-controlled, the other emotionally turbulent – was founded in part upon the envy each felt for the other's temperament.

The breach was caused by the sort of militancy which Teresa Billington Greig thought should be the hallmark of the League: it was at once a protest against a symbol of female subjection and a blow at the process of male government. Women who wished to attend sittings of the House of Commons were required to sit in the Ladies' Gallery where they were screened off from view, as though in purdah, by an iron grille. On 28 October, several League members tried to gain admittance to the Gallery, but only three managed to allay suspicions – the balloonist Muriel Matters; a demure Quaker, Violet Tillard; and a mysterious Helen Fox, who was suspected of being a police stooge. In the Gallery, Muriel Matters chained herself to the grille, while Violet Tillard read out a proclamation to the MPs in the chamber. Anguished attendants tried to remove them but, since the chain could not be unlocked, the grille had to be pulled away from its mounting before they could be taken out. It was perhaps no more than a pebble off the mountain of prejudice, but the League thought it more useful and effective than the faked 'rush' on the Commons staged a week earlier by the WSPU.

In February 1909, the universal affection in the League for Charlotte Despard was given substance by her election to the newly created position of president. Some fifty years later Teresa Billington Greig still had reservations about the wisdom of the choice. 'I suppose she was the best figurehead we had,' she said doubtfully. 'Everyone loved and respected her – she was the sort of person who, though she could get very angry . . . was incapable of doing anything mean or spiteful.' The flaw in choosing her as president was not her temper, but the very strengths of her character – her generous enthusiasm, idealism and intuition.

Cardinal Newman had a theory that committees might be under

the influence of 'daemons – partially fallen, capricious wayward spirits. . . . Hence the action of bodies politic which is so different from that of the individuals who compose them.' Certainly there was scope for daemonic influence while Charlotte Despard was in the chair. So fundamental was her aversion to authority that she refused either to give a lead to a discussion or to rule irrelevancies out of order. Debates dragged on until the original point was lost in the confusion, or, still more disastrously, until she mistook some point of detail for a matter of principle and hurled herself into the argument, drawing everyone into the quarrel on one side or the other. When all semblance of good sense had been lost in a flurry of temper, she would demand in bewilderment, 'Now what *is* the will of the committee? Surely this is a time for action not debate.' At various times every member of the committee threatened to resign, but none more frequently than Charlotte Despard. It was not possible for her to compromise on a position which she felt intuitively to be right, and to their intense irritation the other members of the committee were repeatedly forced to back down rather than lose their president.

As chief tactician, Teresa Billington Greig suffered most; her nerves were already strained by over-work and her irritability grew acute. Frequently absent in Scotland, she relied on the clever but conspiratorial secretary, Edith How Martyn, to hold the fort on her behalf. The treasurer, Sarah Bennett, a plain-spoken, Staffordshire woman, quarrelled incessantly with the secretary whom she rightly suspected of conspiring to force the president's resignation on grounds of incompetence. Individually they were brave and attractive characters, but Newman's daemon was at work when they were in committee. Their ill-tempered meetings made the neat autocracy of the WSPU seem more attractive, but the wider implications of feminism, which never broke surface in the Pankhursts' ordered discussions, were the very stuff of the League's raging arguments.

When Parliament opened in January 1909, Charlotte Despard led a deliberately small deputation of twenty-five women to Downing Street to present the annual protest to the Prime Minister about the omission of the vote from the King's Speech. Some were arrested on the spot and Charlotte followed them into custody that same evening, when she tried to take the survivors to see Asquith at the House of Commons. Publicity was not her purpose on this occasion, for, as she pointed out at her trial, 'Had I wished to create anything in the nature of a riot, I could have done so, but as a matter of principle I tried in every way to keep my intention quiet. I am an old woman . . . I simply wished to see the Prime Minister, and for this I was arrested.'

Although her energy belied it, she was sixty-four, and to the nobility of her bearing was added the pathos of white hair and lined features. When she was sentenced to a month in the Second Division there was an uproar – shouts of 'Shame' came from the public gallery, and the outburst continued until the court was cleared of protesters. One spectator was overcome by emotion as he watched her:

The deeply furrowed face, and the flashing, undimmed eye are photographed on my soul and I am moved to tears, but this court knows no compassion. Are we, who have not done for humanity a tithe of what she has accomplished, to enjoy our liberty . . . while this freedom-loving spirit, this saint of God, is cooped up in a common gaol?

It was an extravagant reaction, but not untypical – there was no doubt that her appearance conveyed a more than ordinary moral force. When she arrived in prison, her former colleague Emmeline Pethick Lawrence was languishing in hospital, a casualty of the WSPU's demonstration during the King's Speech:

I was thrilled to see that stately and commanding figure enter the ward, looking, if possible, more dignified than ever in the quaint uniform of a criminal. Her first act was a calm refusal to take the medicine which the doctor prescribed. 'I have never taken medicine in my life – I do not propose to begin now.' Her word was immediately taken as law. All the officers seemed in awe of her.

After five days the authorities discharged their difficult prisoner on grounds of ill health, although she herself protested that the rest had done her good and 'as a matter of fact I was never better in my life'. Unfortunately for her claim, she at once fell seriously ill. Waiting for a tram after her release early on a snowy morning in March, she had found a group of derelict old women under the arches, and with an impulsive gesture had given them all the money in her purse. Penniless, she had been forced to walk two miles home through the snow, and paid for her kindness with congestion of the lungs.

By the time she recovered, the constitutional struggle between the Lords and the Liberal government had been brought to a critical stage. The battleground was Lloyd George's Budget of 1909, which promised higher taxes on the rich to pay for sickness benefits and old age pensions for the poor. As a Finance Bill, the Budget was supposedly immune to interference from the House of Lords, but the populist measures in it were designed to be deliberately provocative: accepted, it would be a feather in the Liberals' cap; rejected, it would be the basis for an appeal to the country to curb the power of the Lords.

The summer of 1909 marked the end of everyone's patience – Liberals', peers' and suffragettes'. While the Budget was tossed back and forth from Commons to Lords, Parliament had little interest in anything but the crisis, and in exasperation the League decided to concentrate all its energies on Westminster.

Two of its largest branches were in the East Ends of London and Glasgow, a consequence of Charlotte Despard's belief that working women needed the vote most urgently, and of Teresa Billington Greig's suspicion that the government would fear the poor in the streets more than the rich. At the latter's insistence, the League evolved a plan to saturate the area round Westminster with a plethora of meetings, which would take place wherever people were waiting for casual work – in other words, among those half-employed who made up the London mob. At the same time she wanted to substitute for the disappointingly sporadic protests in the police courts, a more direct harassment of government machinery during by-elections; but the opportunity for that form of militancy was still to come.

As the first part of the League's programme got under way in June, the WSPU determined to exercise the old right, guaranteed to all subjects, to petition the monarch. On the 29th a typical demonstration accompanied the petition into Parliament Square, and in the ensuing struggle many women were hurt and 132 arrests were made. It was by now a familiar event and, although the petition was a new way of putting the women's case, the manner in which it was presented added nothing to what had gone before. When thirteen women spontaneously began breaking windows in Whitehall later that day, it represented a watershed: on one side the usual, staged drama, on the other a genuine outburst of anger, which could not be orchestrated into a mere advertising campaign. Disavowed at the time, this anger was bound to recur unless the policy of self-martyrdom began to show results.

By 5 July the League had conducted 243 meetings around Westminster in the space of three weeks, and on that night seven of their assemblies decided to send deputations to the Commons to protest against the Prime Minister's failure to receive the petition. The House sat late over the Budget, so the League hastily set up a rota of reliefs in order that women should be there when Asquith finally left the Commons. When they failed to catch him at any of the exits, they returned the next day, and the next, and did not desist until the Parliamentary recess began on 28 October. It was an extraordinary vigil, which coalesced without planning and gradually acquired the power and emotional impact of ritual.

Some idea of its force was conveyed in H. G. Wells' novel *The New Macchiavelli*:

All through the long nights of the Budget sittings at all the piers of the gates of New Palace Yard and St Stephen's Porch, stood women pickets and watched us reproachfully as we went to and from. They were women of all sorts, though of course the independent working-class predominated. There were grey-haired old ladies . . . north country factory girls – cheaply dressed suburban women – trimly comfortable mothers of families – lank, hungry creatures who stirred one's imagination – one very dainty little woman in deep mourning, grave and steadfast, with eyes fixed on distant things. Some looked defiant, some timidly aggressive, some full of the stir of adventure, some drooping with cold and fatigue. I had a mortal fear that somehow the supply might halt. I found that continual siege of the legislature extraordinarily impressive – infinitely more impressive than the feeble-forcing 'ragging' of the more militant section.

Never was Asquith's hostility to the suffrage more starkly exposed. He refused to see the pickets at the Commons, and when they began to wait for him at Downing Street as well he had them arrested. 'We wish the public would try to understand what this means,' Charlotte Despard wrote in a letter to *The Times*. 'Women, politically unrepresented, have only one constitutional right, that of petition. This right is being denied by the head of the Liberal Government who would rather send women to jail than treat them with ordinary courtesy.' She herself was arrested outside Downing Street, but escaped jail when her fine was paid anonymously.

On 28 October, the day Parliament adjourned and the picket ended, a letter was sent to Asquith informing him that, since he would not receive a deputation, the League intended to 'invalidate a by-election by destroying ballot papers'. Two women, a frail American called Mrs Chapin and the redoubtable Alison Neilans, entered the polling booths where voting was taking place in the Bermondsey by-election, and spilled a chemical solution into the ballot boxes to burn the voting-papers inside. Unfortunately some of Mrs Chapin's solution splashed into an official's eye, which someone then dabbed with ammonia, temporarily blinding him and sending him into convulsions of agony. Mrs Chapin was arrested on the spot and charged with causing grievous bodily harm, and although both women insisted that their chemical was harmless if washed off with water, giving evidence that their hands had been soaked by it without ill-effects, Mrs Chapin was sentenced to four months in the Third Division and Alison Neilans to three. To complete the chapter of misfortunes, the chemical had not in fact been powerful enough to destroy the voting-papers, and the by-election proceeded smoothly.

The attempted sabotage came at a time when the emotional impact of the suffragettes' campaign had been dramatically re-inforced by their adoption of the hunger-strike, the ultimate weapon of self-sacrifice. Marion Dunlop, a member of the WSPU, sentenced in July for the trivial offence of posting proclamations, employed it first to protest against imprisonment as a common criminal in the Second Division rather than a political prisoner in the First. The window-breakers took it up, and all were released within a week. In triumph, Christabel Pankhurst declared that 'we have now learned our power to starve ourselves out of prison, and this power we shall use – unless the government prefer to let us die'. Neither alternative appealed to the government, and in late September they authorized the use of forced feeding to keep their prisoners alive and in jail. The manifest torture inflicted by the forcible insertion of nasal and stomach tubes heightened the agony of the conflict to an almost unbearable pitch. 'If I have to go to prison as a criminal,' Alison Neilans said at her trial, 'then I am obliged to resist – perfectly peacefully – and that will mean forcible feeding, stomach tubes and other barbarous tortues inflicted by those in authority. Look at me. I am now strong, in two or three weeks I shall be a physical wreck.'

In the tense atmosphere, rumour and fact merged and were distorted to fantastic and fearful dimensions. Stones were hurled through windows, Cabinet Ministers were jeered, Asquith was assaulted, and Winston Churchill confided to a friend that the next weapon to be adopted by the suffragettes would be dynamite, the weapon of anarchy. When the police reported that two members of the Women's Freedom League had been practising with revolvers at a shooting gallery, the threat of assassination became too real to be ignored, and two weeks later, in October 1909, the Home Secretary authorized the formation of the Special Branch to infiltrate, and gather information on, subversive groups like the militant societies.

Suddenly the phoney war of militancy had become real. The crude obduracy of Asquith atop his unassailable majority had kicked away any hope of political progress, and there was nothing further to be gained by restraint. But even as the turmoil spread, whipping up in turn a backlash of assault and affray as their enemies took revenge on the suffragettes, the Parliamentary monolith shifted. With the final rejection of his Budget, Asquith called a General Election to break the stranglehold of the Lords, and, as though a plug had been removed, the boiling energies of the suffragettes poured smoothly into the electoral campaign.

Altogether the League fought eighteen constituencies, and, unlike the WSPU who opposed only Liberals, took care to be impartial by campaigning against both retiring Cabinet Ministers and anti-suffragist Conservatives. Although there were rowdy scenes – in Asquith's constituency of East Fife it was noted that 'Miss Urquhart released herself from a violent Liberal by a timely use of jiu-jitsu' – it was evident that the picketing and hunger-strikes had won an unprecedented degree of sympathy for the suffrage cause. Returning from a tour of Liberal constituencies in Scotland, Charlotte Despard wrote to an old friend, Mrs Solomon: 'I have not been able to rest much – our work is so strenuous, fields white to the harvest and labourers few.' As the date of the election approached the tempo of her speaking engagements increased, and in the four days before the poll she fitted in six major speeches and as many smaller meetings in Liverpool and Birmingham, before returning for a last tilt at John Burns in Battersea.

When the result was known, only hyperbole could match her

elation. 'Never perhaps in all history', she announced to a crowd in Trafalgar Square, 'has there been so dramatic an illustration of the Nemesis which falls upon the perpetrators of injustice when the cup of their iniquity is full.' The Liberal colossus was reduced to a stump – in the new Parliament they held 275 seats, just two more than the Conservatives, and they were dependent for their majority on the support of eighty-two Irish MPs. The political log-jam appeared to be broken.

The most obvious beneficiary of the government's weakness was the Irish party, which could press for Home Rule in return for its support; but it was a situation from which any pressure group could profit. Writing for the first time in the League's new paper, *The Vote*, Charlotte told her readers, 'We know that we can bring pressure to bear on the Government of 1910, and we must make it fear us . . . it may well be that those in power may conciliate the women before they engage in another battle.'

As it happened, conciliation came not from the government, but from an all-party committee of MPs under the leadership of Lord Lytton and the journalist H. N. Brailsford, which drew up a Bill designed to be acceptable to most shades of suffrage opinion. It was the third women's suffrage Bill to be introduced since the Liberals came to power, but the difference from its predecessors was apparent when Asquith was reluctant to give it time for a Second Reading* and the Conciliation Committee massed the signatures of 196 MPs to call for an early debate. Living now on the thinnest of majorities, Asquith conceded and, on 12 July, the Conciliation Bill, as it was known, received its Second Reading by a majority of 100 votes. With that overwhelming victory, women's suffrage seemed finally to come in from the streets. The only obstacle to success was the Prime Minister, and even he had promised that 'the House of Commons should have the opportunity of . . . dealing effectively with the whole question.'

Had Asquith's opposition stemmed simply from personal foible his promise might have been taken at face value, but his motives were more complex. As early as May 1908, he had told Mrs Fawcett that he intended to introduce eventually an Electoral

* Bill stages in the Commons were: First Reading (presentation), Second Reading (vote on principle), Committee and Report (individual clauses and amendments), Third Reading (vote on amended Bill).

Reform Bill to abolish plural voting* and introduce manhood suffrage, two measures which might secure a permanent Liberal majority. Obviously, the Conservative House of Lords would veto such a Bill, but at the same time he could not allow any other suffrage Bill to pass, for it was a recognized convention that when a suffrage Act became law a General Election should be called the moment the new register came into operation. With hindsight, therefore, it can be seen that, until the Lords' power was curbed and Asquith's own Reform Bill had been introduced, the Conciliation Bill was doomed to be delayed.

Ignorant of the Prime Minister's calculations, the two militant societies had declared a truce which, with a single interruption, lasted from January 1910 to December 1911. Despite their anger at Asquith's repeated prevarications, they had little option but to accept the peace since both had reached a crisis in their use of militancy. Having whipped up expectations of early success, the Pankhursts had been dragged by their impatient followers to the edge of genuine violence, and while the leaders shrank back from such a course, they possessed no new ideas. 'Mild militancy was more or less played out', Christabel Pankhurst confessed in her memoirs. 'Strategically then, a pause in militancy would be valuable, for it would give time for familiarity to fade so that the same methods could be used again with freshness and effect.'

To the Women's Freedom League the truce was equally welcome because its own militant policy was in a state of disarray, following the injury to the Bermondsey election official. Many members were opposed to the policy of disrupting government business because they wanted the League to adopt the more glamorous massed demonstrations of the WSPU, while others, more cautiously, simply desired to avoid any risk of harming an innocent bystander. At the annual conference in January 1910, the Executive defended its policy fiercely. 'You may go down to Westminster, and you may succeed in getting on to the floor of the House of Commons', said Edith How Martyn, attacking the Pankhurstites. 'That is all right as an advertising protest, but . . . we want to inflict real damage on the political machinery.' And

* Plural voting permitted a man to vote in each constituency where he had a property qualification. Most of these voters were Tory, and Asquith estimated that they cost his party seventy seats in the General Election in January 1910.

Teresa Billington Greig defied the cautious by stating flatly, 'I am very sorry for the innocent bystander, but . . . he is absolutely nothing compared to the winning of liberty for the women of this country.' Her attitude was unacceptable to the majority of delegates, and they voted to prohibit any action which risked injury to onlookers.

Their decision put an end to one strategy, but it was not clear what the alternative was since almost any active protest carried a risk of injury. The confusion became manifest when the Conciliation Bill was wrecked at the end of the year by the constitutional crisis.

To ensure the passage through the Lords of a Bill to abolish their veto, the Liberal government had asked the King to be prepared to create up to 500 new peers, and the King had consented on condition that the question was first put to the country at a General Election. On 18 November, Asquith accordingly announced the dissolution of Parliament, and all pending legislation, including the Conciliation Bill, duly lapsed.

'Here came one of those moments, tests as I think of generalship,' Charlotte Despard confessed to the League, 'when it became necessary for your Executive to act on its own initiative.' Officially, the League was committed to militant action if the Bill failed; but the Executive rightly decided that there was no need for protest since the government was not to blame for its failure. It was clear, however, that non-militancy relieved them of a difficult decision, for all that they could promise by way of militancy was action 'which avoids injury to persons or personal property'.

Unfortunately for the League's policy of self-restraint, Christabel Pankhurst decided that the election was an elaborate plot to prevent the Conciliation Bill becoming law, and called for a militant protest from the WSPU. Since Asquith had already promised facilities for another Bill in the next Parliament, her response was icily condemned by the Conciliation Committee as absurd and harmful to the cause; but its folly was camouflaged by the brutality with which the police handled the demonstration in Parliament Square on 18 November.

In the course of 'Black Friday', as it was known, there were 120 arrests and numerous injuries, but the worst aspect was the sexual undertone of the roughness. A Miss H testified that 'One policeman seized my left breast, nipping and wringing it very painfully, saying as he did so, "You've been wanting this for a long time, haven't you?" ' 'One gripped me by the thigh,' a Miss Freeman reported, 'and when I demanded that he should cease doing such a hateful thing to a woman, he said, "Oh, my old dear, I can grip you wherever I like today".' 'We saw the women go out,' wrote Sylvia Pankhurst, 'and return exhausted with black eyes, bleeding noses, bruises, sprains, and dislocations.' She estimated that three women eventually died of their injuries. The following week, Asquith renewed his promise of facilities for a more flexible Bill if his government were returned, but the women's temper was now so enflamed that they rioted again in Downing Street and Whitehall.

In political terms, the demonstrations were irrelevant – the election proceeded, the Conciliation Bill lapsed, and the militancy died away when its futility was recognized. But in terms of tactics, 'Black Friday' was a turning-point. 'I fear the "raid" is played out,' Charlotte Despard wrote, and her opinion was confirmed by a WSPU member who revealed that 'various girls have been told by their mothers that they might break windows, but must not go on any more raids'. If militancy were needed again, the WSPU could not go back to its familiar dramas. The League, on the other hand, had set its face against destruction or risk of injury. Hitherto it had been the smaller militant society; in future it would be the less militant.

The elections returned an almost unchanged Parliament, in which the Liberals, with two fewer seats than before, still held power by grace of the Irish Party under John Redmond. Within the League, however, the atmosphere in 1911 was very different from the year before. The reverberations of 'Black Friday' had fissured its loose conglomeration of interests into warring camps. Teresa Billington Greig spoke for an influential section in the Executive when she described the raids as 'a policy of wrecking'. Their mindlessness convinced her that militancy should now be entirely renounced because its hubris was preventing the development of a truly feminist movement, and when she was unable to carry her point she resigned from the League. On the other hand, many members who had taken part in the raids were equally incensed by the League's failure to echo the strident voice and tactics of its sister militants.

Charlotte Despard adopted a third way, which satisfied neither side. She too had been appalled by the violence of the occasion, particularly since her old friend, Mrs Saul Solomon, had been among those injured. 'Don't for the present at least go into another demonstration . . .' she urged. 'I speak as the sister and daughter of soldiers when I say it could not be that all should go to the front at once. That would mean the end of the battle.' As usual, the martial language masked a pacific policy. Although she refused to abandon the word, the militancy she had come to believe in was spiritual rather than physical.

As early as January 1908 she had described her refusal to pay taxes as 'a form of passive resistance to the unjust conditions under which women live and work', but in the autumn of 1909 a long series of meetings with the young Indian lawyer, M. K. Gandhi had sharpened her awareness of the potential in this form of illegality.

In South Africa, Gandhi had already encouraged the Indian merchants whom he represented to undertake acts of civil disobedience against discriminatory laws, but by the time he arrived in London in 1909 he had begun to evolve the theory of *satyagraha*, or spiritual resistance, which was to be his life's philosophy. It is worth noting, therefore, that the League's long vigil outside the Commons, and the sufferings of the hunger-strikers, provided him with the first practical demonstrations of the moral force which organized self-sacrifice could exert.

He met both the Pankhursts and Charlotte Despard, but it was only in the latter that his ideas took root. As enthusiasts for Thoreau's teaching, and as members of the London Vegetarian Society, these two already had much in common and Gandhi clearly found her sympathetic. 'Mrs Despard herself is a wonderful person,' he said later. 'I had long talks with her in London, and admire her greatly and much appreciate her advocacy of "spiritual resistance".'

The purpose of *satyagraha* was to win a political reform not by forcing the authorities to yield it, but by effecting a change in their moral outlook. Gandhi was therefore careful to emphasize the dangers of physical resistance:

If the women win power through violent means that will give us no reason to believe that the administration under them will register any great improvement . . . they will practise the same kind of tyranny that they are opposing now, and the masses will remain where they are. If they had based their fight on pure *satyagraha*, they could have changed conditions all over England, and the change would have had repercussions throughout the world.

That was certainly the great aim which inspired Charlotte Despard in the summer of 1910, when she wrote to Mrs Solomon saying, 'We *must* go on, even if this little bill is passed. . . . It is my dream, when the first step is won, to make our League international – for Women's Freedom everywhere, and the lifting up of the oppressed through her.'

Six months later it began to look as if there would not even be a domestic League much longer. Not only did its democracy threaten to degenerate into anarchy, but its revenue had fallen by 20 per cent to £5000 in 1910. 'It is proof of the sad love of mere sensation that funds fall off when there is no active militancy,' she reflected. 'But then our policy is not even understood by our own members.' In the aftermath of 'Black Friday', she tried to lift their attention from the narrow field of tactics to her own, wider horizon. 'It is true that we are demanding the vote,' she wrote, 'but this has never narrowed us down to politics merely. Independence, that royal gift which we have lost, is the goal we must attain if ever we are effectually to serve the world.' But the wrangling continued, and she found herself sadly quoting Mazzini: 'The flag of Democracy is torn in many pieces, and one waves one fragment and one another, and all say that they hold Democracy!'

The difficulty lay in finding an effective means of putting Gandhi's ideals of passive resistance into practice. She had helped to found the Women's Tax Resistance League, but its effectiveness was limited because only single women were responsible for the payment of their own taxes, and even Charlotte Despard herself had no power to prevent the trustees of her marriage and of her husband's settlements deducting tax at source, so that her sole liability was for house duty. The periodic visits of the bailiffs to distrain property from Earnshaw Cottage and Nine Elms certainly made good propaganda, and both Leagues became accustomed to turning out in force at the auctioneers' showrooms when the clocks or jewellery were sold and making it an occasion for impassioned speeches on Hampden and the iniquity of taxation without representation. Yet it was not enough to carry any weight and when the King's Speech omitted women's suffrage once more, Charlotte Despard was ready with another plan.

On the first weekend of April 1911 the decennial census was due to be taken. Charlotte announced her plan to the League: 'I am going to say "No, no. No vote, no information", I am not going to tell whether I am a wife or a widow, whether I have had children or not, or the ages of those in my household, until I am a citizen.' The census boycott was an admirable choice. Its moral purpose was to show 'our deep determination no more to live a lie, no more to pretend to be that which we are not'. But it also allowed Charlotte Despard to voice a long-standing constitutional worry.

With increasing emphasis, she had been trying to show that the State was no longer something so remote that it scarcely infringed the lives, much less the liberties, of its citizens. Compulsory education had been the first invasion of the home, but the social legislation of the Liberals was far more pervasive. In 1909 they had passed a Children's Charter – also known as the Orangebox and Fireguard Act – which made it a crime for babies to sleep with their mothers instead of in a cradle (if necessary made out of an orangebox), and for children to be left alone in a room with an open fire. Another piece of well-intentioned impracticality was the School Medical Inspection Act, which at last caught up with the practice at Nine Elms but which, as Charlotte Despard pointed out, required parents to pay for the treatment of their children. 'In my own two schools, 250 children were found to require treatment, but how are the parents to afford it when they are too poor to feed them properly?' she asked. Scornfully she went on: 'Men, who would not dare to tell their own wives how they should manage their home, dictate to woman at large her duties and responsibilities to her children.' The trend was towards ever greater interference in women's lives, and she predicted that the census figures on women's employment would be used as an argument by those, like John Burns, who wished to restrict the sort of work they should be allowed to do.

Other suffrage societies were invited to join in obstructing the census, but the WSPU declined the invitation and all but the Writers' Suffrage Society withdrew after the Liberals' return to power. Despite the lack of official recognition the idea was, as

Laurence Housman put it, 'well-suited to the non-heroic many', since all that was required of them was absence from their homes when the census form was delivered. At the last moment, the WSPU and other societies gave in to the popularity of the boycott among their members, and joined the League in providing ingenious diversions to keep them from their homes during the crucial weekend. Theatres and halls were booked for all-night entertainments, flat-owners swapped homes and householders allowed themselves to be evicted by party-giving suffragettes; in Lancashire groups of them went bicycling through the night, in Cardiff they walked, and at the Aldwych Ice Rink in London they skated.

By the nature of the protest, it was impossible to estimate how effective it was. The egregious John Burns declared its impact on the overall census to be 'negligible', and in percentage terms the boycott of around 15–20,000 women could only have blurred the second figure after the decimal point. Its greatest achievement lay in rebuilding the sense of comradeship and solidarity which had been ruined by the events of 'Black Friday'; but it remained to be seen whether the League had found a distinctive means of resistance if militancy were ever needed again. The one certain failure of the census protest was in repairing the shortcomings of democracy within the League itself.

After her resignation, Teresa Billington Greig had devoted herself to writing *The Militant Suffrage Movement*. Besides criticizing the Union, it contained a swingeing attack on the League for having 'set itself up a new idol'. 'I do not believe in the worshipping of idols,' she added caustically, 'even the better ones that are human.' In a sense, Charlotte Despard *was* the League. None of her colleagues came anywhere near to matching her in popularity. Edith How Martyn suffered from poor health and shyness in public; Alison Neilans, though courageous, did not have a forceful personality; and Emma Sproson, a working-class woman from Wolverhampton, was direct and energetic enough, but had few ideas of her own. Resignation had removed any other rivals, for no one else had her eloquence and readiness to travel to any part of the country at the invitation of a branch secretary. It is almost impossible to guess at the power that a speaker exerted over an audience more than half a century ago, but undoubtedly Charlotte Despard's speeches had a compelling quality.

At a suffrage rally in Hyde Park in 1910, an eyewitness over-heard a police inspector's comment that 'Mrs Despard has got a big crowd, but that's nothing . . . she always gets a crowd.' Part of the draw was her appearance:

. . . there was something Attic about the pose. The arms were raised Cassandra-like, the whole, thin, fragile body seemed to vibrate with a prophecy, and from the white hair the familiar black veil streamed back like a pennon. An old woman, I suppose, as years go, but the eye is undimmed, and the figure youthfully upright. . . . The face can look stern and forbidding . . . contempt and anger can curl that lip at the broken promises of politicians, but the general austerity of the features is mitigated by the gentlest of smiles.

Still, there must have been something more than her dramatic appearance to make people invite her back time and again, and to explain why, on the eve of the General Election in December 1910, she managed to draw a full house in Newtown, Wales, when Lloyd George was speaking across the street in a smaller, half-empty hall. The secret, perhaps, lay in what one witness called her 'inward flame' and another her 'visionary tenderness'; certainly, she found her most appreciative audiences in South Wales and Scotland, where strong preaching had trained the palate. Yet for mystics and non-mystics alike the heart of her popularity was a profound and optimistic assurance, drawn from Shelley and Marx, that mankind was inexorably struggling towards a higher civilized and spiritual state. Well aware that her ideas were dismissed as utopian, she argued that feudal lords and slave-owners had once thought feudalism and slavery to be natural states, but, for all that, progress had buried both. Asquith thought it natural that women should be voteless dependants of men; but one day his notion too would be an historical curiosity, and who should maintain on that day that the equally 'natural' state of capitalism could not be utterly transformed? 'Human nature is dynamic,' she insisted. 'It changes, it moves, great forces act upon it . . . old moulds are broken and new moulds are ready for the expanding life.' Implicit-ly she believed that mankind was rebellious, and she welcomed as the symptom of a moral imperative every act of rebellion by child, woman or man against the established order. 'The peace of sub-mission is finally the peace of death. In life, and only in life, is to be found the freedom out of which harmony and honourable peace can grow. For life we are striving, and in our strife there is hope.' It was the credo of a fine, fighting faith, whose magic enthralled the Women's Freedom League.

Her unique position, her daunting energy and dominating personality continually overwhelmed those about her, and at times the League resembled a one-woman band. When the League treasurer resigned and the editor of *The Vote* fell sick in the spring of 1911, Charlotte took on both their posts for several months, thus magnifying her already massive influence and playing havoc with the League's administration.

Although it ranked highest among Charlotte Despard's interests, the League did not exclude others from her attention. She continued to speak at ILP branches, and to attend meetings of various women's trade unions, such as the Shop Assistants' and the Caterers' of which she was president. Meanwhile, in Nine Elms, the schools still had to be inspected, the children fed and nursed, the Despard Club organized and the mothers instructed in hygiene. It would not have been possible without Rosalie Mansell who, according to Teresa Billington Greig, did most of the spadework, while her employer 'queened' it. Almost without thinking, Charlotte Despard gradually piled more and more burdens on to her.

As a school manager and a member of the League's Executive, Rosalie Mansell acted as her *alter ego*, as well as running the clinic, kitchen and club in her absence. From 1905 she had also been foster-mother to a baby girl named Vere, the result of a love affair between a cavalry colonel and a hospital nurse during the last months of the Boer War. Through the intervention either of her brother or of Rosalie Mansell, Charlotte had adopted the baby, but the demands of public life had left her little time to be guardian in more than name. The pressure of responsibility placed on Rosalie Mansell eventually proved too much for her, and her slow collapse precipitated the entire League into almost fatal crisis.

Like many nurses at the time, Rosalie used laudanum as a tranquillizer. As the tensions mounted, she increased the dose until she was addicted. By the end she was taking it intravenously, and so openly that the baby Vere developed a phobia about needles. But her employer seemed aware of nothing more than an uncharacteristic inefficiency which was gradually confusing her already complicated schedule of engagements. Her missed appointments and unforeseen absences from the Executive tried its long-suffering members beyond endurance. Her waywardness as chairman had driven five members to resign in the previous six months, including such distinguished figures as Margaret Nevinson, a Poor Law Guardian, Anne Cobden Sanderson, likewise a Guardian and an influential political hostess, and Maud Arncliffe Sennett, who soon set up her own suffrage party in Scotland, the Northern Men's Federation. The latter's explanation for leaving might have served for all the others: 'wearying of the waste of time, talk and mock procedure, and of the lack of *grip* at the head . . . I resigned.' The president's indecision, exaggerated by the effects of her secretary's breakdown, made it almost impossible for the Executive to function, and at last her frustrated colleagues rebelled. In the autumn of 1911 she offered to resign on some obscure point of principle and, to the horror of the League at large, her resignation was immediately accepted. Letters and resolutions of support for her flooded into headquarters, but her colleagues were already quite well aware of her popularity; in the end, it was the golden future of the new Conciliation Bill which persuaded them to reconsider.

The Bill had received its Second Reading in May with a record majority of 255 votes to 88, and then, like its predecessor, it had been stalled by government business. Once more the barrier was the Parliament Bill to abolish the Lords' veto, but on this occasion, when Lord Lytton protested to Asquith, the Prime Minister had replied with a specific promise to make available as much time in 1912 as the Bill required to become law. With the success of the Bill apparently assured, the Executive decided that they could allow Charlotte Despard to remain in office for the few remaining months necessary for woman's franchise to become law.

Their confidence was almost universally shared. 'From the moment the Prime Minister signed this frank and ungrudging letter', *The Nation* decided, 'women became, in all but legal formality, voters and citizens.' Even Christabel Pankhurst had been won over: 'It is a pledge,' she said, 'upon which we can base the confident expectation of taking part as voters in the election of the next and every future Parliament.' The only shred of doubt was expressed by Charlotte Despard. At the Kensington Town Hall in June 1911, she informed her audience of a rumour that the government intended 'to introduce an election reform Bill . . . to amend the franchise laws for men while this injustice is still done to us, and I say this is abominable'.

The abomination remained a rumour, and unaware that Asquith, having successfully abolished the Lords' veto, now intended to proceed with his Reform Bill, the women allowed optimism to overcome their wariness. For the last time, the two militant societies cooperated with each other in work and celebration. They lobbied against the introduction of wrecking amendments to their Bill when it reappeared in 1912 – the only danger, it seemed, to the certainty of success. Charlotte Despard and Christabel Pankhurst appeared together to celebrate the release of Clemence Housman, sister of the poet, who had been imprisoned for not paying tax. Both societies protested against sex inequality in the National Insurance Bill, which would exclude almost three million women servants from sickness benefits; and both demonstrated against the award of a £400 salary to MPs while the women who were taxed to pay for it were not allowed to choose who would receive it.

Charlotte Despard, however, was almost alone in her enthusiasm for the rash of strikes which broke out that autumn among miners and transport workers. She made her home into a headquarters for the striking railwaymen of Nine Elms and, when Mary Macarthur brought some 15,000 women workers out on strike in Bermondsey, she enlisted herself as an aide, raising money, distributing bread and wondering joyfully whether 'the people's eyes are opening at last'. Already she was looking beyond the Conciliation Bill to the areas of divorce reform, education and above all equal wages, in which enfranchised women would work a revolution. Watching Labour, too, as it began to show its strength 'like the symbolic figure of Samson, conscious of its power, but not yet trained to use it', she did indeed seem to see, breaking in front of her, the dawn of the long-awaited day.

On 7 November, Asquith met a deputation from the People's Suffrage Federation, an organization without past or future, but a convenient excuse for his announcement of a Bill to abolish plural voting and to enfranchise every male citizen, regardless of property. The only concession to the women was that the Bill would be open to an amendment on women's suffrage.

The news smashed the suffragettes' high hopes. No one

supposed that, having passed complete manhood suffrage, the Commons would enfranchise only a tiny number of women, nor was it possible that they would be consistent and include complete female suffrage. *The Times* described Asquith's announcement as 'the explosion of a mine beneath the Conciliation Bill'. Helena Swanwick of the NUWSS declared that 'the Bill has been blown into the air', and, in Lloyd George's gloating words, 'the Bill has been torpedoed'.

In his first month of office the Prime Minister had declared his intention of bringing in such a Bill, and, as Winston Churchill justly observed, 'Asquith's opinions in the prime of his life were cut in bronze'. The years of agitation in the streets and of discussion in Parliament had, it seemed, achieved nothing, and almost twelve months to the day after the violence of 'Black Friday', Christabel Pankhurst alerted her troops with the cry: 'War is declared on women!'

8

The explosion of the Electoral Reform Bill heralded the most convulsive phase of the suffrage campaign. In the course of the next three years the WSPU was led inexorably by its narrow political ends into a cul-de-sac, while the League was able to develop its broader aims into the beginnings of an effective policy for the women's movement as a whole. Their divergent courses were marked almost before the echoes of the explosion had died away. Christabel Pankhurst had seen it as a declaration of war, but the more cautious Charlotte Despard warned her followers, 'Never go into battle merely to prove you're not a coward.'

The difference became more explicit when all the suffrage societies were summoned to a conference with Asquith and Lloyd George on 17 November 1911. Christabel Pankhurst took the opportunity to deliver an ultimatum of immediate militant action unless the government itself introduced a Bill to enfranchise women. Charlotte Despard, on the other hand, made a moving appeal to avert 'what I have always most earnestly deplored, a sex war'. 'I plead here for the weakest and most helpless women,' she said, '. . . the unmarried mother, the so-called illegitimate child, the widowed mother working night and day for her child. There is nothing more hopeless and pathetic than the position of these poor women.'

It was a similar plea, presented by Sylvia Pankhurst's deputation of working women, which in June 1914 was to soften perceptibly Asquith's hostility to the suffrage, and on this occasion too it produced a noticeable impact. Helena Swanwick of the NUWSS, who was present, stated that 'Mrs Despard was remarkably effective, and the two Ministers liked her hugely. I have never heard her so good.' Certainly Asquith went out of his way to be conciliatory, stressing that the support for women's suffrage that existed in the Cabinet and Commons would ensure the government's acceptance of such an amendment to its Reform Bill. In place of his usual outright opposition, he confined himself to a refusal 'to be responsible for the authorship of a measure which I don't conscientiously believe has been demanded in the interests of the country'. It was true that Asquith had the devious mind of a lawyer, but he also had the social conscience of a Liberal, and the only sincere appeals made to it in all the suffragettes' agitation were made by Charlotte Despard and Sylvia Pankhurst.

When its president told the League that 'we still have two chances – the Manhood Suffrage Bill may be amended, nor is the Conciliation Bill dead', she was not being falsely optimistic. Almost two-thirds of the Cabinet and a similar proportion of the Parliamentary party were committed to women's suffrage, while Lloyd George, who had opposed the Conciliation Bill, now promised to introduce the women's amendment to the Reform Bill and advocate it both inside the House and out. The psychological shock of Asquith's announcement had been devastating, but politically women's suffrage now had a greater chance of success than it had ever had in the past.

Unfortunately, in the worst misjudgement of her career, Christabel Pankhurst decided to destroy the Conciliation Bill, because of Asquith's refusal to introduce a government-sponsored measure for women's suffrage. The day after the conference, the windows began to go in the High Streets and in government buildings. 'The broken pane', said Emmeline Pankhurst, 'is the most valuable argument in modern politics', and the case made by shards of glass was reinforced in December by the telling advocacy of burning pillar-boxes. In February 1912, C. E. Hobhouse, an otherwise undistinguished Minister, provoked the suffragettes' ire by comparing their vandalism unfavourably, for scope and ferocity, with that wrought by men in 1832 and 1867. Within a week, hardly a window in Whitehall and the West End had not been holed by stones or shattered by hammers. The scale of destruction stung the government into action. The Pethick Lawrences were arrested for conspiracy, the WSPU's offices were raided and their paper was censored, but their leader, Christabel Pankhurst, managed to escape to Paris from where she continued to direct operations.

In the shadow of this limelighted orgy of revolt, the League relapsed into hopeless confusion, pulled forward by its Pankhurst faction and back by the constitutionalists, while its leader endeavoured to pursue her own course of non-violent militancy. In an article published in January 1912, entitled 'The ethics of civil disobedience', she argued that 'it is a woman's *duty* to resist an unjust state, as Thoreau did the slave-owning American government', but, as both Gandhi and Thoreau himself had shown, 'the passive form of resistance is preferable'. She reminded the League that they had decided to be militant only if the Bill failed, and the methods she suggested were tax resistance, hampering the law where it affected women and children, and protesting at sexual discrimination in the courts. The firebrands derived little comfort from this, and many defected to the Pankhursts' army, while the constitutionalists, alarmed by the tidal wave of hostility set off by the WSPU's violence, would have preferred to abjure any kind of law-breaking. The differences which had been brewing for a year now began to come to a head.

Many of the provincial branches, especially in the north-east, shared facilities and functions with the WSPU, and they bombarded the leaders with appeals to enlist in the Pankhursts' campaign. In London, the majority of the Executive, enraged by the WSPU's deliberate attempt to destroy the Bill, wanted to launch an open attack on their activities. Meanwhile the president's inability to descend to the drab procedures of committee-work – agenda, reports, resolutions and amendments – made the Executive a minefield from which few decisions emerged, and those usually mutilated beyond effectiveness. Bereft of guidance, the local branches drifted into a state of near-anarchy, refusing to pay their fees or even to allow professional organizers from headquarters to enter their area.

As the date of the Conciliation Bill approached, the situation within the Executive deteriorated. There was acrimony when Charlotte Despard instituted, without consultation, a project in which local branches were to set up watch committees to monitor cases of sexual discrimination in the courts. There was even ill feeling about the genuine advance made when the Labour Party conference in February at last adopted women's suffrage as part of its policy.

The decision was important, for once one political party had taken up the cause, others would have to declare their positions. It represented a considerable triumph for trade unionists like

Keir Hardie and George Lansbury, and Labour women like Charlotte Despard, who had kept the cause alive in its ranks. At a joint meeting of the League and the Labour Party in the Royal Albert Hall, Ramsay MacDonald promised his audience that 'we shall support women's suffrage with might and main, even if by our support we shall turn the Government out'. Carried away by the union of her two great loves, Charlotte Despard suggested to the Executive that the League should become the women's branch of the Labour Party. The proposal was pointedly ignored and, when one of her colleagues later asked whether she intended to pursue the idea, she replied angrily, 'I shall say what I think fit, and if the League does not like it I shall leave.'

In March, the Liberal *Daily Chronicle* gave vent to the frustration felt by many suffrage sympathizers at the Union's violence: 'All sensible people', it said, 'are being forced to the conclusion that there can be no women's franchise legislation under the present conditions.' There were more well-publicized defections from the Bill's supporters, and an unfounded rumour that Asquith would resign if it were passed helped to swing the Irish party against it. Faced with the probability of a defeat engineered largely by the Union, the League's Executive decided to keep any protest small and strictly law-abiding.

At the end of the debate on the Conciliation Bill on 28 March, the previous year's majority of 288 to 55 was seen to have been converted into a deficit of 208 to 222. With the instinct of a homing pigeon, Charlotte Despard raced from the Lobby, where she had heard the news, to the plinth in Trafalgar Square. She was flanked by Rosalie Mansell and Kate Harvey, a deaf physiotherapist who had become one of her closest friends. To the excitable crowd in the Square, their arrival promised trouble, but, before she could take up her familiar stance below Nelson's column, the police moved in to arrest her. A constable caught her by the arm, but Kate Harvey held her round the waist while Rosalie Mansell tried to push him away. Rosalie was knocked to the ground but, just as the police were about to drag Charlotte Despard off, a group of young women pushed them apart and succeeded in putting her in a taxi before the police could recover.

Shaken physically, but nor morally, she appeared the next day at the official protest meeting organized by the League in the

Essex Hall. 'The defeat of our Bill is an insult,' she shouted. 'The time for compromise is past . . . and it is now necessary to return to militant tactics.' To the fury of the Executive members, who had heard nothing of her plans, she then outlined a new scheme for an economic boycott. Among the suggestions, which she un-wisely passed on to a group of reporters, were a ban on expensive clothes and a refusal to patronize milliners.

Overnight the League was dubbed 'the Hatless Brigade' (hats having about the same relationship to respectability as brassières in a later time), and it became the object of much heavy-handed mirth in the weekly journals. It was the last straw so far as the Executive was concerned. Having flouted their prohibition on illegal protests, their president had invented policy and made them all a public laughing-stock. At a conference held in April to discuss the League's future, all the frustration and wounded pride that had built up at every level of the League burst venomously into the open.

The main butt was Charlotte Despard, who was accused of being autocratic, incompetent and bad-tempered. Her principal qualifications for being leader, one colleague observed, lay 'in the admiration and enthusiasm of her followers. We must all admit that devotion in women has never been accompanied . . . by any discrimination as to the object of their devotion.' Emma Sproson remarked that 'she has always more or less intimidated the Executive Committee'. But the most serious charge was laid by Edith How Martyn: 'The insuperable difficulty in our work', she said, 'is that the President claims and exercises entire personal freedom to disregard the decision of the Executive Committee, and her unrestrained actions and speeches render serious political work impossible.' Even Alison Neilans, the most courageous and compassionate of her colleagues, was driven to admit that 'One might love and revere the Queen, but one might not like to work with her.'

The accusers themselves were barracked as they spoke, and, when they had ended, were in turn damned for being obstructive, vacillating and too willing to be cowed. Charlotte Despard hardly bothered to defend herself. 'I cannot be tied up,' she said. 'I can-not be told, "you must do this, you must do that". That is abso-lutely impossible for me. I must be myself.' She was neither helpful nor conciliatory, but she was truthful. It was the spirit which she had developed in childhood, preserved in a cocoon through marriage, and held couched like a lance against the windmill of injustice ever since. Her power lay in being untamed. Sensing that, perhaps, and certainly loving her for the warmth of her character, the conference decisively confirmed her as president, and accepted the resignation of the seven Executive members most adamantly opposed to her.

The triumph was total, for not only were her enemies routed but in their place came the loyalest of friends. The Executive was now dominated by women who had come into the movement in response to her utopian dream of transforming society, and who were in a sense her disciples. Among them were Alix Clarke, whose volatile temperament and nervous thirst for adventure drove her to run some of the League's most vigorous branches in the heart of anti-suffrage Wales; Anna Munro, a shy and stubborn young woman, who was a fervent believer in passive resistance, and was twice jailed for her conviction; and Charlotte Despard's cousin, Isabel Tippett,* who was as short-tempered, idealistic and philanthropic as she. At headquarters, an ebullient South African, Nina Boyle, was put in charge of tactics; the administration was entrusted to the competence of Florence Underwood; and the post of treasurer was occupied by Dr Elizabeth Knight, who supplemented a flair for fund-raising with surreptitious contributions from her massive income from Knight's Castile Soap. Finally, Charlotte Despard had at hand, acting as press secretary, her closest friend, Kate Harvey.

Like her leader, Kate was a widow. Despite the handicap of complete deafness, she had brought up three daughters singlehanded and at the same time made her house in Bromley a home for handicapped children, where she practised as a therapist. This formidable combination of energy and efficiency had come into Charlotte Despard's life on 12 January 1912 (a date she later commemorated fondly as 'the anniversary of our love'), when she had just received a letter from Edith How Martyn accusing her of being a dictator. The charge had been particularly wounding since she took pride in not imposing her opinions on others, and in acute distress she had resolved to resign.

In common with many others, Kate Harvey had first been

---

* Isabel was the mother of the composer, Michael Tippett.

attracted to the League precisely by Charlotte Despard's vision of it as a spiritual crusade, and now, brimming over with indignation, she had argued that it was her moral duty to stay. Moved by her angry loyalty, Charlotte had allowed herself to be persuaded, and then soon discovered that other sympathies bound them together. Kate loved deprived children with an intensity as powerful as hers; she was a tax resister and had suffered the indignity of distraint; and she had the same ambition to see liberated woman liberate the world. It was, in Charlotte's words, 'an ever to be remembered day', from which sprang an almost engulfing love, the warmest personal relationship she had known since Max's death. They stayed in each other's houses, took holidays together, and Kate Harvey's three children became Charlotte Despard's honorary grandchildren. It was impossible that the love of two such intense natures should be easy: Kate's sensitive personality was continually gashed by some thoughtless act committed by her friend in her restless thirst to awaken the people, while the latter often felt that she was being judged and found wanting. For all the misunderstanding, it was the most important love of Charlotte Despard's widowed life.

Their conversations were serious, not to say high-minded, and turned frequently to spiritual matters, for one of the most important bonds between them was a common belief in Theosophy, the ancient wisdom.

Theosophy had been founded in 1875, one of the hundreds of cults which took hold in Europe and North America among the ruins of the old omniscient faith. Its first president was Madame Blavatsky, a Russian mystic who chain-smoked, told coarse jokes and claimed to have received her esoteric knowledge from a Master of the occult world whom she had encountered one moonlit night beside the Serpentine. Many thought that her claim and behaviour were no more than might have been expected of a Russian exile who had made her way by her wits from a job in the circus and a Cairo flowershop to the leadership of a well-financed cult. Her magical feats were notorious, as was the judgement of the Society for Psychical Research that they were elaborate conjuring tricks; and there were many, including Emmeline Pankhurst, who regarded her as an impostor. On the other hand, her followers testified that she was a seer, genuinely inspired by the purest spiritual knowledge, and they maintained that the scandalized world had been misled by appearances. Certainly, she was a woman of singular personality, who had succeeded in synthesizing from the occult, the Hindu Vedas and Darwinian theory, a faith that was optimistic, purposeful and coherent.

Just as different species had changed in the course of several generations, so, the Theosophists held, the soul evolved through a series of lives until it achieved perfection and was released from the Wheel of Life. All living matter possessed this dual nature, spiritual and material, which was in fruitful conflict; for the onward progress of the soul could best be achieved by working on the world around it. While this implied individual responsibility, Theosophy, like all Darwinian philosophies, also took the improvement of the species, in both spiritual and social aspect, to be inevitable. This universal impulse towards betterment was termed 'the world-mind', and, as one of its symptoms was taken to be the gradual replacement of a competitive, masculine ethos by a feminine, caring instinct, it was appropriate that, next to Madame Blavatsky, the most influential figure in the Theosophist movement should be another woman, Annie Besant.

Born in 1847, Annie Besant had separated from her husband and made a career as a propagandist for Charles Bradlaugh's secularist beliefs and the socialist ideas of Edward Aveling before becoming Madame Blavatsky's disciple in 1888. For twenty years she had been the foremost Theosophist in England, investing its tenets with a pronounced theme of social concern; but in 1909, soon after becoming president of the Society, she was persuaded that a young Indian boy, Krishnamurti, was the vehicle for a new manifestation of God, and all her beliefs were at once coloured by that presumption.

In the autumn of 1909, Charlotte Despard attended a series of lectures in which Annie Besant warned the world to prepare for 'the coming of a new world in which truth and righteousness and justice shall be the moving forces'. It must be said that the lecturer was inclined to believe that the preparation could best be accomplished by an autocratic regime. To the astonished editor of *The Vote* she suggested that George V might establish personal rule over the British Empire, since 'if the office of Kingship were made a great one, great souls would be sent to fill it, as in the case of the Mikado of Japan, a most advanced soul'.

This aberration did not hinder the growth of a strong friendship between the two women, whose backgrounds had much in common; nor did it prevent Charlotte Despard from adopting Theosophy as the basis of her own ideas. 'Unspeakably it has helped me,' she once wrote, '. . . because in dethroning materialism it still holds fast to reason.' Until then, socialism had answered her need for an all-embracing explanation of society's problems, but it had left unsatisfied the mystical side of her nature. Margaret Bondfield had noticed that she still used the planchette to consult the spirit of Mazzini, while her diary showed that she continued to trust the prophecy of her automatic writing that 'great upheavals . . . and a Coming' were imminent. Yet it had been a secret and slightly ashamed interest, for she liked to think that she was guided by pure reason (although it might be truer to say that, having arrived at a decision, she was gratified if it transpired that reason led there too). The occult and socialism had coexisted uneasily; neither was viewed favourably by Catholicism; and none of the three gave any comfort to the women's movement. Only when she discovered Theosophy were these disparate enthusiasms drawn into one undivided vision, which saw Catholics, suffragettes and strikers as manifestations of the same irresistible spiritual force.

'With storm-darkness and perplexity it may be,' she wrote in her pamphlet, *Women and the New Era* (published in 1911),

but with unfailing certainty, the new social movement advances, impelled onwards by a strange unrest.

'Blessed are those', said the initiate Christ, 'who hunger and thirst after righteousness.' It seems to me that such a fever is upon us, and looking for a reason, I find it in the thoughts and emotions which the last century has been building up.

In one of the most striking of Shelley's parables, he compares the cumulative power of thought to the growth and fall of the avalanche:

> Flake after flake in heaven-defying minds,
> As thought by thought is piled, till some great truth
> Is loosened, and the nations echo round,
> Shaken to their roots, as are the mountains now.

Great truths are being loosened today, and the forces through which this is coming to pass are familiar to us: the woman-force, the labour-force, the child-force. These, moving with ever-increasing momentum, are building up energy, breaking down prejudice, so that presently the Truth, for which the world is waiting, may stand revealed.

Her metaphysics might seem to have little relevance to the hard pragmatism of Westminster politics – to Asquith's estimates of seats lost through plural voting, to the calculations of Lloyd George and Winston Churchill of votes to be gained through a wider franchise, and to Redmond's shrewd strategy of squeezing Home Rule from a minority government – but it was, if anything, the petty arithmetic of Parliament which was out of touch with the pervasive, spiritual malaise of the country. In 1903 Kipling, the bull-horn of imperialism, had damned the ethics of Conservatism as 'Arid, aloof, incurious, unthinking, unthanking, gelt', and had read in the minds of its rulers the scathing syllogism:

Because we know we have breath in our mouth, and think we have
    thoughts in our head,
We shall assume that we are alive, whereas we are really dead.

After four years of Liberal government, H. G. Wells, the prophet of reform, echoed the same frustration through the mouth of his hero in *The New Macchiavelli*: 'For my own part, since I love England as much as I detest her present lethargy of soul, I pray for a chastening war – I wouldn't mind her flag in the dirt, if only her spirit would come out of it.'

That longing for some emotional cause with which to break up the dead conventions of society appeared in different forms – aesthetically, with the Post-Impressionist Exhibition of 1911; constitutionally, with the Ulster rebellion against the Home Rule Bill; sexually, with women's revolt; and industrially, with the syndicalist movement. Each of these, but especially the last, represented the affirmation of irrational impulse against the constraints of custom and ordered civilization.

It was not the least of Charlotte Despard's merits that in her sibylline utterances there was a genuine comprehension that the crisis which the Liberal government and a liberal society had reached was moral rather than political. Her clearest statement came in August 1913, when a strike by Dublin tram-drivers under Jim Larkin had resulted in riots, when Bonar Law had guaranteed 'the support of the whole Unionist party' for any measures taken by the Ulster rebels, 'whether they are constitutional or . . .

unconstitutional', and when London was in the grip of a transport strike some of whose leaders were avowed syndicalists, as hostile to the government as any Orangeman. Charlotte Despard offered her own explanation of the universal disrespect for law and order:

In a society where it is commendable cleverness to rob human beings ... of their strength, their vitality, their joy in the earth ... where it is a crime to snare a pheasant and a venial offence to assault a child – what can we expect the law to be? Can it be deemed wonderful that it fails in maintaining order and in conquering the respect of the people?

This was the language of the nineteenth-century Radicals, but for the women seeking the suffrage it had a particular and entirely up-to-date relevance; for, in the eighteen months since the League set up its watch committees to monitor the courts, their surveillance had uncovered an astonishing perversion of social values.

Initially the investigation had been concerned with simple disparities in sentencing. In a typical example of drunk and disorderly behaviour, where the couple were found to be equally guilty, the woman was fined twice as much as the man; and, in a case where a couple was found guilty of improper conduct, the man was fined but his female companion was sent to prison for a month. Behind these obvious examples of unfairness there gradually appeared a far more disturbing picture.

To judge by the sentences imposed, theft stood only below murder as a serious crime; begging and soliciting came next, on a par with sexual assault on a child; while physical assault on a wife ranked just above baby-battering, which carried the lightest punishment. The longest sentence discovered by the League in a case of wife-assault was nine months, imposed for manslaughter when the wife died of fright as she was being throttled. The most severe sentence for baby-battering was four months (again for a case of manslaughter), and the more usual penalty was a fine or a month's prison. By comparison, a woman servant who stole a watch and chain was given three years' penal servitude, a sales assistant who took 1s 7½d from the till at Lipton's grocery was sentenced to nine months, and the lightest sentence recorded for theft was three months for stealing three hens.

While these sentences may not seem altogether surprising in the light of the excessive veneration of property in that era, it is less easy to explain the lenient view the courts took of sexual assault on children. The maximum sentence in the police courts was six months, but it was rarely awarded; more typical was the three months given to a man for indecent assault on a five-year-old semi-paralysed girl, and the four months for criminal assault by a recidivist; for first offenders, fines or a simple binding-over were common. The longest sentence, given in an Assize court, was eighteen months, pronounced by a judge who described the case as 'the worst of its kind I've come across', and who later in the day sent a man to prison for three years for stealing a saw from a rubbish dump. His values were not exceptional. Patrick Innes, the Recorder of Sandwich, stated in court that an assault on a little girl was not an ordinary crime, like theft, but one which 'the most respectable man might fall into'. His remarks were echoed by another judge who, after hearing a case of assault on a seven-year-old girl, said: 'This is the kind of thing that can happen to any man.' Even the father of an eight-year-old girl assaulted in Glasgow appeared relatively unmoved by the crime; according to the League's reporter, he simply remarked, 'It's no sic' a dreadful thing is it?'

In one sense it was not. When two-thirds of all the families in a major city like Glasgow lived in two rooms or less, there was no place for childhood innocence; sexual promiscuity among children and by adults on children was a commonplace, and the National Society for the Prevention of Cruelty to Children thought that as many as 37 per cent of criminal assaults were incestuous. To that extent, social attitudes to paedophilia were moulded by the dreadful housing of the poor, which made it impossible to segregate adults and children at night. But, as the judges' comments suggest, such tolerance was not confined to the poor.

It is hard to reconcile the public and pervasive sentimentality about the innocence of children with the condoning of sexual assault upon them; but the hypocrisy would seem to have arisen directly from society's attitudes to women. Treating woman as child-like and at the same time erotic encouraged a confusion of thought which saw the girl child as woman-like and sexually tempting, precisely because she was innocent and manipulable. That confusion enabled a rapist to claim that his seven-year-old victim had given him 'all sorts of encouragement', and allowed the courts to regard such offenders and those guilty of indecent assault as the victims of temptation rather than the perpetrators of crime.

The importance of the League's watch on the courts, in which they were soon joined by other suffrage societies including the WSPU, lay in its challenge to the most fundamental assumption buttressing male superiority – that, by reason of their greater physical strength, men would constitute themselves the natural protectors of women and children, and so justify having direction over them. It was the essence of the liberal tradition that power was a responsibility to be used rightly. The concept invaded the habits and thoughts of every stratum of society, and it guided the rule of household and Empire alike.

In April 1912, the eminent bacteriologist, Sir Almroth Wright, wrote a notorious and widely ridiculed letter to *The Times*, explaining the suffrage campaign as the outburst of 'sexually embittered women . . . that half-million of our excess female population . . . which had better long ago have gone to mate with its complement of men beyond the seas . . . there is mixed up with the women's movements much mental disorder.' The daftness of his strictures obscured the significance of one passage in which he caught the emotion which lay at the heart of the opposition to women's suffrage:

The law which the militant suffragist has violated is among the ordinances of that code which forbade us even to think of employing our native Indian troops against the Boers; which brands it as an ignominy when a man leaves his fellow in the lurch and saves his own life; and which makes it an outrage for a man to do violence to a woman.

There could be no society more enlightened than one based upon the tolerance and self-denial of the most powerful. It was that superiority which set Britain apart from Germany (where Might was Morality) and which justified her possession of Empire, so that the law, the code, the chivalry that was so essentially Christian might be spread across the earth. In the eyes of Sir Almroth and others of like mind, the suffragettes had broken the unwritten bargain by which, in return for some circumscription of their independence, British men gave protection and justice to women, as to Nigerians, Indians and Chinese. In so doing, they threatened to undermine the most liberal civilization in history.

In practice, that civilization was as perfidious as it was noble;

paedophilia and misogyny in relation to women were paralleled by racial intolerance and bullying in relation to the colonized and by exploitation and cruelty in relation to the poor. Yet the flaw in the liberal tradition was not so much its hypocrisy as its structural inability to put matters right. The code to which Sir Almroth Wright referred governed the behaviour only of the powerful towards the weak, not that of equals. Through the centuries, social injustices had in the last resort been reformed by the injured classes gaining the necessary power; and the powerful had accepted the process, however reluctantly, as justified by the terms of the code. But the demands now being made would have required so much power to be ceded to the weak that the structure within which the code operated would have had to be destroyed. If women were to be equal to men, the natives to the colonizers and workers to employers, there would be no more chivalry, no more enlightened imperialism, no more *noblesse oblige*. The old liberal tradition, committed to acting justly *de haut en bas*, had little room left for manoeuvre. On the one hand, the powerful – in the form of the Conservatives and Ulster colonists – were ready to rebel rather than allow power to be given to the colonized in Ireland; on the other, the weak – in the form of the unenfranchised working class – found it more natural to use the language of socialism, which claimed justice as the right of all rather than the duty of the strong.

Placed in this context, the women's movement could be seen to share with the colonized and the poor the frustation of making demands which could not be met within the gounds of the old order. It was natural, therefore, for Charlotte Despard to identify allies in the Home Rulers of Ireland and the strikers who paralysed the docks in 1912.

When Tom Mann and Ben Tillett brought the London docks to a halt, she tried to explain to the League that strikers and women had been enslaved by the same process of imperial deterioration 'from conquest to luxury, founded upon servile manhood and servile womanhood'. 'I was oppressed by the small size of the children,' she wrote, after making her usual donation to the distress fund for strikers' families. 'The worst evil is not the brief, economic effects of the strike, but the perennially filthy conditions of the housing.'

Unlike other suffragettes, she bore the Irish party no ill will for voting against the Conciliation Bill, for where Home Rule was concerned she felt herself to be Irish. 'For years I have longed for the redemption of my people,' she exclaimed when the Executive voted to opposed the Irish MPs in retaliation at the next election; 'no majority will ever make me oppose Home Rule.' She had made her first purely political visit to Ireland in 1909, when she spoke to James Connolly's Irish Socialist Republican Club in Dublin; but after the Home Rule Bill was introduced in 1912 she campaigned frequently throughout the country for 'the Home Rule of men and women together'. It was a happy coincidence that the green, white and gold of the League's flag were also the colours of the Irish tricolour.

It was not easy for her followers to appreciate that apparent enemies were fundamentally allies, but to make her point Charlotte Despard was ready to deny her own cause. 'I am not a feminist – indeed I hate the very word', she exclaimed to a Glasgow audience. 'It is my earnest hope that the present women's movement will prove to be a passing phase and that the day is not long distant when it will merge with the men's movement.'

The impetus of the women's movement, however, was still provided by Christabel Pankhurst, who was driving it in a very different direction. She allowed no other cause to distract her from the vote, and in the years after her flight to Paris it became plain that despite the violence she inspired, she was a conservative actuated by a stern belief in the values of the chivalric code.

In a series of articles written in 1912 for her new paper, *The Suffragette*, she described how men had abandoned the knightly ideals of purity and self-restraint and allowed society to be destroyed through the ravages of venereal disease. Her allegations, later published in a volume entitled *The Great Scourge*, claimed that 80 per cent of the male population was infected and that this was the cause of the high levels of infant mortality and female sterility. The moral, pithily rendered as 'Votes for women and chastity for men', was that women were needed in power to restore the old values which men had betrayed. It was not for nothing that the inner guard of the WSPU had been given the title of 'the New Crusaders'. The historian George Dangerfield detected a whiff of lesbianism in Christabel Pankhurst's condemnation of male sexuality, but it was closer to the stink of brimstone – Jonah damning the evils of Nineveh, or Savonarola the corruption of Florence –

and it was quite in character that, when the First World War broke out, she should describe it as 'God's vengeance upon the people who held women in subjection'.

Christabel Pankhurst ruled the WSPU through Annie Kenney and, later, Grace Roe – the prototype of the New Crusaders – and no breath of criticism for her strategy was permitted. In October 1912 the Pethick Lawrences were expelled and in January 1914 Sylvia Pankhurst followed. When Asquith's Reform Bill was at last introduced in January 1913, the Speaker ruled that, because the Bill had not been drafted widely enough, a women's suffrage amendment would be out of order. After that example of male duplicity, the last restraints were dropped. With arson, slashed paintings and yet more shattered glass came the suffragettes' reply, and when they were imprisoned their endurance of the torture of force-feeding sanctified their acts of violence. In April 1913 the government passed the 'Cat and Mouse Act', which enabled the authorities to release hunger-strikers until they were healthy enough to serve the rest of their sentence. In addition, suffragettes were banned from meeting in public places like Hyde Park and the WSPU's paper, *The Suffragette*, was proscribed and its staff arrested. But these measures only incited the victims to further violence.

In June 1913 Emily Davison threw herself under the King's horse in the Derby, and the movement had its first authentic martyr. But the constant, living martyr was Emmeline Pankhurst. Sentenced to three years in prison in February 1913 for conspiracy to burn Lloyd George's house, she was taken to Holloway half a dozen times and was released as often, after hunger-striking, to appear like the very genius of revolt at suffragette meetings beneath the eyes of the police, inciting her followers to still more outrageous feats. The legend that still dominates the suffrage campaign was created in those years when she seemed, like a frail Samson, intent on pulling down the edifice of government even at the cost of her own life. 'I have seen the exhibition of qualities which I consider to be as rare and precious as anything which a nation can possess,' Lord Lytton told the House of Lords. 'I have seen those qualities given to a cause, as great and as noble a cause as you could find, but given in such a way as to defeat the very object that they sought to obtain. . . . And that to my mind is a tragedy.'

Politically women's suffrage was utterly destroyed, inside and outside Parliament. A year after the Conciliation Bill had been defeated by thirteen votes, a similar Bill went down by forty-seven votes and candidates now spurned the support of suffragettes because they were such an electoral liability. The League suffered when its meetings were broken up by anti-suffragists and when its help was rejected by the Labour Party at the Keighley by-election in November 1913, but, because its target had always been more than the vote, it escaped the sense of futility that dogged its sister militants.

The League was directing much of its activity towards the reform of legal abuses, which lay with particular weight on women. Following the example of its president, it regularly took up the cases of young mothers convicted of infanticide, urging MPs and newspapers to treat the crime, wherever possible, as manslaughter rather than murder. *The Vote* fulminated against the practice in police courts of relying on the testimony of a single policeman to convict for prostitution and pointed out that, as the accused in such cases was invariably designated 'a common prostitute', the magistrate was from the start liable to be prejudiced against her.

The most successful part of the League's legal strategy was the campaign organized by Nina Boyle to have women officials in court during the cross-examination of child witnesses. Usually all women, including relatives, were cleared from court during cases of rape or indecent assault; where children were involved as victims or witnesses, such cases very frequently failed for lack of evidence because the child, questioned by a male barrister before an all-male court (in one instance for six hours at a stretch) was unable to give a coherent account of what had happened. The League's deputations to the Home Secretary and Lord Chancellor achieved little, but individual judges were persuaded not to clear their courts. As other societies took up this cause there was a perceptible movement towards accepting women's presence during cases of indecent assault, and, by no coincidence, towards stiffer sentencing of offenders. In May 1914 Nina Boyle put forward the idea that women officers should be recruited to take evidence and stay with assaulted children in court, and from that suggestion there evolved the first policewomen's force in Britain, which the League instituted in September 1914.

The League was responsible for another innovation in 1913,

when it complained about the absence of honours for women and made good the deficiency by awarding its own. Among those on this first honours list were Ellen Terry, Dr Elizabeth Garrett Anderson and Lady Gregory, and, unlike the suggested reforms in the law, the idea was well, if condescendingly, received by the press – 'a charming and graceful gesture', the *Daily Chronicle* termed it. These were sighting shots in a long battle, but all the League's proposals in time became standard practice as women voters, magistrates, police officers and lawyers gradually altered the masculine values of the country.

Its stable organization and purposeful strategy resulted in a startling growth in the League's membership during the brief period before the outbreak of war. In the last half of 1912, 500 new members were enrolled and seven new branches formed, and the following year another eighteen branches were added, with 1200 members. This was as swift an increase as any in the League's history, but in terms of income (£3120 in 1913) and membership (about 7000 in all) it was still only about one-eighth of the Union's size.

Almost half the League's membership was in Scotland. 'There is a special vitality, an unwavering spirit of hope among the Scottish members,' Charlotte Despard remarked after one of her frequent tours. In law and education there were some areas in which Scotland was more advanced in its attitude to women – a widow was, for instance, guaranteed provision from her late husband's estate, and women graduates were awarded degrees from the universities – and politically this was reflected in the attitude to the suffrage taken by town councils and newspapers. The presence of Asquith at East Fife and Churchill at Dundee produced rowdy scenes at elections, but in general the League members in Scotland tended to be law-abiding rather than militant. Whereas the north-of-England branches tended to be linked with the WSPU, in Scotland the ties were rather with Mrs Fawcett's NUWSS and other non-militant societies, with whom the League organized a marathon march from Edinburgh to London in October 1912 to carry a petition to the Prime Minister. There was one notable tax resister in Isabel Bunten, but otherwise their methods were constitutional – vigorous lecturing in the holiday resorts, lobbying the town councils and postcarding their MPs.

Although militancy was discredited as a political weapon, the

League still described itself as militant. Charlotte Despard's view that violence was unethical and irrational had been accepted as policy in the summer of 1912, but civil disobedience 'not merely to annoy the powers that be [but] to give them an object lesson' remained an option. After the Speaker's ruling in January 1913, Charlotte Despard, Isabel Tippett and Nina Boyle made for Trafalgar Square. Ringing bells to attract crowds, they popped up one after the other on different sides of the plinth while policemen raced round it to shoo them away. All three were arrested and given the customary choice of fine or jail, but after two nights in Holloway Charlotte Despard's fine was paid by some anonymous well-wisher and she was released. In April another demonstration, against the passage of the Cat and Mouse Act, brought her another prison sentence – her fourth since the suffrage agitation began – and she was now a trifle blasé about the procedure: 'Day at the police court: the usual thing . . . the ordinary sentence: I went to Holloway with my dear Kate Harvey.' After a sharp row with the governor the next day, she discovered, to her baffled fury, that her fine had once again been paid and she was free.

When Hyde Park was put out of bounds to the militants, Anna Munro and Nina Boyle made a point of conducting Sunday meetings there and were twice imprisoned. Specific occasions such as these produced a steady trickle of prisoners to keep the League represented in prison, but by 1914 they were almost at a loss for 'object-lessons' to give the government. On the eve of the war they were discussing two highly impracticable schemes. The first, which might be called the Lysistrata tactic, involved blackmailing the government by threatening a drive to teach birth control to the working class. It was suggested that the authorities, already seriously alarmed by the falling birthrate, might cave in and grant the vote rather than allow such dangerous knowledge to be disseminated among its breeding stock. 'Of course it is a serious step,' said the originator of the idea; 'for once you start it you cannot stop it.' After heated discussion, several compelling arguments defeated the suggestion – it would take too long to have an effect, it would cause domestic strife, and, depending on the point of view, either it was immoral or the information should be made available anyway for social rather than political reasons. As might have been expected of a Catholic, Charlotte Despard was staunchly opposed to the scheme, and in the course of the debate she recalled the judgement she had passed on a woman who once confessed to her that she used artificial contraception: 'My friend,' she had said, 'you will never be happy with this going on, you are at the present time your husband's harlot.'

Charlotte Despard preferred her own scheme of making a run on the bank's gold reserves, as the men had done to win the first Reform Bill. The war came before her idea could be acted upon, but almost certainly it would have failed because women did not control enough capital to make an impact, and because the supply of gold was far greater in 1914 than in 1832. There were by then no quick solutions left, only the lengthy process of hampering, hindering and protesting.

Tax resistance remained the best example of such militancy and, after the passage of the National Insurance Act, the popularity of this tactic increased to the point where the secretary of the Women's Tax Resistance League estimated that there were 'more than ten thousand resisters'. Not all were suffragettes, for a large number were women who simply ignored or disliked the business of buying a weekly stamp for their servants. But those who were convinced supporters of the suffrage tended to be self-employed, and the majority of them were members of the League. There, were doctors like Elizabeth Knight and Isobel Patch, and writers like Evelyn Sharp – the latter two, who were bankrupted by the Inland Revenue as late as 1917, had a claim to be considered the last of the militants. It was another League member, Dr Wilks, who exposed an absurdity in the tax law when she sued for the return of property distrained to cover her unpaid taxes. She won her case on the grounds that her husband was the one responsible for the debt; but he, an impoverished schoolmaster earning a quarter of her income, was quite incapable of paying her tax and was accordingly sent to prison. The anger aroused by this manifest unfairness was wittily orchestrated by Bernard Shaw, who explained that it was impossible for a husband to force his wife to disclose her income, and equally impossible for him to believe her if she told him anyway. The ridicule and the fury persuaded the Inland Revenue to let the matter drop, and the wretched Wilks was set free.

The most famous insurance resister was Kate Harvey, whose long battle occupied the attention of the press, partly because of her determination, and rather more because the servant whose stamps she would not buy happened to be called Asquith. When a distraint warrant was issued against her in 1912 she barricaded her house, and eight months passed before the bailiffs could force their way in with a crowbar. The following year she still refused to pay and, with a defiant 'I would rather die first', set about building a better barricade. On this occasion the bailiffs needed a battering-ram to get inside, and the courts, deciding to make a example of her, sentenced her to two months in prison.

For the first time in her public life a sense of entirely personal anguish overcame Charlotte Despard's stern sense of duty. Her enthusiasm for work evaporated, and each day her pain was reflected in her diary. 'The miss of my darling always greater. . . . I think of her first at noon and latest at night. . . . Sad and first thoughts always of *her*, my darling . . . feeling of deep depression. . . . The days are dragging, very hard to realise that she has not been in a fortnight.' Eventually the damp cell in which Kate Harvey had been put made her so ill that she had to be released a month early, and there was anger mingled with her friend's relief: 'Then at last the dear face, it seemed changed, she has suffered cruelly. . . . I was so glad it was all over.'

No one else aroused so intense an emotion in her; indeed, in the course of her suffrage career she had taken on such a public life that there sometimes seemed little place left for personal feelings. Her Surrey neighbours shunned her; one little girl who lived near by remembered that 'an aura of disapproval hung around that house, why we never understood – all we could think was that Mrs Despard must be a witch'. Her intimates in the suffrage movement were so much younger than she was that they tended to be admirers rather than equals. Even her long friendship with Mrs Saul Solomon, the widow of a Governor of the Cape Colony, which dated from voyages to India in the company of Max, had at last succumbed to public events. Although she had followed the Pankhursts after the split, Mrs Solomon's trenchant enthusiasm for the women's movement had endeared her to Charlotte, who once wrote to say: 'Wherever you may be in body, your heart and soul will always be with the oppressed and with those who are struggling to free them.' But in 1913 the Union's vandalism became more than Charlotte could tolerate and, in the coolness that developed, she and her 'beloved friend' ceased to communicate.

A few other friends remained from the days of her marriage; but, since they had no interest in socialism or the suffrage, their occasional meetings, snatched amidst the jostle of protest and lecture, had about them a sense of unreality. When she stayed with Max's old friend Arthur Hirschel, the diamond merchant, at his cottage in Sussex, the conversation centred on gardens in general and his in particular, of which he was inordinately proud. 'I told Arthur that when he was my age it would be about right,' she remarked after one meeting in 1913; but time, to which she seemed immune, had everyone else in its grasp. A week after joking with him she noted, 'he looks worn', and, three months later – 'Great shriek of sorrow! I heard the news of the death of my very old and dear friend.' Among others of her own age, she found that Sir Richard Stapley, an architect, was 'looking very old and is nearly blind', while Hans Geiler, an industrialist, had been paralysed by a stroke; she was genuinely pleased that Nora French, her sister-in-law, who was more than fifteen years younger than she, should still be looking 'wonderful for her age'.

In the Victorian manner Charlotte paid dutiful visits to her relatives, most of whom found 'dear old Aunt Lottie', with her mad ideas and bizarre dress, a joke if not an embarrassment. A figure of fun to the younger generation, she was an irritation to her sisters, with the exception of the youngest, Katie Harley. She alone had enlisted in the struggle for women's suffrage, although as a member of the NUWSS's Executive she hardly saw eye to eye with Charlotte. Nevertheless, in their fleeting encounters Katie showed a genuine warmth – unlike her others sisters – in the exchange of news and the reminiscences of 'old, old times'.

Charlotte's brother Jack, whom she continued to hold in the warmest affection, was now Chief of the Imperial General Staff, and the duties of preparing the army for war and preventing mutiny in Ulster forbade any meetings. Only after his resignation over the Curragh incident in March 1914 did he pay her two brief visits, on one of which the presence of his latest mistress kept their conversation to generalities. Charlotte gave no sign of being aware of the relationship, and by then it would have been strange if she had even let the topic enter her mind.

Since her discovery of Theosophy, with its all-encompassing explanation of the mechanism of humanity, a thin missionary frost had begun to settle on her mind. Universal laws rather than individual relationships occupied her attention. She felt passionately about people in general rather than in particular. She was even inclined to picture herself less as a being than as an instrument of the world-mind, the bearer of a message. In this vaulted state of mind, the sharp emotion she felt for Kate Harvey rang discordant and distracting echoes.

They were both women of strong convictions, intuitive in their responses, idealist in their aims; but their approach was crucially different. In her fierce, silent world, Kate Harvey could only deal with one person at a time, and the needs of that person occupied her to the exclusion of all else, but Charlotte was no longer capable of that single-minded attachment to an individual. Repeated misunderstandings arose out of her determination to speak at a meeting or attend a demonstration even at the expense of Kate Harvey's private arrangements, and, although Charlotte agonized about the conflict, the public commitment almost invariably won out. 'Long talk with KH,' she wrote in 1913; 'she cannot bear my militancy – it goes to my heart because *she* suffers. May I do the right!' Doing the right in this case turned out to be a militant protest against the ban on suffragette meetings.

These were flaws in an otherwise warm affection, but a potentially far more serious cause of dispute arose over Charlotte's ward. When Rosalie Mansell eventually left to be cured of her addiction at the end of 1912, Charlotte became responsible for Vere, now a mischievous, emotionally insecure ten-year-old whom a succession of schools had failed to control. Although she wanted to sympathize, Charlotte constantly resorted to stiff lectures on proper behaviour, almost like one of her own dreaded governesses – 'you shouldn't boast . . . never forget how much people have done for you . . . do try to be a little more thoughtful.' 'I can't say she felt motherly love for me,' Vere wrote many years later. 'I never remember her hugging me or nursing me, though she may have done so when I was very small, but she gave the love and protection she knew of, and as I never had anything else I didn't miss it.' She was frequently exasperated by the girl and bothered by her own impatience, and she was conscious too that Kate Harvey expected her to devote more time and attention to Vere's difficulties. But she was an old and busy woman, and she had an urgent message to deliver to the world.

The apocalyptic note which she had struck in her first Theosophical pamphlet was repeated more forcefully in her next publication, *Theosophy and the Women's Movement*, which appeared in 1913:

In the development of civilisation the love-instinct must predominate, and so women will have to play a large part in the reconstruction of society which will follow the era of destruction which seems to lie in front of us. Let me put the position clearly. Revolt is in the air. Against dire poverty and its hideous humiliations the heart of humanity is rebelling.

The need to knit the strands of revolt together drove her to add, to the endless list of League branches that wanted to hear her, Theosophical lodges, socialist churches and striking workers. There was a miscellany of trade-union, tax-resistance and anti-White-Slavery organizations to address. In June 1913 she travelled to Budapest for an International Congress of Women and spoke to large crowds on the coming upheaval: 'I was astonished by our reception', she wrote, 'and the feeling there is about militancy.' She returned with the Congress's message that everywhere women were looking to Britain for a lead, and the sense of urgency became greater still.

A few days in November suggest the crowded life she was now leading:

16th After mass to Regents Park for open-air meeting of WFL; to Caxton Hall where large assembly [of the League]; Rev. Hatty Baker preached, Ibsen reading . . . then we broke up and went to Downing St. Meeting very impressive, four arrests.
17th Ealing Broadway; fair [League] meeting for a wet night.
18th Vote conference; Nine Elms mothers meeting; left early to go to Actresses' Franchise meeting . . . then to Shop-Assistants' Union meeting at Clapham, spoke on Women as Citizens.
19th Caxton Hall; [League] meeting good and enthusiastic; Albert Hall, a grand and excited meeting; disturbances from students, quietened by Larkin who was simply splendid, then Tillett who was fine.

In an attempt to slow the pace, Kate Harvey took her away on holiday to Switzerland; but on her return Charlotte found the Battersea building labourers out on strike, and the lack of food for their children persuaded her to set up and help administer a distress fund for those in need. It seemed that for every family aided there was another furiously indignant at being left out, and so another wives' committee was formed to unify them again, as the earlier one had done. As if that were not enough, her involvement with the Shop Assistants' Union required her to address meetings of the striking shop-girls; she could not refuse a request from an old friend of the ILP, John Scurr, to speak on his behalf at a by-election in Bethnal Green; and the insistent claims of Irish socialism were making themselves felt. It was impossible for her not to join Connolly on a socialist platform in Edinburgh, or to avoid forming a Catholic women's committee in Battersea to provide holidays for the children of Larkin's tramway strikers,* or to remain silent at a Trafalgar Square demonstration in April against the Ulster Unionists' incitement of 'brothers shooting brothers' – but silent she had to be, for by then her voice had given out.

She had in fact almost worked herself to death, and although Kate Harvey immediately took her away on holiday again the infection in her throat spread and for a few weeks she lay seriously ill and barely conscious. 'Illness is a new experience for me,' she wrote in the first days of returning lucidity, 'and I have had some strange thoughts . . . of those who suffer, the great multitude without alleviations, and I vowed, if recovery came, to devote myself more than I have to their service.' She chafed against the confines of her sick-bed, and it was not until June that she could write: 'I am with great gladness able to shake off invalid ways . . . stimulated by the papers I began to throw together a leader, "Is it war?" '

There were so many wars to choose from – the sex war, the class war, the spiritual war – but it hardly mattered which. To a child of the Darwinian era, brought up in security, knowing that progress was the inescapable lot of mankind, the approaching conflict could only presage an upward stage in civilization's history.

The little burst of energy was premature. Still weakened by illness, Charlotte decided to take a long holiday with her Irish cousins, the Franks, who lived in County Cork. News of the outside world hardly penetrated there: 'They bathed, I paddled and read the melodramatic papers . . .' was her entry for 29 July 1914.

---

* Jim Larkin, the leader of the Irish Transport Workers' Union, led a series of strikes in 1913 and 1914 which provoked widespread violence.

Two days leater her holiday ended, and the deafening thunder of assassination, mobilization and declaration burst upon her when she arrived back in London. On 4 August she recorded: 'Today there was no further room for doubt. Germany has broken the neutrality of Belgium and Great Britain has sent an ultimatum.' The one war she had not considered had broken out, and the era of destruction had come with a vengeance.

9

When war was declared for 'that scrap of paper' which guaranteed Belgian neutrality, the malaise of liberal society was abruptly replaced by a sense of exhilaration and purpose. It was the apotheosis of the chivalric code: to keep one's word no matter what the cost, to protect the weak against the strong and to fight, not for personal gain, but for justice. That Grey's secret diplomacy and the dark understandings of the French and British military staffs had left little alternative was of no account. In the fervour that now intoxicated the nation there was a vein of ecstasy, as though life's inner aim had been revealed. As the recanting pacifist, Gilbert White, wrote: 'To have something before you, clearly seen, which you know you must do and can do, and will spend your utmost strength, and perhaps your life, in doing is one form at least of very high happiness . . .' Compared to the confusion, the deadlock, frustration and inconsequence, of the previous years, war became the most glorious assertion of humanity.

Without sharing in the general elation, the vast majority of women in the suffrage movement accepted without hesitation that the demands of their country superseded all other considerations. On the day that Britain's ultimatum was sent to Germany, Charlotte Despard and Millicent Fawcett attended a meeting of Women for Peace; but, when the ultimatum expired, Mrs Fawcett told the NUWSS: 'Women, your country needs you . . . let us show ourselves worthy of citizenship, whether our claim to it be recognized or not.' Accordingly suffrage work was suspended, and their energies were directed towards relief projects for the unemployed and for refugees, and most notably towards equipping and staffing the Scottish Women's Hospital, which was sent to Serbia. The reaction of the Pankhursts went beyond the NUWSS. They not only ceased to be suffragettes, but of all women became the most vociferous in their support of the government's war efforts. 'Militants will fight for their country as they have fought for the vote', the *Suffragette* avowed, and their strident hounding of young men into the army bore no little resemblance to their attempts to hound the government into giving women the vote. But it was more than resemblance – it was precisely the same impulse at work.

As Christabel Pankhurst's espousal of chastity had already suggested, her anger at male society stemmed from its betrayal of the chivalric values in which she believed more strongly than any. The war now offered men the chance of redeeming themselves – or, as her mother put it: 'I want men to go to battle like the knight of old who knelt before the altar and vowed that he would keep his sword stainless and with absolute honour to his nation.' If militancy could not instil purity, then Kitchener, the celibate warlord, would.

While the Pankhursts believed the war to be the saving grace for a corrupted society, Charlotte Despard took it as its final condemnation.

So long as materialism – physical force – is the order of the day, so long as the spiritual consideration, which women and honest workers of both sexes could bring to the government, is absent, we shall have these epidemics of armed strife, this war hysteria. We must keep our own flag flying and emphasise our demand to have a voice in decision.

And so the League continued alone to hold weekly suffrage rallies in London's parks, to proselytize in holiday resorts and to bombard the government with deputations and petitions whenever suffrage reform was mentioned. 'Wear your badge!' a regular notice in *The Vote* insisted. 'Never go without it! Our best service for the country is still our demand for citizens' rights.'

It was not their only service. On the outbreak of war a spontaneous boycott of clothes and luxuries occurred – ironically, the very action that Charlotte Despard had long advocated – and the number of people out of work suddenly doubled. In many families the husband had already gone off to join the army and, since military allowances were slow to come through, the distress was acute. A relief fund of £4,500,000 was raised, under the patronage of the Prince of Wales, for the dependants of servicemen, but it was distributed through the Soldiers' and Sailors' Families Association on the grudging principles of the Charity Organisation Society, and local distress committees had to sustain both those who fell outside the fund's scope, and those averse to the SSFA's officious procedure.

Like the NUWSS and Sylvia Pankhurst's East London Federation, the League formed a relief organization, the National Aid Corps, to direct contributions and volunteers to help in this emergency. It set up three workshops for unemployed women to make children's clothes after a 'hygienic' pattern designed by its president, but its most distinctive contribution was to call for recruits to form a corps of Women Police Volunteers, who would act as special constables and also pay welfare visits to soldiers' families.

When war broke out, Charlotte Despard had been living in Nine Elms for more than twenty years; and in that first bright summer, the young men who hurried off to enlist were the 'old boys' of the Despard Club, whom she had gathered in off the streets as babies, nursed in the clinic, inspected at school and supervised in their boisterous, cigarette-smoking adolescence. In the first month, over 300 of them exchanged their constricted, uncertain existence in Nine Elms for the excitement and economic security of the Army, and they left behind wives and children without so much as the occasional earnings of a costermonger's barrow to sustain them. She was not taken unawares when the first victims of the chivalrous impulse proved to be women and children. Her own immediate reaction to war had been to order 200 pairs of children's boots and a stock of clothing material. But the need was more pressing than she had anticipated. Not only were army allowances slow to come through; they only amounted to 11s 1d for the wife and 1s 9d for each child – little more than Poor Law relief. And the economic disruption had destroyed the livelihood of home-workers who were dependent on orders from milliners and dressmakers. In Nine Elms there was no margin of safety, and many of 'her' families came close to starvation

Admirably direct in a crisis, Charlotte Despard brought in a large supply of dried milk for the most urgent cases, expectant and nursing mothers, and distributed milk and milk puddings to stave off the worst effects of famine. With less immediately successful results, she helped to set up local distress committees in the area; but they bore the hallmark of all her committees and their good intentions were much handicapped by ill-tempered argument. Fortunately the League had learned how to cope with the vagaries of its president. The National Aid Corps took over the supply of milk and was soon feeding about seventy mothers daily, while other volunteers under the direction of Isabel Tippett revived the cheap meals service for children which had lapsed on Rosalie Mansell's departure. Tables and benches were installed, a vegetarian cook was hired to provide broth and suet pudding and, after a series of mishaps in which her customers loudly refused to eat vegetable soup and the cook resigned in high dudgeon, the restaurant eventually served about 250 meals a day at a penny a plate. Finally a nursery was opened for children whose mothers were sick, and the provision of all these amenities, together with the still-continuing clinic, had such a marked effect on the children's health that even in 1917, when the high cost of living and shortage of food had produced a general infantile debilitation, sickness among Nine Elms schoolchildren averaged no more than 5 per cent, against a national figure of 16 per cent.

The creation of this minute welfare state confined Charlotte Despard for a time to Nine Elms. There were rarely enough helpers in the restaurant, so she took her place ladling out soup and controlling the uproar of a hundred children: there were boots to be distributed, clothes to be handed out, sick children to be visited, and above all there was morale to be sustained in fatherless, husbandless homes. Like a wandering friar in habit and sandals she patrolled the shabby streets of Nine Elms, consoling and counselling. 'My constant cry is "Don't worry, it's so bad for the children",' she wrote. 'And very often a smile comes, and we have a little talk, and I know that, for the moment at least, the burden is shifted.' There should, she suggested in a letter to *The Times*, be 'two or three amusing people posted in every area from where soldiers have gone to give a lead and lighten the prevailing gloom'. Thirty years later the BBC took on that job, but in 1914 there was only the traditional remedy, and suddenly the newspapers were lashing up a scandal about soldiers' wives drinking away their husbands' allowances.

Before the end of the year the British Expeditionary Force, under its commander, Field-Marshal Sir John French, had almost perished in holding the line at Ypres, and as the optimism of August vanished, a wave of hysterical anger was directed at those who stayed at home. Young women with nothing better to occupy them handed out white feathers signifying cowardice to men of military age in civilian clothes, and others turned vengefully on the wives of the soldiers themselves. 'Day by day women come to us, assuring us they and their children are starving and pleading for larger grants from the society,' wrote an SSFA official in October. 'And all the time puffing in our faces fumes of whisky, gin and the like.' Quite sensibly Charlotte Despard pointed out that, if women were going to the pubs, it was for the comfort of company as much as of drink, and the solution was to provide pubs without alcohol;* but it was not a time for sense to prevail. In November a deputation of ladies from the SSFA, led by the Duchess of Marlborough, made an official complaint to the Home Secretary about the drinking, and the government responded immediately by placing all servicemen's dependants under police supervision and stipulating that no allowance should be paid to a woman deemed 'unworthy' of it. In December the Commanding Officer in Cardiff went further. Using his powers under the Defence of the Realm Act (DORA), he ordered all soldiers' wives to be off the streets by 7 pm under a maximum penalty of three months in prison, and immediately court-martialled five women who disobeyed the edict, sentencing them to sixty-two days in jail. Other area commanders were less extreme, but up and down the country they arbitrarily imposed curfews of varying sorts on all women, which ranged from banning them in pubs after 6 pm to forbidding them to approach within a prescribed distance of military camps. To add insult to injury, the SSFA published a letter from General Smith-Dorrien, in which he advised them to 'Tell the women and girls, they can serve their country best by leading quiet lives, thus setting an example of self-restraint.' It was still recognizably the nineteenth century speaking, but the voice had developed a rough edge in extremity.

If the League had needed any justification for its decision to keep the suffrage flag flying it was provided by these discriminatory measures. There was in fact nothing to substantiate the SSFA ladies' allegations. Apart from a short jump in the first week after the declaration of war, the figures for drunkenness among women had not increased, and the League could show that in Glasgow, for instance, only eight women had been convicted for

* In March 1915 the teetotal Despard Arms was opened, and operated successfully near Hampstead for four years.

the offence in the first four months of the war. Nina Boyle wrote an angry protest to the Prime Minister against the sex discrimination in pubs and the police surveillance of dependants which, she noted, was 'class legislation of a peculiarly intolerable kind as we understand that the wives and families of officers will not be subjected to these indignities'.

Two months later, in January 1915, the League organized demonstrations in Edinburgh and in its familiar haunt of Trafalgar Square, where it was joined by the East London Federation and two other small societies to protest against the discriminatory regulations and police surveillance. Quite logically, both meetings ended with a call for the vote. Later, Charlotte Despard and Sylvia Pankhurst took a deputation to the War Office and won some partial redress when they were assured that the orders imposing a night curfew had been suspended, but the surveillance and withdrawal of allowances continued.

To encourage resistance at a local level, Charlotte Despard became president of the Soldiers' and Sailors' Dependants' Society, which, in Preston, succeeded in having the orders withdrawn by showing that they were unnecessary and only encouraged gossip and rumourmongering. There were not many such successes, and in the end it was the need for women workers – who had to be out late, were economically independent and could not be denied some of the indulgences granted to male workers – that made the regulations redundant.

The employment of women police was the first crack to be made in the barrier surrounding the preserve of male jobs. The volunteers who answered Nina Boyle's call in August 1914 were trained in jiu-jitsu and court procedure, and wore a uniform of long skirts and Norfolk jackets of blue serge, topped by a straw Panama hat. In November two of them were sent at the request of the authorities to help the police in Grantham, and soon afterwards another pair began service in Hull. Ironically, their first job was to enforce the hated curfew on women, and Nina Boyle, who deemed the ordinance illegal, withdrew the League's support after three months, leaving the development of the force to its two earliest recruits, Damier Dawson and Mary Allen. Nevertheless, it was a portent that the peculiar demands of modern war should so soon have required the presence of women in a man's job.

By the beginning of 1915 the brief slump at the start of the war had ended, and with a return to full employment the League's two workshops could be closed down. In February the first effects of the huge diversion of manpower into Kitchener's armies began to be felt; Edinburgh Corporation, for instance, was driven by the dearth of men to advertise for 'women of respectable parentage and patriotic feeling' to work as tram-conductors. As male drivers, teachers, ticket-collectors and office-clerks put on khaki, women were taken on in their place, and it was these very visible 'substitutes' who most exercised the popular imagination. But modern war also required modern government. The creation of a new bureaucracy, to oversee military allowances, price controls and the mass of regulations controlling the use of labour and materials, opened up a vast new market for female workers. The 200,000 typists and messengers taken on in government offices were virtually ignored, but the 600,000 women who, from the middle of 1915, began to work in the nationalized munitions industry were never forgotten. Without them the army on the Western Front would have continued to suffer that initial scarcity of shells which, from Neuve Chapelle in March 1915 to Loos in September, left it to attack undamaged trenches defended by uncut barbed wire. The munitions workers were not only an integral part of the military system, they were almost subject to military discipline; for their terms of employment were controlled by a Munitions Tribunal and they were unable to leave their jobs without its authorization. The myth of 'man, the fighter and protector' was clearly in need of adjustment.

The social system against which Charlotte Dexpard had been battling for so long received its death blow in 1915 and 1916, but the tragedy in which it perished overshadowed any pleasure she might have felt. The casualty lists from France brought Nine Elms its quota of sorrow, and for her there was the particular pain of sharing her brother's distress at the toll of his troops. She hungered for his success as urgently as the deep-dyed Pankhursts, but did not hesitate to broadcast her belief that British women should feel that 'the women of Germany, Austria and Hungary are as much our sisters as the women of France'. In place of national and class frontiers, they must found 'a strong European Federation' based upon the sisterhood of women and the brotherhood of workers, which would remove the cause of any further war. In that direction lay the proper course for the new order, but to her despair, it seemed that the new was in danger of inheriting the worst features of the old.

'The great discovery of the war', she wrote in 1916, 'is that the Government . . . can force upon the capitalistic world the superlative claims of the common cause.' It was certainly true that the government had nationalized factories, controlled transport and food and broken up monopolies in a way which would have been unthinkable two years earlier. Yet it winked an eye at the stupendous profiteering in which companies indulged, taking advantage of wartime conditions. In 1915 the British & Argentine Beef Company showed profits up by 600 per cent; in 1916 United Collieries and the Scottish Iron & Steel Company each reported profits of 400 per cent; and Bonar Law revealed that he had made £1000 from a £200 investment in a ship that was sunk: 'there was scarcely a magnate', wrote the novelist Compton Mackenzie, 'who had not waxed fat as a lobster on corpses.'

In the same year, 1916, the Board of Education concluded that one in six schoolchildren was 'so physically and mentally defective as to be unable to derive reasonable benefit from the education which the State provides'. To Charlotte Despard the answer was plain. 'Take over the milk as you have taken over the munitions,' she wrote. 'See that the municipalities distribute it at a fair price.' Instead, the government had suspended regulations requiring the inspection of milk and permitted it to be distributed without any tests for purity, although samples showed that 10 per cent was tuberculous. As a result 60,000 people, mostly children, continued to die each year from TB, with countless others permanently incapacitated.

This was the inheritance of the nineteenth century, and it was intolerable to Charlotte Despard that the government should be blind to the need for new priorities. 'In heaven's name, let us not mince matters,' she cried in the crisis of 1916. 'Now at the eleventh hour, let us be true to ourselves and to one another. . . . We have allowed slum landlords, spirit dealers, sweaters of labour and the adulterers of food and drink their own sweet way for too long.' The habits of the old way were not to be eradicated so easily. The terrible toll in France had forced the government to some reforms, but it continued to ignore among the casualties of war the 100,000 children who were killed annually in their first year, with as many more left crippled by rickets, TB and other diseases.

If the authorities' attitude had not altered in these matters, it might at least be thought that their outlook on women would have changed for the better. When the first appeal was made for women workers in March 1915, the League had written to Asquith asking that, in return, women should be enfranchised. He replied, in pre-war style, that he 'could not consider introducing legislation on the contentious subject of women's suffrage during the course of the war'. A little over sixteen months later, in August 1916, the Commons were debating the urgent need to revise the Parliamentary register so that young servicemen who had no vote could be included on it. When Asquith spoke, it was to announce a spectacular reversal of all his previous utterances: 'I am bound to say that [the suffragists] presented to me not only a reasonable, but, from their point of view, an unanswerable case.'

It appeared to be a notable conversion, and Charlotte Despard concluded in her diary: 'practically our battle is over'. But closer examination showed that the change of attitude did not go deep. Asquith had more to say:

If you are going to bring in a new class of electors, on whatever ground of State service, ... the women of this country have rendered as effective service in the prosecution of the war as any other class of the community.... What is more, and this is a point that makes a special appeal to me, ... when the war comes to an end, and the process of social reconstruction has to be set on foot, have not women a special claim to be heard on the many questions which will arise directly affecting their interests, and possibly meaning for them large displacements of labour?

Clearly, the vote for women was to be a reward for taking on a man's role in an emergency, and a comforter for the return to their proper function in normal times. It was not to be a recognition of equal citizenship.

To avoid controversy, the whole question of a wider franchise was considered first by an all-party committee headed by the Speaker, and its report did not appear until March 1917, by which time Lloyd George had replaced Asquith as Prime Minister. Two months later, on 25 May, almost precisely fifty years after John Stuart Mill first introduced a woman's suffrage amendment, the government brought in its Representation of the People Bill, which, among other things, proposed to enfranchise women over thirty who were on the Local Government Register, or whose husbands were. Warmly bathed in sentiments similar to those expressed by Asquith, the clause survived an attempt to remove it by 385 votes to 55, and thereafter the suffrage societies could watch the government pilot home the measure for which they had fought so long.

The League watched its progress with mixed emotions. 'We do not exult,' its president observed; 'our true feelings lie deeper.' They were a mixture of suspicion and recognition that their business was far from finished. Under the Bill, less than half the 13,000,000 adult women in the country would be eligible to vote; but it was reluctantly accepted that the age and property limitations were politically expedient, so that the 11,000,000 eligible men should not seem to have been outnumbered from the outset. That was a battle for the future; the immediate one was to win a genuine rise in the status of women. The condescending praise for their war work ladled out by journalists and politicians was merely, Nina Boyle suggested, '. . . a thin veneer overlying much distrust and genuine fear . . . a pinchbeck recognition without value or stability, save that it has secured at a certain psychological moment the passage of a women's suffrage clause into the Government's Act'.

As an indication of wartime society's real sentiments, the League took more seriously the popular demand for the reintroduction of the Contagious Diseases Acts. These, originally enacted in 1866 and 1869, had empowered a magistrate to order any girl suspected of being infected with venereal disease to be designated a 'common prostitute' and subjected to compulsory medical examination. Altogether more than 100,000 women were subjected to this degrading process, but less than 10 per cent were found to be infected. It had taken Josephine Butler seventeen years to convince Parliament that the Acts were not only grossly unfair to women but quite ineffective in containing the disease. They had finally been repealed in 1886, but it took only three months of war before the Plymouth Watch Committee called for their re-enactment. The League's intelligence service proved swifter than the government's, and an outraged deputation of Charlotte Despard, Nina Boyle and Sylvia Pankhurst reached Downing Street before the news. Consequently, they were required to explain the nature of the provocation before they could protest against it, but having done so they retired with the Prime Minister's promise that the government had no intention of reintroducing the Acts.

By 1916, largely as a result of Kitchener's decision to train the recruits for his New Armies away from their home areas, but partly also because of the influx of imperial troops to Britain,* the incidence of venereal disease had more than doubled compared to pre-war rates. However, in the locker-room mentality of military commanders there could be no doubt that it was women, not men, who were responsible for spreading infection. For all their fair words, as Nina Boyle pointed out, the newspapers took the same view, 'talking of the responsible men of the nation, once they become soldiers, as if they were innocents, unworldly helpless lambs who require shielding from the world'. Thus *The Observer* could, in the same issue, offer good wishes to the women's suffrage clause and call for 'an extension of the Defence of the Realm Act (DORA) to deport all women from camp areas who cannot give a proper account of themselves'.

In February 1917 it became clear that the government was of like mind. A Criminal Law Amendment Bill was introduced which proposed to make all women suspected of having the disease liable to compulsory examination. Thus, while women's suffrage was proceeding through the Commons, it was accompanied initially by a Bill which suggested that at the deepest level official attitudes had not altered since the mid-Victorian era.

The League's reaction was swift. Overnight all interested bodies were summoned to a meeting at Central Hall, Westminster, and there a campaign was set on foot to persuade MPs that the argument which Josephine Butler had wielded a generation earlier still held good. Twice the government tried to rephrase the offending clauses to meet objections, but they were eventually forced to abandon the Bill for lack of time. Undeterred it brought the Bill back in 1918, and, when it was once more delayed, the original intention was achieved by promulgating Regulation 40d of the DORA. This allowed a magistrate to remand in custody any woman accused of having infected a serviceman, and if examina-

---

* In large towns the rate, according to a Royal Commission on the subject, was 25 per cent, compared to 10 per cent in 1913. It was (and no doubt remains) a fact that the licentiousness of soldiery was greater away from home; thus, in 1921, 21 per cent of the British Army of the Rhine were infected, compared with a mere 4 per cent of the troops at home.

tion found her to have the disease she was liable to six months' hard labour. 'Damnable, lying hypocrisy', Charlotte Despard stigmatized it. 'The accused is sheltered, he can tell his story secretly, with none to contradict him, and the maligned victim has no redress. Can women be blamed for feeling that of all the cynical, one-sided laws that have ever been passed, this is the worst?' Week by week, *The Vote* reported the cases of women hauled up in court on the word of men – strangers, fiancés, husbands – with whom they had quarrelled or broken up. It is impossible to say how many were remanded in custody for examination; over 300 had actually been prosecuted by the end of the war, but only about a third were found guilty.

This most extreme manifestation of sexual hostility was accompanied by other instances of general, if less harmful, discrimination. It could not be overlooked that those much-lauded workers in the National Shell Factories were paid 50 per cent less than men, that cost of living bonuses were halved for female civil servants, and that, despite the government's specific promise, few of the women who stood in for men received their wages. Even so, munitions workers, earning up to £3 a week, enjoyed an economic independence they had never known before, and their high spirits and extravagance provoked the kind of sour misogynism that surfaced in the government's Criminal Law Amendment Bill, which would have made it a crime for a girl under nineteen to wander through the street and behave in a riotous manner – a crime for which she would have been liable to imprisonment until her nineteenth birthday.

While the government veiled its hostility with praise, organized labour took no pains to conceal its dislike. The skilled unions, particularly the Associated Society of Engineers, had fought against the dilution of craftsmen by the employment of women, and only Lloyd George's promise of a return to pre-war practices when peace came had overcome their opposition. The hostility was not diminished when it was found that, after a relatively short training, a woman could exceed a skilled man's production: the Glasgow industrialist, William Beardmore, reported that, 'The actual output by girls with the same machines, and working under exactly the same conditions, and for an equal number of hours, is quite double that of trained mechanics.' Since women's wages were a third less than men's, the engineering industry enjoyed soaring profits, and the unions became grimly convinced that the presence of women in the factories after the war would result either in lower wages or in higher production targets. The unions had no greater love for the 'substitutes': the only statement of policy that the TUC made in wartime about women's work was that bus conductresses should be dismissed 'on moral grounds' after the war.

'When the war is over', Charlotte Despard suggested in 1914, 'we may see a European concert or better a World Federation represented by a great International Council to . . . [arbitrate] on the questions that may threaten to divide the nations.' To bring that moment a little nearer, she had joined the British section of the Women's International League, which was formed in April 1915 by the Women's Peace Congress meeting in The Hague. There was nothing incompatible between women's suffrage and the WIL – indeed, the latter was at first largely composed of former members of the NUWSS who had rejected Millicent Fawcett's order to abandon suffrage work – but it was initially impossible for Charlotte Despard to give any time to this new League. While her brother was in command on the Western Front she did not feel that she could publicly criticize the government's military operations and in fact she added her voice to those appealing for women to help in the war effort; but his removal from command in December 1915 released her from any obligation to guard her tongue.

When the government introduced national service for single males in January 1916, the infant peace movement began to draw her attention more insistently. Meetings of the No Conscription Fellowship appeared in her diary, she joined the National Council against Conscription (later the National Council for Civil Liberties), and a more openly critical note appeared in her speeches. 'I love fighting', she told an audience of Tonypandy miners in April 1916; 'fighting for better conditions – not against the flesh but against spiritual darkness in high places.' The symptoms of darkness had started to spread rapidly – the abolition of habeas corpus, the threat to shoot conscientious objectors in non-combatant units who refused orders, the imprisonment of strikers on the Clyde and the prevalence of rule by regulation through the DORA, military commanders and tribunals. 'We have to keep our eyes very wide open – curious Acts pass through very rapidly now,' she told the miners. 'The women have not been represented in the past – you men are not represented now.' And she ended with a warning that, in terms of civilization, 'I don't think Germany has produced much since she became a military nation, and if we turn ourselves into a military nation we shall not produce much either.'

Barely three weeks after this speech the Easter uprising in Dublin served to trigger off more serious examples of militarism than she had feared. Like most of the people in Ireland, she was not struck by the significance of the occupation of the Dublin post office and other key areas until after the brief revolt had collapsed and its leaders, including James Connolly, had been executed. It was the news of the murder of Francis Sheehy-Skeffington, a pacifist and suffragist, shot down while unarmed by a British officer, that provided the clue: 'This', she exclaimed, 'is *militarism*!'

In the very week of the Dublin rising, a British army of 9000 men in the town of Kut surrendered to the Turkish army, and the government used these two disasters to impose conscription on all males up to the age of forty-one. Following so closely on the executions in Ireland, conscription aroused in Charlotte Despard her first serious doubt that the war must necessarily bring about progress. Britain itself seemed corrupted and most of its people, made fearful by Irish treachery, the surrender at Kut, the imminent (as it seemed) capture of Verdun and German victories against Russia, were only too willing to accept whatever measures the government imposed.

Staying with a League member in Portsmouth, she quarrelled with her hostess: 'the awful Mrs Johnston is a jingo of the first water!' she wrote angrily. 'I fear I became rather excited and infuriated; how frightful it is when *women* talk of reprisals.' At Nine Elms she quarrelled with Father Flanagan: 'Alas! he is like most of the clerics, and maintains that we are fighting for righteousness, and that war must go on until the enemy is humbled.' Most seriously, she also quarrelled with Kate Harvey.

In August 1916 the two women had bought a holiday home near Hartfield in Sussex, which they named 'Kurandai'. Situated on the edge of Ashdown Forest, with moorland rising up beyond the garden, it recreated that secret childhood plot which had always represented happiness for Charlotte Despard – a garden in the midst of wilderness. Wherever she lived in the country she cultivated roses, delphiniums, hollyhocks and tulips, delighting in the succession of blooms and scents which each month brought out; but it always seemed that she needed some wild ground close at hand, as though it were essential to have an escape route from the well-tended flower-beds. In Kurandai she enjoyed a vicariously domestic life, surrounded by Kate Harvey's three daughters and, later, the handicapped children whom she brought down for fresh air. Significantly, the bitterest argument in their friendship broke over the conflict between the peace movement and the one personal responsibility that was directly hers – for her ward, Vere.

Vere was by now a high-spirited girl in her teens – rather too high-spirited in the opinion of Kate Harvey, who felt that her taste for practical jokes was having a bad effect on her own daughters. Vere, she decided, was being denied love and attention and, in a typically direct way, Kate Harvey could not help letting her friend know. It was difficult advice to take. Charlotte recognized its truth, repeatedly telling herself, 'I must try more, only *love* will save my child', but there were committees to be attended, articles to be written and lectures to be prepared. When Vere was too rowdy she was banned from Kurandai altogether until she showed that she could control herself, and as a general rule the child was packed off whenever possible to school, to friends or back to her mother. Although the latter lived in London, it had always been decided while Rosalie Mansell was in charge that the woman's heavy drinking made her a bad influence. Now, Charlotte Despard allowed herself to believe that Vere would be better off spending more time with her natural mother.

At length Kate Harvey remonstrated with her friend, and Charlotte recorded wearily in her diary: 'She does not understand – I have my duty to the people.' It was a priggish defence, and Kate Harvey was provoked to riposte with bitter congratulations on her popularity and the splendid times she must have with everyone at her feet. Charlotte was wounded to the heart. 'All is dead between us,' she wrote sadly; 'something beautiful has gone.' Still, she did not waver: 'from my point alone I must be true to my duty', she decided, and in the last resort she was prepared to jettison her one close friendship in order to devote herself to her public life.

She could never resist an invitation to join a committee,

although, as Helena Swanwick, president of the Women's International League, briskly remarked, 'she was no good at all on a committee where she found it impossible to bring her mind to bear on a resolution'. In 1916 and 1917 she was on the councils of the Women's Freedom League, the Women's International League, the Battersea branch of the No Conscription Fellowship, the National Council for Civil Liberties, the Theosophical Society, the London Vegetarian Society, the Battersea Labour Party, the Women's Labour League, the Home Rule for India Committee and the Women's Peace Crusade. These required her presence at between twenty and thirty public meetings a month, in addition to her regular attendance at the Nine Elms Settlement. 'I think I see [Kate Harvey's] point,' she wrote, after reflecting on her friend's bitter attack. 'I have taken on too much: if I am to have my child I must give her true, alive thought.' Yet the wide open spaces of public life invariably drew her from domestic concerns, as the moorland lured her from the garden.

The paradox of the philanthropist neglectful of those closest to him is familiar, but it was precisely because Charlotte Despard was prepared to dump all other claims that she was so valued. 'She is pre-eminently great,' Nina Boyle once said, 'morally and physically, because she does not care what results come out of the things which she holds as convictions.' If she was asked to address a peace meeting in Swansea, it was certain that she would be there, even if it meant a cross-country train journey through the night from Newcastle, a long walk in driving sleet and the threat of a riot at the end of it. A journalist described her, frail and ancient, at one such meeting in 1917: 'She seemed to belong to an age of samplers, embroidery and wax fruit.' But she did not falter in the face of a jeering crowd. 'We don't want German peace terms,' they shouted. 'We want *our* terms.' 'You will have neither their nor your own terms,' she retorted. 'You will have God's terms.' There was a flummoxed silence for a few moments, broken by a voice which muttered, 'You'd better get out of this before you get hurt.' 'I am not afraid of Englishmen', she cried. 'None of you will hurt me.'

Her confidence was justified. Although the issues were more urgent, she never suffered the violence that had been stirred up by her suffrage speeches. The threat of physical hurt always remained, of course, and when a neighbour reported that two men 'big as trees' had called for her at Nine Elms while she was out, she had little doubt that they had intended to do her harm. 'What is to be, is to be', she reflected. 'If my message is not to go out, I cannot help it, so only I can serve.'

In the face of such stern intransigence, Kate Harvey gave way, tacitly accepting that Vere would have to be sacrificed to the greater good. Nevertheless, their confrontation in the autumn of 1916 marked the point at which Charlotte Despard admitted the unconditional supremacy of her public life over the most pressing of private considerations. On the one hand it was selfish of her, and Kate Harvey's reference to her love of public acclaim was not unfair; but on the other hand she was engaged on the most noble of all missions – the struggle for peace. Not by one second did Charlotte Despard help to shorten the war, yet, by sacrificing all for that end, she managed to give purpose to the morality for which so many lives had been lost.

At Asquith's prompting, conscientious objection to military service could be claimed not only on religious but on moral grounds – it was, he said, 'a question of a man's heart and conscience' – and the tribunals which heard such claims could impose either non-combatant service, 'work of national importance' or a complete exemption. The conflict between national need and personal conviction brought into the open the two forces which Charlotte Despard identified with the old and new orders. They can perhaps best be illustrated by some of the exchanges between tribunal and objector.

At Battersea, a clergyman asked the objector what he would do if a German attacked his mother with a bayonet. 'Do you believe in God?' the objector replied. 'Look here, young man,' his questioner said sharply, 'impertinence won't do you any good. You must know that I am a clergyman.' 'Then you do believe in God,' the objector answered. 'Don't you think then that my mother's life would be much safer in His hands than in mine, stained with my brother's blood?' More curtly, the same conflict emerged at the Oldbury tribunal, when the chairman asked incredulously, 'Do you really mean to say you wouldn't kill *anybody*?' 'Yes', said the objector. 'What an awful state of mind to be in,' the chairman exclaimed. And one of the pleasantest and most eloquent examples came from Wandsworth jail, where a crowd of conscientious objectors began singing hymns and 'the Red Flag' in the dining-hall, to the visible annoyance of the murderers, burglars, rapists and robbers peacefully eating their meal. 'March those noisy devils out of here!' roared the Assistant Governor. 'I won't have them disturbing the decently behaved, respectable prisoners.'

Such encounters made concrete what Charlotte Despard used to refer to as 'the war of the spirit against the flesh'. It was the same war which pitted the women's movement against the government, but with each case she became more convinced that the objectors were now the ones in the front line.

Unlike any other war, the Great War was remarkable in that each of the combatant nations in Europe which asked for peace did so because its civilian population had refused to sustain the war, rather than because its armies had been defeated. Since the prime military goal was never directly achieved, it is perfectly possible to see the war through Charlotte Despard's eyes as a struggle to persuade the people to seek peace. Thus the victors were Lenin, Liebknecht and the nationalists of the Austro-Hungarian Empire.

The first and greatest of these victories was prefigured by the March revolution in Russia, which overthrew the Tsar and established parliamentary democracy with universal suffrage. The House of Commons sent its congratulations to the Duma (the new Soviet State Council), as did Tom Mann, the syndicalist; and Emmeline Pankhurst was almost as delighted as Charlotte Despard, who struggled for words to express her excitement. 'My sisters,' she wrote in an open letter to Russian women, 'I cannot use the ordinary commonplaces. To say that I congratulate you would be out of place. Rather – I am with you – we are one.' In her enthusiasm it seemed quite possible that a revolution which had succeeded in breaking the iron hold of the most notorious police state in the world could well take hold in Britain. She joined an *ad hoc* group called the United Socialists, which planned to set the idea in motion through a grand conference of socialists.

The 'Great Labour, Socialist and Democratic Convention' met in the unreal setting of the Coliseum Picture Palace, Leeds, and passed four resolutions hailing the Russian revolution, applauding its peace proposals, calling on the British government to establish a truly democratic state after the Russian model, and setting up local workers' and soldiers' councils, or soviets, to achieve real democracy. Ramsay MacDonald told the audience that the working class had regained the initiative seized by the ruling class at the beginning of the war; Dora Montefiore called on the people to 'dig their trenches and consolidate themselves in order to abolish wage slavery and bring in the co-operative commonwealth'; and Charlotte Despard cried, 'Let us in Heaven's name do something, arrange something, whereby in combination we shall show our power and make the power of the people tell.' None of these deserved to be called a plan of action, and the conference as a whole applauded the Russian revolution rather as a step towards peace than as an example to be followed. MacDonald was acutely embarrassed to be placed in charge of the provisional committee organizing the workers' councils, and most of the trade-union leaders followed his example in ducking out of any active role.

There were enough idealists present to make an attempt at putting the resolutions into effect. Sylvia Pankhurst took the ideas back to the East End and founded the Workers' Socialist Federation, and Willie Gallacher used them to inspire the Clyde shop-stewards' committee, which at times almost resembled a soviet. Charlotte Despard, the only woman elected to the provisional committee (on the strength of an inspiring speech about the loss of freedom in speech, political association and wage bargaining), took the responsibility for forming a soviet in Newcastle. It met in July, a pandemonic occasion on which servicemen invaded the theatre where delegates were meeting, and choruses of 'Rule Britannia' intermingled with 'The Red Flag', the sound of breaking chairs, scuffled fights and earnest pleas for unity and brotherhood from the speakers on the stage. Charlotte Despard denied that they wanted peace at any price – 'an honourable end to the war' she said was the objective – but soon afterwards the stage was rushed, bringing an end to the only meeting of the Newcastle soviet. Similar scenes occurred in Swansea and, with particular violence, in London, for the execrations of the yellow press had goaded people to fury against the soviets, less for their revolutionary than for their pacifist tendencies. By the end of the year, Lenin's peace overtures to the Germans had destroyed the last vestiges of popular support in Britain.

The failure of the soviets cast a cloud over Charlotte Despard. For the first time she began to feel her age, and when she went on holiday that summer it was with the meagre hope that 'the fresh air and rest will make me strong enough for another winter'. Death was much on her mind; as her diary put it, she was 'thinking much of the other side'. Old friends like Felix Moschelle and Sir Richard Stapley had recently died, and, saddest of all, her youngest sister, Katie Harley, had been killed in March. She had been serving with the Scottish Women's Hospital in Serbia when a shell exploded nearby and she was struck by a splinter. Her death left Charlotte with no other intimate but her brother Jack. 'He is, I think, dearer to me than anyone else,' she confessed after one of their meetings. But these were rare occasions, for he was still on active service, in command of Home Forces, and it was not desirable that he should be seen in public with his pacifist sister. Each of their meetings was a landmark, 'a day to be written in red letters' she would say, but the intensity of joy made the absence of other personal feelings the more noticeable. When she hurled herself back into the peace movement that autumn it was with the driving urgency she had shown just before the war broke out.

The one remaining token of the Leeds convention was the Women's Peace Crusade, which in July had assembled 14,000 people on Glasgow Green to acclaim the peace policy of the new Russian regime. Its founders included Ethel Snowden, Helena Swanwick and Charlotte Despard, all members of the WIL, and a former stalwart of the Freedom League, Muriel Matters. With a potent mixture of socialism and Christian morality, they worked to build a peace constituency from Quakers, red Clydesiders, nonconformists and ILP pacifists. Morally and politically, the message accorded closely with Charlotte Despard's personal beliefs, and she preached it with the passion of a sacred text. 'Brotherhood' was the title she gave to her talk, and it referred to the brotherhood of the pre-Babel peoples, as well as the brotherhood of workers: Christ, as an adept of ancient and occult knowledge, had left with his immediate followers the secrets of the early harmony, she said, and it was only the corruption of Christianity and the greed of capitalism that had obscured his teaching and permitted war to be waged. 'I should like the words "alien" and "foreigner" to be banished from the language', she would declare; 'we are all members of the same family.' The terms of peace did not enter her scope; the supreme need was to recognize the common brotherhood of the warring nations, and only then could the terms be discussed.

She was now possessed by a fear that civilization itself might not survive the terrible era of destruction. 'It is urgent', she wrote in 1917: 'if, indeed, it [peace] is not immediately supplied the whole civilised world will find itself in a maelstrom of ruin from which there will be no escape.' The fear grew until it haunted her permanently. 'All the time there was the great ache at one's heart', she admitted in 1918, 'for the piteous tragedy in which western civilisation seems to be ending, but in truth we do not want the old state of things to go on.'

Beside this catastrophe, the claim of women, already half won, had to give way, and the success of the Representation of the People Bill shone with a very thin gleam. When the House of Lords accepted the Bill on 10 January 1918, Charlotte Despard wrote bleakly: 'The first phase of our battle is over . . . it is with no exultation or rapture of gratitude that we acclaim our victory, but rather with wonder that such an elementary act of justice should have been so long delayed.' Even in such unpropitious circumstances it was a cold reception to give to the triumph of twelve years' labour, as she herself seemed to recognize when she remarked in her diary: 'How strange! a year or two ago we would have been full of exultation, – now – .' Another cause had at last overshadowed the importance of the vote, and in October 1917 she had asked to be relieved of the presidency of the Freedom League.

She was persuaded to stay on until the victory conference met in February 1918, but then she announced her irrevocable decision to leave. Her work for the Women's Peace Crusade was a calling which could not be denied, she said, any more than she had been able to refuse the call of socialism and the women's movement before it. Her decision was not altogether regretted by those who felt that the League was becoming associated with her pacifism, but it was a hard blow nevertheless, since she was, as everyone accepted, the very embodiment of the League. She did not cut her links entirely, for she remained a member of the Executive; but to all intents she was now abandoning, amid cascades of praise, the organization she had founded more than eight years earlier.

The Women's Peace Crusade now occupied her as the League had done in those far-off days. Three times in the last year of the war she traversed Yorkshire and Lancashire, twice she toured Scotland and Wales and the Midlands, and she made repeated forays around London. Like other pacifists she discovered that, the further she went from the capital, the more warmly her cause was accepted. Her diary for a few days of one such tour in January 1918 conveys the mood and audience which were typical of her Crusade meetings:

January 6th. Keighley, Yorkshire. I delight in the family with whom I am staying. Morning and afternoon went with them to the Baptist Mission Service: afternoon held our Crusade meeting in a large dingy hall – packed! At first there were signs of disturbance, but it passed and I had a very attentive meeting.

January 7th. Stayed with another Yorkshire family, father a railway worker, all keen ILPers, much enthusiasm for peace. Hall not so large, but well-filled with a most sympathetic audience.

January 8th. To Blackburn. Almost all women in the 'Friends' meeting house – rapt attention. A fine young factory girl was in the chair – her sweetheart is in prison. I am finding a fine, spirited audience in these women of the north.

January 9th. To Bolton. Met by WPC secretary, an eager-eyed girl, one of her brothers is a Conscientious Objector in Wakefield prison. Atmosphere of enthusiasm and determination at the meeting which helped me.

January 10th. To Nelson. The Great Hall held a large and very enthusiastic crowd – the Peace resolution was passed by acclamation. Stayed in a worker's pleasant little home; his son is a CO in Dartmoor.

January 11th. Snow falling persistently and I bought a pair of man's galoshes to put over my sandals – these make me impervious to weather.

January 13th. To Accrington. Heavy snow blocked the tram-lines. Earnest little crowd in the ILP rooms – many women; they flocked round me after it broke up to ask what they could go. A meeting is to be held to start a Crusade here.

By the end of the war there were about a hundred branches of the Crusade in existence, with perhaps fifty members each; but the number of sympathizers was far greater. Over 4000 people gathered on the links at Leith to hear Mrs Despard speak in October 1917; 60,000 signed the WIL's peace petition; more than 100,000 bought copies of her pacifist pamphlet, *An Appeal to*

Women; and the Union for Democratic Control, to which all pacifist-inclined bodies were affiliated, estimated the membership of its affiliates to be 650,000.

As Charlotte Despard's diary suggested, these were for the most part people without influence, idealists outside the main structure of society; but they had a powerful ally in the rising tide of resentment in the labour movement. It was provoked by conscription, the high cost of living and government directives controlling the movement of the workforce. In January 1918, the Labour Party conference, which Charlotte Despard attended as a delegate for Battersea, gave expression to their feelings by adopting a resolution urging the government to seek peace by negotiation. More powerful yet was the impetus which the American President Wilson gave in the same month by offering his Fourteen Points as the basis for a negotiated end to the war.

When German armies, reinforced by troops from the Russian front, poured through the Allied lines in the spring of 1918, the peace movement gathered strength in Britain, and Cabinet Ministers were forced to tour the country in a furious effort to shore up the national resolve to continue fighting. Throughout those months, Charlotte Despard was torn by alarm at the German success, but her faith in the power of international socialism was unabated. However belligerent their governments might be, the people, she believed, were peace-loving.

On 5 May, Labour Sunday, she went to Finsbury Park to celebrate the centenary of Karl Marx's birth. The meeting had been banned, but since a crowd had gathered she took her place on the platform:

I spoke for about a quarter of an hour to a spirited meeting before a posse of police arrived. I insisted on putting our resolution, and it was passed with acclaim, then bodies of men in blue, on foot and on horseback, came pouring in. We fell back singing The Red Flag and cheering the Revolution.

It was a stirring moment, and perhaps as close as she came to winning her pacifist war. A month later the German tide had halted, and as the current began to flow towards the East, similar scenes in Berlin and the industrial cities of Germany heralded the end.

The voices of peace became more insistent – from America,

from neutral countries and from Germany itself – but they were dismissed as 'a mare's nest' by Balfour, on behalf of the government. 'Heavens, how they cling to their war!' Charlotte Despard exclaimed in horror. But the politicians were now safe, for as the prospect of victory came closer, the industrial unrest which had made the peace movement so formidable turned its attention to mundane matters of wages and production targets.

When the first strong rumour of peace came in October, Charlotte Despard almost fainted from relief – 'I had not realised until then', she said, 'the weight, the awful tension that had been upon us' – and when the fighting continued, each casualty became an unforgivable murder. She was staying at Kurandai when the spreading revolution in Germany and the Allied advance at last brought the nightmare to an end.

Glorious sunrise, red streaming under a canopy of clouds. Feeling a little strange and sad, I went up to the moorland alone. I took it very quietly, resting from time to time, and tried very hard to steady my thoughts. There were many changes, breaks of palest blue between the clouds, some of which were very heavy, and woods and meadows in the distance lighted up. The air, the silence, the breadth of everything helped, but I was not quite calm.

The madness was past and, from the vast amphitheatre of chaos, the world slowly descended to the puny chessboard of peace.

An election had been confidently predicted before the year's end, whether or not hostilities had ceased, and political campaigning had been added to her engagements since July. The centre of Labour's affairs was a seedy club in Gerrard Street, named the 1917 Club in honour of the Russian revolution, and there Charlotte Despard found herself promoted to the informal councils of the Party's leaders. That pacifists like MacDonald and Snowden should have been ready to discuss peacetime strategies with her was understandable, but from right across Labour's spectrum her public standing was recognized by the flood of invitations from Parliamentary candidates asking her to speak for them. In Battersea itself she was appointed to the selection committee responsible for finding candidates for the two constituencies into which the borough was now divided.

John Burns was still the sitting member, and his organization continued to exist in skeleton form, but full employment had weakened its hold on voters, and, more importantly, his own will to power had spent itself. 'Strange to meet him again', she wrote when he appeared before the selection committee; 'he is now white-haired and with a furrowed face.' Having resigned from the government in 1914 in opposition to the war, Burns could not stand on Lloyd George's coalition ticket; but, when he refused to accept the principles of the Labour Party's constitution, the Battersea committee declined to accept him as a candidate. The denial of the candidacy was almost the only power left to the local party after thirty years of Burns' rule in Battersea. Ward leaders, councillors and officials were Burnsites first and Labour second, and the majority of them followed the lead of the most powerful figure in the Tammany Hall organization, Sam Brogan, who immediately endorsed the coalition candidate. Gutted of its leadership, the local party at first announced that it would take no part in the election, but then, as a last resort, the committee appealed to Charlotte Despard to accept the candidacy. 'A curious surprise,' she wrote. 'At first I refused, but it was pointed out that this was the only way – or hope – to save the seat for Labour, and so I gave in.'

The Act permitting women to become MPs had been squeezed through Parliament in the last days before dissolution, and seven others beside Charlotte Despard stood in this first election for which they were eligible. Only one, Christabel Pankhurst, received the endorsement of the coalition, and she was given a straight run against Labour in Smethwick. No fewer than four former members of the Freedom League were in the fight, but it was Charlotte Despard who commanded the most enthusiastic support.

She certainly stood in need of help. Her opponent was backed by the Conservatives, the Liberals and a breakaway part of the Labour Party. Endorsed by the coalition, he had the right to employ its two most potent slogans – 'Hang the Kaiser' and 'Make Germany pay. Squeeze her till the pips squeak.' His manifesto was simple: 'We have won the war,' it read, 'but we have not yet won the peace. Would it be safe to give a voice in the settlement of the victory to a Pacifist? Remember that the path of duty is the path of safety.' As if this were not sufficient he also put it about that, since Mrs Despard supported the Bolsheviks who had made peace with Germany, she was little better than a German herself.

Against this, she could only put her long residence in Nine

Elms and the Irishness of the Despards and the Frenchs, but her manifesto did at least talk about recognizable issues such as the need for better housing, free secondary education and free milk for children. She had the official support of some trade unions and the main Labour Party, but it was doubtful if the rank and file would follow suit. 'She is undoubtedly a contestant to be reckoned with,' *The Times* commented, 'but as she is credited with opinions which belong to the extreme wing of the Socialist Party, it is not expected that anything like the full Labour vote will go in her favour.'

For the first week of the campaign her opinions were in any event scarcely heard at all, since an attack of bronchitis prevented her speaking. When she did recover, she immediately began to fulfil her promises to speak for other candidates. The League did what it could, canvassing and addressing the voters in her absence; but instead of gratitude it earned only her blame for providing too many women speakers: 'How often one has to say "Save me from my friends",' she said peevishly.

Handicapped though it was, her campaign suddenly caught light a week before polling day:

For the first time I felt the heat and passion of the election were being felt . . . three big meetings, all good, the [Latchmere] Baths were overflowing and full of enthusiasm, and for the first time I heard the note of opposition strong. Hang the Kaiser, Indemnity! I dealt with them as straightly as possible and the audience were with me.

Incautiously, the League allowed itself to be carried away. ('Judging from the interest and enthusiasm aroused,' the helpers reported, 'we anticipate a great victory for Mrs Despard.') Her opponent repeated the smears, little boys trailed her in the streets shouting 'German' at her, she accused him of underhand tactics, and then it was all over with nothing to do but observe the novel spectacle of women queueing up outside the polling booths.

There was a fortnight's delay before the results were announced, during which she firmly told herself, 'I must not look forward.' But she could not help seeing that the *Nation* had listed hers as one of several seats where a Labour victory could be expected. On 28 December she went to Battersea Town Hall to hear the result. 'A painful day ever to be remembered', she recorded. Her opponent was elected by 11,236 votes to her 5634, and worse was to follow when she joined Ramsay MacDonald and Philip Snowden at the 1917 Club. Both had lost their seats: 'news of Labour defeats *poured* in, none but the Jingoes had a chance'. Not a single pacifist was elected, and it became apparent that, compared to the others, she had polled well. Nor was there any comfort to be derived from the women's results. Only one had scored a victory – Countess Markiewicz, the sister of Charlotte Despard's friend, Eva Gore-Booth – but she was in Holloway, and, as a Sinn Feiner, refused to take her seat.

On every count, Charlotte Despard tasted the defeat of the causes she held most dear, but she refused to be dismayed. 'The forces that make for freedom seem to be in abeyance, but they are not dead,' she informed her supporters; and, as the New Year began, she started to prepare for the next election – canvassing, talking to women at the mothers' meetings, and visiting them in their shops and homes. In importance it amounted to no more than a pebble, but she had in mind a mountain. On the first page of her diary for 1919 she inscribed a passage from Æ (George Russell)'s *National Being*:

Sometime in the heroic future, some nation in a crisis will be weighed and will act reasonably rather than passionately, and will be prepared to risk national existence rather than continue existence at the price of killing myriads of human beings, and it will oppose moral and spiritual force to physical force, and it will overcome the world by making gentleness its might, as all great spiritual teachers have done.

IO

In old age a certain rigidity of mind is inescapable. Years have been invested in a way of life, and to alter it and the outlook that goes with it would seem like a confession of failure, not simply of the moment but of an entire life. Locked into habits and ideas from which they cannot escape, the old are, as a rule, left behind in an accelerating society and, because the pattern of thought which once was sound is made irrelevant, they are often driven into the isolation of their memories or an ineffective querulousness about physical infirmity and the impatience of the surrounding world. For them, in Chateaubriand's famous phrase, 'old age is a shipwreck'. In some, there is a serene acceptance of inevitable change, and in a fortunate minority, there is the discovery that the outside world corresponds to the 'set' of their ideas. To this last category Charlotte Despard belonged.

While most of her generation lamented the destruction of the old way of life, she, with socialism as her religion and Theosophy her science, welcomed its passing as the darkness before the dawn. When she returned to the automatic writing which had flowed from her pen at the beginning of the century, she rediscovered in the haphazard words the prophecy of 'a Coming'. What was then obscure had become clear long since; quite evidently it pointed to the avatar whom Annie Besant had discovered in the person of Krishnamurti, and for whose revelation the Theosophical Society had been preparing itself since 1911. Opinions differed about the sort of world he would usher in. Annie Besant seemed to favour an immaculate aristocracy of adepts and advanced beings to order affairs; but Charlotte Despard could only visualize it as a classless commune, and thus saw in the advance of socialism a confirmation of the avatar's coming.

Her relatives found Aunt Lottie's millenarianism quite as barmy as her penchant for being arrested as a suffragette, but the polite family conversation which hid their private thoughts also concealed Charlotte's firm conviction that she held the key to the world's turmoil. She had never doubted her own insights, and now in her grand old age the question of doing so never arose; her only interest was in finding the evidence to support her theory. Each event was examined microscopically to yield up its secret symptom of the future, and she sifted through other people's minds, especially if they were young, like an interrogator in search of a hidden clue. 'She had a kind of vampire quality,' a friend, Alison Howden Litster, remembered. 'After a half-hour of conversation with her, one felt like a squeezed lemon. She asked a lot of questions and kept digging into one's answers until she had extracted some information she wanted.'

When the answers were to her liking she could listen for hours, and 'an elderly Swiss woman with a wonderful scheme for regenerating the world' was allowed to keep her up long past bedtime, but 'poor, little Miss MacLure', who wanted to talk about her spiritualist experiences, received short shrift: 'I was obliged to speak very plainly to her – she is off on the Cosmos and spirit interviews with Isaac Newton and Mrs Snow [a deceased member of the League], when she ought to be considering how to earn her living.' No doubt it was sound advice, but coming from one who had held regular consultations with Mazzini's shade, it had a crotchety ring, and the trait was still more marked in her attitude to the adolescent Vere.

Once upon a time, in her youthful sixties, Charlotte Despard had written, 'I don't think the good, conventional child has any conception of . . . the gay spirit of adventure that attends the steps of the born rebel.' Some fifteen years later she was grumbling like a governess about 'my poor rebellious Vere': 'I had a painful scene with the poor child who is full of rebellion' – 'The outburst came when I told her to brush down her fringe' – and so on. Vere was clearly a difficult child. She had not settled at any of her schools, and after her sixteenth birthday she failed to stay with any of the women farmers whom Charlotte Despard persuaded to employ her. Occasionally her guardian lamented, rather helplessly, 'O am sad at heart for the poor thing, she should be having a joyous time'; but she no longer reproached herself, as she had once, for failing to give Vere the absorbed attention she could give to causes. 'I had not time for a long talk,' she wrote after placing her at another farm; 'still, I fear that she thinks everyone is to blame but herself.' With that she put the matter from her mind, for there was quite simply no longer room in it for the demands of a growing child.

With the narrowing of sympathies came other frailties of old age. In the winter of 1914 she had fallen heavily, hurting her back and left shoulder, and, although she had apparently recovered, the pain returned whenever she became tired or depressed. From her mid-seventies, her diary recorded a succession of awkward collisions and tumbles, and the frequency with which she forgot bags, keys and lecture notes testified to a failing memory. When she could no longer read in poor light, she was persuaded to buy spectacles; but she never wore them and always succeeded in losing them. The most telling symptom of her years, however, was simply that the cancellation of a speaking engagement, instead of causing disappointment, now gave her a sense of relief – 'like a hard-up person', she said, 'who suddenly finds himself with money'. If she had ever felt inclined to accept physical limitations, she would quite probably have begun to dwindle away after peace had come.

Since her resignation from the presidency of the League she had more time to read, and this she did without discrimination, devouring newspapers and poetry, mystical and Marxist tracts, and Irish history in any form. Tagore's *Gitanjali* almost rivalled *The Revolt of Islam* as her favourite verse – 'simple Indian jewels', she wrote, overflowing with the child's adoration of the Father/ Mother God'. Mysticism exerted an ever-growing hold, and it was irresistible when linked to an Irish theme. Constantly she returned to Æ (George Russell)'s *The National Being*, which described Irish – indeed all – political change in spiritual terms, and she copied passages from it for her guidance: '. . . though we think of revolution, we know that the patient marshalling of human forces is wisdom. . . . The individual may be reckless, the race never can be so.' His emphasis on gradualism and spiritual growth encouraged her to devote more attention to her Catholic faith, and it gave her particular pleasure to read a book on Christ's life 'which shows that *He* was a great social reformer'. With the permission of the parish priest she installed an altar at one end of the club room in Nine Elms, where mass was celebrated weekly; and she began to make it a practice to meditate each morning on a text drawn either from the Gospels or from Theosophist writings, or on occasion from a leader in the *New Statesman*. There was no reason why she, like other activists in old age, should not eventually have diverted all her energies from politics into religion.

She was seventy-five, and found a growing pleasure in tending the garden at Kurandai and in doting briefly on Kate Harvey's adopted family of crippled children. Her own little bungalow was now being built close by in a glade filled with daffodils in spring, and staying there she admitted to herself, 'My little hermitage begins to feel like home – I have had so many, this I think must be the last.' Yet a week later, when she returned to the noise and grime of Nine Elms, she was surprised to find that, 'in spite of the sweetness of what I have left, I don't think I was sorry to be back in the hurly-burly'. Although age had begun to touch her, it did not affect her capacity for outrage and compassion.

The house at 2 Currie Street remained a haven for unfortunates, usually 'my girls' of the Despard Club, who were now old enough to be pregnant or overburdened with children, or 'old boys' who, as discharged soldiers, needed cash or a reference for a pension. The Nine Elms Settlement was still run by the League, and what Mrs Despard could not cope with was attended to there. Her forays out into the streets and alleys continued to provoke a volley of complaints from her to the Borough Council about dilapidated houses and defective sanitation, and Howlett, the slum landlord, was still hounded about the state of his property; but she was forced to admit that a generation of public housing and building regulations had 'improved matters beyond comparison since the old days'. In the immediate aftermath of the war, when a short boom provided full employment even in Nine Elms, it was the suffering abroad that captured her attention.

Until Germany actually signed the peace treaty at Versailles in June 1919, the Allies maintained their wartime blockade on strategic materials; and since Germany would not use its Merchant Navy to ship food alone, the people of Central Europe suffered a famine which exceeded the worst privation of the war. Even when ships were made available, the lack of raw materials made transport inside the countries difficult, and produced unexpected crises such as an absence of rubber teats for babies' feeding bottles.

In the depths of the Sussex countryside, such problems had seemed far away, but sitting in her little, overcrowded flat in

Nine Elms, above the children shouting in the street and in the club room below, she read the reports with horror. 'The account of the awful suffering in Vienna is appalling,' she wrote in March 1919. 'I threw it down choked – and we continue the blockade – it is almost unbearable.' Never less than single-minded in her indignation, she became so obsessed by the plight of the Viennese children that Kate Harvey, who loved her capacity for outrage, was driven to forbid her to mention the subject of famine again. Charlotte dismissed this outburst as 'a little cloud', and turned for support to the Freedom League; but they, while sympathetic, were too concerned with restrictions on women's employment to give their full attention to Central Europe. 'Their usefulness I think is over,' she declared in a temper, and broke her last official links by resigning from the Executive. Only the Women's International League gave the subject the high priority she demanded: 'This League', she noted with satisfaction, 'is more alive than the WFL, and has, I believe, work before it.'

Its first and most practical accomplishment in peacetime was to raise £6000 for relief, and, with this money, to send food and other aid, including a million rubber teats, to Central Europe. When the delegations from a dozen different countries met in Zurich that May for the second congress of the WIL,* the British party proved the most ferocious in its criticism of the blockade and the negotiations at Versailles. Charlotte Despard was among them, and her passionate denunciation of the cold politicking which entailed such cruelty was received with exceptional acclaim by the starved, defeated women of the Central European delegations, whose countries were at that moment being stigmatized with the guilt of being solely responsible for the war. In the emotionally charged atmosphere, her transparent sincerity and compassion pierced the barriers of language, and that evening her room was filled with flowers and grateful messages. When the Congress came to elect four representatives to communicate its desire for an easing of the peace terms to the statesmen at Versailles, her name was by popular acclaim added to the list.

It was of course hopeless to imagine that the Big Three, locked between their own rivalries and the promises they had made to

---

* At the congress it merged with the League for Peace and Freedom to become the Women's International League for Peace and Freedom.

their electorates, would give heed to the little deputation of women, but, by a stroke of good fortune, Charlotte Despard and Chrystal MacMillan found among Lloyd George's entourage Lord Robert Cecil, an old friend from suffrage days, who received them sympathetically. With his assurance that Lloyd George was in fact trying to moderate the harsh terms demanded by France, they had to rest content, for all efforts to see the wizard himself were fruitless. Jane Addams, the head of the WILPF, had an interview with President Wilson, but Clemenceau, whose character—'dry in soul and empty of hope', in Keynes' phrase—left the deepest imprint on the Treaty, refused to accept so much as a message.

The ineffectuality of their mission had a significant effect on Charlotte Despard. When she returned to Nine Elms she picked up the pattern of political activity where she had left it: long sessions in draughty Labour committee rooms to vet candidates and formulate policy, and constant patrolling through the rubbish-strewn streets to canvass support and turn out voters at local elections. It was unglamorous work, the very blades of grass-roots politics, but as the year continued she began to have doubts about the value of democracy itself. In this, as in so many of her intuitive responses, Charlotte Despard was the paradigm of that particular line of idealism which has already been traced from Shelley through the socialism of the 1880s and 1890s to the ILP, and which in the 1920s and 1930s was to flourish among communists and fellow travellers. Like others of her cast of mind she had believed that President Wilson could inspire the European democracies to reach beyond the narrow loyalties of nationalism to some wide principle of humanity. 'Each part of the final settlement must be based upon the essential justice of that particular case,' he had said, but in the event justice was made to serve French chauvinism, Italian aggrandizement and British colonialism. The map of Europe might be changed out of recognition, but it was redrawn in the same nineteenth-century spirit of self-interest from which the war had originally been bred.

In the deliberations of the Western democracies, idealism played no part, but in the East it apparently flourished in the Marxist form developed by Lenin, and to Charlotte Despard the gravest indictment against parliamentary government was its murderous hatred of communism. In Russia the Allies aided the White armies of Kolchak and Denikin against the infant Soviet

Union; in Hungary they helped the autocratic Admiral Horthy overthrow the communist regime of Bela Kun, and in Germany the Social Democrats combined with the army to wipe out the Spartacists and murder their leaders, Rosa Luxemburg and Karl Liebknecht. Amid such deeds, the creation of the League of Nations, the sole act of idealism, appeared to be window-dressing – 'a Capitalist fraud', in Charlotte Despard's opinion.

Before the war Charlotte Despard had decided that Liberalism had failed, but after Versailles she suspected, and lectured on her suspicions, that democracy itself had failed. The reason, she suggested, was that 'our democracy has been political rather than economic. . . . We must get rid of this infamous and stupid government and start afresh, trying to build up an economic democracy.' This required the nationalization of all wealth and its redistribution on a basis of equality. It was not far removed from the beliefs she had held as a member of the Social Democratic Federation, but socialism itself had moved and, after the Bolshevik revolution, had concerned itself almost exclusively with the steps to revolution rather than with the aftermath. Essentially the only question for the entire Left at that time was the choice between direct action and constitutional action as a means of gaining power.

The question was most fiercely debated in the British Communist Party, which was formed in May 1919 from an amalgamation of the British Socialist Party (formerly the Social Democratic Federation), the Clydesiders' Socialist Labour Party, and a variety of other groups including the Workers' Socialist Federation. This last was, in the words of the Party's official history, 'formed, led, (almost owned) by Sylvia Pankhurst', but her 'super-revolutionary' zeal to do away with Parliament, unions and all existing assemblies was sharply rebuked by Lenin. Such institutions should be infiltrated, he said, and the proper use of direct action should be to intensify the class-struggle with the particular purpose of raising social consciousness. It was, therefore, open for left-wing members of the Labour Party to believe, as Charlotte Despard did, that the revolution itself would come about without violence, simply through the constitutional means of elections and committees and the direct means of strikes and union action. Her own views were crystallized by reading Jean Jaurès' *Studies in Socialism*: 'I think it makes it perfectly clear that the old forms of Revolution are over, that it will not come until the Proletariat are prepared, and that meanwhile the best method is to strengthen the associations and gain political power.'

The Labour Party was officially committed only to the use of constitutional action, but since it did not ban communists from its ranks until November 1922, the question of direct action was debated there also. Thus, although Charlotte Despard was communist in all but name, and spoke at a Communist Party rally in 1920, there was no necessity for her to leave the Labour Party. How well she followed the Leninist line may be seen in her vigorous efforts to improve the efficiency of the Labour Party in Battersea.

Showing a surprisingly practical grasp, she insisted on professional, full-time organizers and a permanent headquarters, and since she herself paid for both in the first two years after the war her voice carried weight. She secured the appointment, as organizer of the Women's Section, of Mrs Ganley, who later became one of the first communists on the London County Council; and, although it is hard to tell where Charlotte Despard's influence ended and the left-wing railway unionists' took over in the choice of candidates for parliamentary and local elections, it was certainly she who defeated a last attempt by John Burns to reassert his old authority in that area. The end result was a local party heavily weighted with communists and fellow travellers, and in 1922 it selected as its parliamentary candidate, Shapurji Saklatvela, who was returned at the November election as one of the first two communists to sit in the House of Commons.

Successful as the constitutional tactic undoubtedly was in Battersea, it did not satisfy Charlotte Despard's romantic thirst to see the Promethean spirit among the workers. Direct action – that is, striking for political ends – was what she hoped for, but in her eagerness she was liable, as she had been in the 1890s, to mistake a wage-strike for the beginning of the millennium. As prices and rents climbed in the autumn of 1919, the Triple Alliance of railwaymen, miners and transport workers threatened concerted action, but only the National Union of Railwaymen actually came out. Coincidentally, police in London and Liverpool were also striking on behalf of an abortive union and, in Nine Elms, railwaymen and police pickets stood shoulder to shoulder. As the doyenne of Nine Elms, and as a long-time friend of the police strike-leader, ex-Inspector Syme, Charlotte Despard was swept up in the current. The Despard Club became the NUR strike headquarters, and for a thrilling week she shuttled between crowded meetings of the union and the police. 'A feeling of Hope in the air', she wrote. 'It is felt that Trade Unionism is being attacked. The two forces [Labour and Capitalism] seem really to be face to face at last. Is it the beginning?' She was in the course of an exercise in meditation, and there was nothing incongruous in her noting that 'Yesterday I meditated on organising comradeship, today on the presentation of God the Father.' Unfortunately, the railwaymen's leader, J. H. Thomas, had more materialist ambitions and settled for shorter hours and a wage rise. Disappointment was not a new experience for Charlotte Despard. She drew comfort from an impression that 'the strike has done much to quicken the feeling of brotherhood', and she took as the themes for her winter lectures, 'Solidarity' and 'The Ascent of Man'.

Her disenchantment with democratic forms of government was accentuated by a visit she paid to Hungary in the summer of 1920. She had been there first in 1913, when she was struck by the generous provision for orphans and the children of unmarried mothers; but on her return, as the representative of the Save The Children Fund, she barely recognized that pleasant orphanage and hospital. 'What a difference,' she wrote. 'Now nothing here for comfort – new-born babies wrapped in coarse sacking made from paper fibre. . . . I knelt and drew a tiny tot to me. She pressed her face against my soft cloth, smiling like an angel. Alas! it is motherhood the world needs.' She heard at first hand of the crimes committed by Admiral Horthy's White terror squads. 'Communists and Jews are being hunted down,' she told the *Manchester Guardian* afterwards. 'The Whites will simply stop a man in the street and ask if he is a Jew, then flog him or worse.'

Although the word was hardly known, Horthy's regime was undoubtedly fascist, and the support which the Western democracies gave to it confirmed her determination to see communism triumph.

When the most effective example of direct action occurred, shortly after her return from Budapest in June, her joy was unrestrained. Having expelled a Polish invasion sponsored by the French, the Soviet Red Army began to march on Warsaw, so alarming the Allies that in early August Lord Curzon announced that any further advance would lead to war. Since 1919, British aid to the White Armies in Russia had provoked a smouldering 'Hands off Russia' movement, frequently addressed by Charlotte Despard; but now it burst into flame, and within a few days 300 local councils were formed to oppose the threat of war against the Soviet Union. On 9 August, Charlotte Despard wrote triumphantly: 'For the first time in History Labour is showing its strength. If compulsion of any kind against Soviet Russia is attempted, six million trade unionists will down tools.' In the face of the threatened national strike, organized by an unofficial action committee but commanding almost universal trade-union support, the government shuffled down, denying any intention of hostile action. War weariness, as much as any ideological sympathy, explained the spontaneous resistance, but motives were less important than the dramatic example of government giving way when confronted by a united labour force.

Long anticipated and long denied, her dream of Labour forcing its ideals of equality, compassion and peace upon a cynically materialist government seemed to have approached the realms of reality. The trade-union movement, 6,500,000 strong was greater than ever before. Sympathy for the political Labour Party had grown enormously since the 1918 election, and she could trace its power at first hand in Battersea as the local party recorded triumphs in the LCC and borough council elections. Nine Elms itself had 'changed beyond recognition from the old days', and the new Labour Medical Officer of Health was anxious to take over and expand her clinic and meals service. She was at last on the winning side and, apart from the MOH's wish to include meat on the menu for the meals service ('that we cannot allow'), there were no shadows on the evening road of her long life, which now stretched ahead, straight and well lighted by the bright prospects of her dearest cause.

Three days after the success of the 'Hands off Russia' ultimatum, and while Lloyd George still fulminated against the unconstitutional and undemocratic interference in government policy which it represented, Terence MacSwiney, Mayor of Cork, was arrested for being a member of Sinn Fein, and began a hunger strike. For seventy-four days he starved in Brixton jail, an ordeal which focused the attention of every Irish exile on the insurrection taking place in the homeland. By the time MacSwiney died, on 25 October, the course of Charlotte Despard's life had been turned from the relatively straightforward road of British socialism into the tangled byways of Irish politics.

She had from the start supported Sinn Fein's campaign for Irish independence. It was an emotional, mystical attachment, largely fixed by Æ's blueprint for an Ireland 'based on a social order, democratic and co-operative in character. . . . To make normal that spirit which is now only manifested in abnormal moments should be our aim.' When Æ wrote to *The Times* in April 1918, protesting against the attempt to introduce conscription to Ireland, she commented approvingly: 'This country ought by this to be convinced that Ireland is and will be recognised as a nation.' She joined the Irish Self-Determination League and worked energetically for the release of Maud Gonne MacBride, who had been imprisoned for her anti-British activities. In the 1918 General Election, Redmond's Home Rule party was swept away and Charlotte Despard was delighted when Sinn Fein, having won 75 of the 105 Irish seats, constituted itself the Dáil Éireann – the Parliament of an independent Ireland – and elected Eamonn de Valera, the senior survivor of the Easter uprising, as its President. 'To the ordinary thinker there is no issue,' she wrote; 'Russia is Bolshevik and Ireland is Sinn Fein.'*

The issue, however, was disputed, and most strenuously, by her brother Jack, now Lord French, and Viceroy of Ireland since April 1918. 'One must try to understand what the real Irish National aspirations are and how to get into, and keep trust with, them', he said at the time of his appointment. 'But before one can even begin to put the garden in order, one must *weed it out*.' On his arrival in Ireland he had immediately arrested the Sinn Fein leaders and banned the party, and he had no hesitation in judging its declaration of independence in January 1919 to be an act of rebellion. When the infant republic's supporters began to raid police stations, he ordered further arrests and the internment of suspects without trial.

'Jack is taking tough measures,' his sister noted apprehensively

* At this time Sinn Fein represented all those who wanted an independent, united Ireland. Its aims never altered but the defections – in 1921 of those who supported the Treaty with Britain, and in 1927 of de Valera – left it a mere rump of idealists who acted as a political limb of the IRA.

but, with her curious ability to compartmentalize contradictory emotions, she continued to think sentimentally of him as 'my Jack Viceroy, mavourneen', while giving active support to the Self-Determination League, which was Sinn Fein's front organization in Britain. When she visited Dublin in April 1919, however, he was already a virtual prisoner in Viceregal Lodge, and she thought it better to stay with Maud Gonne.

At that date, only Lord French and the fieriest of the IRA seriously considered that the sniping campaign might turn to war, but Yeats gave voice to a general foreboding in the lines he wrote in February 1919:

> Things fall apart, the centre cannot hold,
> Mere anarchy is loosed upon the world.
> The blood-stained tide is full, and everywhere
> The ceremony of innocence is drowned.
> The best lack all conviction, while the worst
> Are full of passionate intensity.

Among the most passionate was Maud Gonne, the infatuation of Yeats' early life, who had once drawn him towards Irish nationalism. In his play, *Cathleen ni Houlihan*, she had taken the part of Cathleen, who stood for the indomitable spirit of Ireland; and her passion and glorious appearance forever identified her in the role. Nationalism was still the vent through which her protean energy poured, and, although she was now over fifty, the uplifting beauty that had bewitched Yeats and the imperious stature that had dominated Dublin crowds still contrived to embody the ecstasy and grandeur of patriotic emotion. Since the execution of her husband, John MacBride, after the Easter uprising, anglophobia and Sinn Fein had driven all other interests from her consideration, and six months in prison only served to sharpen the intensity of her feelings.

While Charlotte was staying with her, Yeats came to dinner and must have groaned inwardly for the two women were kindred spirits, egging each other on to new heights of passionate intensity. The encounter was not repeated and, when Maud Gonne and Charlotte Despard later shared a house together, it was noticeable that Yeats took elaborate care never to visit his former love if there was any chance of running into her companion.

By the end of the year, Lord French had dismissed the Inspector-

General of Police, who opposed his hard-line policy. He thus made possible the recruitment of British former soldiers to bring the badly demoralized police up to strength. These recruits began to arrive in March 1920, and soon became known – first familiarly, then balefully – as 'the Black and Tans'. A new administration was installed in Dublin Castle whose views harmonized more closely with the Viceroy's, and from the early summer the sniping campaign became more obviously a running battle.

Much encumbered with Battersea politics and Austro-Hungarian starvation, Charlotte Despard's attention was distracted from Ireland, although each beat of the accelerating tattoo of murder and reprisal there caused her anguish among the turmoil of other events. It was the long fast of Terence MacSwiney that concentrated her mind. Still buoyed up by the unions' success in preventing the government from interfering in the Russian invasion of Poland, her first instinct was to appeal to her trade-union audiences 'to prevent, if even by direct action, what was going on', and to lobby the Parliamentary party to take up the cause. The Labour Party was not unsympathetic, and later in the year called for 'the withdrawal of the British army of occupation', but the gap between sympathy and action was one which she could not tolerate in this instance. When her friends in the Commons fobbed her off, she wrote angrily: 'There now seems little hope of stirring up B[ritish] Labour to take, as they should do, drastic measures, and so the horror continues.'

As the slant of her interest became known, it grew more difficult for her to ignore the position which her brother occupied, for messages began to arrive from Ireland beseeching her to intercede with him. In September Maud Gonne wrote asking her to use any influence she had with Lord French to secure the release from prison of her sixteen-year-old son, Sean MacBride; but Charlotte's appeal to her brother met with a cold silence. She reminded herself that her 'poor brother is a mere figurehead now' – which was true, although largely because the new men were putting into effect the stern policy he had advocated, and so the Lord-Lieutenancy could revert to its original ceremonial function. His silence was not that of helplessness, but of the new bitterness which arose in the autumn of 1920 from the creation of Republican 'flying columns' to ambush police patrols, and from the reprisals of the Black and Tans. In such circumstances, Lord French found it impossible to regard his sister's activities lightly, and only the fact that they were confined to England saved them from being, in his eyes, open treachery.

On 25 October any restraints which Charlotte Despard still felt disappeared. 'Terence MacSwiney, patriot and martyr, is dead, that is the one thought,' she wrote. It was no longer a matter of protesting against the horrors, but of enlisting in a cause. Her schedule of lectures in the following week called for her to speak on Hungary and the plight of refugee children, but the subjects were almost crowded off her notes by reflections on the martyr's death. When she returned to Nine Elms after her tour, it was to find three letters asking her to intercede with her brother against the execution of Kevin Barry, the 'young lad of eighteen summers who fought to free old Ireland', as the ballad describes him, but by the time she received the appeals he was already dead. On her next tour, her message was more forthright still: 'With all the force I could command . . . I indicted Lloyd George and his colleagues, Walter Long and Bonar Law, for murder most foul.' She joined demonstrations and spoke to massive crowds gathered outside Wandsworth jail where other Irish prisoners were kept, and whether she was called upon to lecture on unemployment or Theosophy she was drawn as though into a vortex by the subject of Ireland.

Out of deference to her brother's position, she had not visited Ireland since the beginning of the troubles, but she could not long be kept out now. On the last day of 1920, she was visited by Dorothy MacArdle, the Irish historian and a member of Sinn Fein, who brought first-hand news of the situation. The story she told was of a growing madness: on the one side uniformed terrorists, on the other young men courting martyrdom in order to provoke yet wilder reprisals. 'She fears, as I fear, something desperate, then a massacre, following by the stifling of all spirit,' Charlotte Despard noted. It was as though the nightmare she had feared during the Great War were to be repeated in Ireland. There could, in consequence, be no question as to her proper course, and almost the last words of that year shaped the rest of her life: 'I promised to go if it would help.'

11

For most of Charlotte Despard's life, Ireland had been an ideal land, and she scarcely knew it in reality. There had been frequent holidays in the grand house at Montrath belonging to Max's relations, the Franks, and there had been a series of suffrage tours before the war, but she was no more Irish than she was working class. Now, thirty years after she had set herself to identify with the poor, she was about to make a similar attempt to merge with the Irish, and the impulse was the same: to lose herself in a cause whose rightness could not be doubted

She could feel no enthusiasm for the juggling of tactics and priorities which occupied the energies of enfranchised workers and women. To one whose mind reckoned only in absolutes, anything less than immediate transformation was intolerable. But she was forced to conclude that 'the change will not come quickly as the English are naturally conservative . . . the Anglo-Saxon race lacks vision'. The Irish on the other hand did not equivocate. Their goal was liberty without delay. And so, with scarcely a backward glance, Charlotte Despard allowed herself to be drawn into their struggle.

Officially she went to Ireland in January 1921 as the guest of the Irish Women's Franchise League, but her hostess was Maud Gonne. Ostensibly she travelled on a tour of inspection, but with her hostess as her guide it was in truth the collection of evidence for the prosecution. Motoring through Cork and the south-west, they undoubtedly took risks, for the area was under martial law, and both soldiers and police were on knife-edge alert. A few months earlier, in the most daring stroke of the war, Michael Collins and his men had shot dead twelve British intelligence officers, and on the same day a party of 'Black and Tans' searching for armed men in a football crowd were fired on from the grandstand and, shooting back, killed a dozen onlookers. In December, part of the main street of Cork was set on fire by a company of 'Black and

Tans', enraged by the shooting of one of their number; and, a week later, one murdered a young man and an old priest in the roadway. The military authorities themselves admitted that 'the troops are getting out of control, taking the law into their own hands, and that, besides clumsy and indiscriminate destruction, actual thieving and looting . . . are occurring'.

Two elderly ladies of subversive opinion, travelling through country which simmered with rebellion, could hardly consider themselves safe, but they held a trump card which they played whenever their car was waved down by the tense young men manning military roadblocks. Afterwards Maud Gonne gleefully wrote to a friend: 'It is amazing to see the puzzled expressions on the faces of the officers and the Black and Tans who continually hold up our car, when Mrs Despard said she was the Viceroy's sister.' With this password they penetrated the most sensitive areas – 'places I should never have been able to get to alone', Maud Gonne admitted. They returned with evidence of deliberate terrorism and destruction of property by military and police, 'carried out scientifically,' Charlotte Despard told reporters, 'with the object of cracking the Irish spirit and Irish industry'.

There was no lack of justification for her charge, since the destruction of buildings suspected of housing gunmen had been officially authorized in an attempt to channel the destructive temper of the Crown forces. A Labour Party commission of inquiry later came to a similar conclusion, but what gave her indictment its peculiar force was the same influence as had permitted her to gather the evidence. Such a statement, coming from the Lord-Lieutenant's sister, was a powerful piece of propaganda, and it was recognized as such both by Sinn Fein and her brother.

Grieved though she was that her beloved Jack should regard her action as treacherous, Charlotte had reached one of those moods of stubborn certainty which 'pushed' her from one cause to another. There was work to be done in Dublin. The children and wives of the Sinn Fein prisoners were in a pitiful state, and the White Cross, Maud Gonne's relief organization, desperately needed help. The appeal of children in distress was one which Charlotte Despard could never resist, but there was more to it than that. In the excitement of revolution, when everything seemed possible, from the recreation of Gaelic civilization to the establishment of a socialist republic, idealism was the common currency, uniting all shades of opinion. The Ireland in which she found herself was no longer a figment of her imagination. Not only did it exist, it housed a people who spoke the language of her inmost thoughts. Rather than be separated from them, she chose to resign from Britain.

For the next six months she passed to and fro between Dublin and London, cutting the ties that held her to the one and spinning the web of acquaintanceship that drew her to the other. From her sisters she parted with cold affection, their attitude strongly suggesting that exile was the proper penalty for her betrayal; and, although Jack had returned to England, having retired in May 1921, he refused to see her. The tributes paid by her friends in the multitude of leagues and associations to which she belonged touched her, but she was not sentimental enough to be deeply moved by a committee's good wishes. The close links with Kate Harvey had already been weakened, and were broken now without bitterness: 'We had many, many lovely days of work and pleasure together,' Kate Harvey recalled later in a letter to her, 'and we have memories that we may have roses in December. Ours have lovely colours and sweetest scents.' The house and her share of the land at Kurundai were made over to Kate Harvey, in the same way that her house in Currie Street was given to the Nine Elms Settlement until the council could take it over.

The hardest parting was from the people of Nine Elms. Individually and spontaneously they came to her house or stopped her in the street to express their sorrow at her departure – her 'old boys' from the Club, the women who had attended her mothers' meetings, the children from the clinic, the railwaymen who had used her house as a strike headquarters. An illuminated scroll was presented to her 'as a token of appreciation for her life-long work and devotion to the cause of humanity – particularly on behalf of the Labour and Socialist movement in Battersea', and there were more artless presentations from the schoolchildren and the factory girls of Crosse & Blackwell. It was the harvest of thirty years' service and kindness.

'My people', she had called them, but it was a proprietorial rather than an associative phrase. She did things for them rather than with them, and she was marked out from them by her wealth and upbringing in a manner which neither her goodness nor her eccentricity could disguise. 'You could always tell she was a lady', one of her neighbours remembered. She had long abandoned the old dream of merging among the poor – 'I am not a hand-worker, that is not my good fortune, perhaps,' she once told Lloyd George. Yet the abrasion of poverty had had its effect in scouring off the encrusted habits of her marriage, so that what emerged was that curious mixture of adolescent characteristics – idealism, selfishness, rebelliousness, enthusiasm and an unassuageable desire to reform the world – which was the quintessential Charlotte Despard. To leave her second birthplace caused her great sorrow, she said, 'but the call of the native land is urgent . . . the suffering there demands my service for the years that may be left to me'.

She was Irish. A green filter obscured all alien hues – the Scottish mother, the half-English father and the long generations who had grown fat in the pastures of Kent. 'I have to go to Ireland,' she cried to the members of the Freedom League who gathered for her birthday celebrations. 'It is the call of the blood, and cannot be denied.' 'Mrs Despard is a most remarkable woman,' Maud Gonne commented approvingly, 'and intensely Irish in feeling.' To have impressed so favourably the *ne plus ultra* of nationalists was a dangerous achievement. Countess Markie-wicz, née Constance Gore-Booth, had also discarded her English heritage, and of her, Sean O'Faolain, her biographer has written: 'She was not the first to go more Irish than the Irish themselves, nor the first to take literally all that we blathered (with many but secret reservations).' Curled up behind the language of idealism which had thrilled Charlotte Despard in Dublin were secret reservations so weighty that when they began to emerge she was utterly bewildered and in danger of being destroyed.

When she returned in July 1921, staying at first with Maud Gonne in Dublin, the fighting had ceased, and Sinn Fein and the British government were beginning to negotiate the terms of the peace treaty. The Government of Ireland Act, passed in December 1902, had established two Irish parliaments, one for the six northern counties and the other for the remaining twenty-six; elections to them in May 1921 had returned Republicans for almost every constituency in the South, while in the North the Unionists captured 38 of the 50 seats. Northern Ireland was, therefore, in operation as an independent entity before the status of the South had been established.

The protracted negotiations with the British government over the South's exact status split Sinn Fein apart, and in January 1922 de Valera resigned as President when a majority of the Dáil voted to accept terms by which the republic was to be known as a Free State, but was to remain within the British Empire. The question of the border with the North was to be settled by a Boundary Commission, but that was bitterly opposed by the IRA, which emphasized that its oath of allegiance was not to the Dáil but to a united republic of thirty-two counties.

As the Free State came closer to civil war, Northern Ireland was racked by sectarian riots, whose violence was a reflection of the Protestants' sense of vulnerability in their fledgling Province, and the Catholics' confidence in help from the South. Since the Treaty negotiations had begun, IRA gunmen had come north in large numbers, while the Province had taken over from Britain the armed Special Constabulary. The 'B' Specials, 25,000 part-timers recruited from the Orange Order, were distinguished for the fervour of their Protestantism. Both sides claimed provocation for the disturbances – the murder of a police inspector in Lurgan, or the expulsion of Catholic workers from the shipyards – but, wherever the blame lay, in 1922, the first year of the Province's life, over 200 people were killed and more than 1000 wounded. The proportion, judging from a small sample, was two Catholic casualties to one Protestant, and the semi-official harassment of the minority religion sent a stream of Catholic refugees flowing southwards.

They provided Charlotte Despard with the first taste of the intractable problems which beset her new country. She and Maud Gonne had established a reception centre for them in Dublin, where they tried to find food, housing and, if possible, work; but the increasing number of refugees who appeared after the passage of the Special Powers Act in 1922 strained their resources to the limit. Angered by the stories of Protestant discrimination, Charlotte Despard went to Belfast a month later to investigate conditions for herself. She visited Ballymacarett, a Catholic enclave around St Matthew's church in East Belfast, and Ardoyne, a similar community in the west of the city, and in this latter area witnessed the sort of incident which was responsible for the exodus of Catholics from the city:

Having visited many panic-stricken families and inspected their houses, riddled with bullet-holes, I stood talking with some of the women. Everything was quiet. The people stood about in little groups before their doors. The children were playing. Suddenly there was a pistol shot; it was fired from an armoured car. Panic followed, the children ran in to any open door. I was drawn by trembling women into the cottage of an ex-soldier – a man who had fought in Belgium and Gallipoli. Volley after volley, from rifles and machine guns, swept the streets, and this went on with brief intervals for an hour and a half.

When she could leave the district, she asked for an interview with Sir James Craig, the Prime Minister, but was referred to the Minister for Home Affairs, Sir Dawson Bates. Although Bates could hardly refuse to see the sister of the Earl of Ypres, Freeman of Belfast and adamantine enemy of all Republicans, he took the opportunity of telling her that she was a disgrace to her family, and by way of revenge she published their conversation in an open letter to Craig:

... in spite of interruptions from himself and a gentleman in his office I told Sir Dawson Bates [of what I had seen] and asked for protection for the Catholic workers.

His reply was: 'We give protection to all law-abiding citizens.' 'Not to Catholics,' I said. 'Irrespective of creed,' he answered.

I gave instances of the brutality of the 'Specials' and asked for their withdrawal. 'The "Specials",' he said, 'are a fine body of men, who have been doing their duty under exceptionally trying circumstances.' He then turned his back, and refused to say any more.

Even that brief exchange showed some of the overlapping and deeply entangled divisions within the Province – between Catholic and Protestant, worker and capitalist, dissident and police. The new state had no tradition to give it stability, and its survival depended on the rigid enforcement of order; but measures like the Special Powers Act of 1922, which entangled the overlapping categories still further, could only store up trouble for the future. 'Go on as you are doing,' Charlotte Despard told Craig in her letter. 'Give your legalized gunmen carte blanche to shoot, maim, and insult their fellow-townsmen and to destroy their homes; keep thousands of men idle, and, as sure as day succeeds night, retribution in an awful form will come to you.'

From the harsh reality of one emergent state, she returned to that of another with equally confused loyalties and implacable hostilities. Even before she had gone to Belfast, tensions in the South had been raised when some men of the IRA forcibly seized the Four Courts, Dublin's centre of justice. They were allowed to remain there until the result was known of the election held on 24 June to ratify the terms of the Treaty with Britain. Less than a third of the electorate had voted for Republicans opposed to the Treaty, and four days later the newly elected government of William Cosgrave ordered the bombardment of the Four Courts.

At once Charlotte Despard, Maud Gonne and Hanna Sheehy-Skeffington persuaded the Lord Mayor to come with them as a peace committee, and for a few hours the shelling ceased while they negotiated with the besieged and the government. When the IRA refused to surrender their weapons, the guns began to fire again, signalling the start of a year-long civil war of nightmarish quality in which both sides made torture and assassination a commonplace. As the war spread, de Valera and the anti-Treaty Sinn Fein were drawn into the fight alongside the IRA, and in response Cosgrave passed the Public Safety Act, as draconian a measure as the Special Powers Act in the North. Some 12,000 suspects were imprisoned under its terms, and the women who had formed the peace committee now turned to new work.

The moving spirits of the Women's Prisoners' Defence League consisted of its president, Charlotte Despard, its secretary, Maud Gonne, and Hanna Sheehy-Skeffington, the widow of Francis Sheehy-Skeffington who was murdered in 1916. Politically they supported de Valera, although all had been in favour of the Treaty and deplored violence; but the impulse of their actions was humanitarian. They provided information, where possible found jobs, or gave financial assistance to prisoners' families – who frequently did not know where the men were held and, unless they had other resources, faced the grim threat of the Poor Law. It was not in the nature of the three women to let the scandal of internment pass quietly, and, as both Charlotte Despard and Hanna Sheehy-Skeffington had been suffragettes, their tactics took a familiar turn. 'We have had processions, poster parades, vigils at prison doors, letters to papers, home and foreign,' Charlotte Despard wrote of their campaign, and on one occasion they made a noisy interruption of the government's business.

On 21 September, Kevin O'Higgins, the Free State Home Minister, was introducing a clause of the new constitution to the Dáil when, according to newspaper reports, 'Mrs Despard, standing at the rails overlooking the floor of the House, shouted out a protest against the alleged barbarous treatment inflicted on untried prisoners':

The Home Minister, disregarding the interruption, continued his speech, but Mrs Despard also continued to address the Assembly, declaring that she spoke as an Irishwoman representing thousands of prisoners' relatives. The contest, which went on between the two speakers, to the amazement of the many visitors in the Gallery, as well as to the whole House, brought the intervention of the Speaker who declared that, as Mrs Despard was breaking the rules of the House, he would have to order her removal. She retorted, 'I am breaking the rules of this House because of this system, and because it is impossible for the truth in regard to these prisoners to get out in any other way.'

After she had been taken out, shouting and struggling, the majestic figure of Maud Gonne rose, made her protest and was removed, and in due course Hanna Sheehy-Skeffington followed the same procedure and suffered the same fate.

It is impossible to measure the importance of their work. Politically it was negligible, morally it was vital. Amid the barbarities of civil war, when captives were shot out of hand, tortured, castrated, and in one case tied in a group to a mine with a short fuse, when prison guards paying off old scores sent many inmates mad, and as many more to the sanity of the grave, and when the government itself executed hostages in reprisal for murders on the other side, the women gave a persistent voice to the standards of more humane times. They were as unwelcome, as unhelpful and as absolutely necessary as a bad conscience.

Yet it was hard to believe that their puny efforts could have much effect when such a rage infected the country, and Charlotte Despard, who had hoped that suffragette tactics might soften the government's approach, had to find comfort where she could. 'Possibly if we had held our tongue things would have been even worse than they were,' she wrote doubtfully. 'But we know the agitation has kept up the courage of our boys and girls in prison.'

That small success in itself was too much for the government, and in January 1923 it banned the WPDL as an illegal organization. Ignoring the ban, the women continued to parade and to hold a regular Sunday meeting on the ruins of Gresham's Hotel in O'Connell Street, and neither the police nor the odd stray bullet singing off the stones prevented them broadcasting news about the prisoners. Later, when the police drove them from the ruins, they set up portable platforms until the authorities gave up, saying, according to Maud Gonne's version, 'those damned women make more trouble than the meetings are worth'.

In April, Maud Gonne herself was arrested and sent to prison, where she immediately began a hunger-strike. 'Moved by a sudden resolve,' Charlotte Despard wrote, 'I waited outside Kilmainham [jail] – strange nights and days, bitterly cold. . . . Oh the bitter cold and the *length* of those nights.' Beside the prison gates the seventy-eight-year-old woman maintained a constant vigil for almost two weeks before her friend was released. By the time they had both recovered, the civil war was over, but for the rest of her life Charlotte Despard paid for her heroism with crippling arthritic pain in her shoulder and back which periodically incapacitated her.

Although she now had to ration her strength, the demands of the WPDL did not cease once the uneasy peace had come. Arrests and imprisonments without trial continued, and those already interned remained behind bars. Because of rivalry between the IRA and Sinn Fein, there was at first no pressure exerted for their release except by the women; but they, using the sort of non-violent militancy practised by the Freedom League, gradually built the 'Free the prisoners' slogan into a huge and emotive movement. It is a curiosity that suffragette tactics which were aimed directly at the government only had an effect on the country at large but finally achieved their ends precisely by that indirect means.

In the autumn of 1923 the internees at last began to be released, and each train into Dublin bore numbers of confused men, sometimes wounded, often homeless and always hungry. Members of the WPDL set up a rota to meet the trains, while their headquarters became a rendezvous and information centre for prisoners' families. Throughout the winter Charlotte Despard met trains, comforted relatives, collected food, money and clothing and attended the Sunday ritual in the ruins of O'Connell Street. The punishing regime strained her frail strength, but Maud Gonne had set a standard of dedication which she felt impelled to emulate; indeed, it sometimes seemed that to be put off by anything less than the most crippling of arthritic attacks or the most dizzying of giddy spells would be unpatriotic.

Their work earned both Charlotte Despard and Maud Gonne the popular honorific 'Madame'. It had first been applied to Countess Markiewicz, who was manifestly foreign not merely in title but in her piping upper-class English tones. Thus it conveyed both popular esteem and a popular conception that these two were not Irish. As patriotic Irishwomen, Madame Despard and Madame MacBride must have been dismayed by the mistake, but what was worse, they, who were as fervent in their Catholicism as converts should be, were generally regarded as Protestants. This did not diminish the affection felt for them by Catholic Republicans; in some ways it exaggerated the feeling; but it did effectively classify the women as beings apart and thereby doom Charlotte Despard's democratic wish to take her place among the Irish people. Maud Gonne, however, suffered no loss by such a classification, for it simply reinforced the mythic impact of her personality.

Of all the dominating women to whom Charlotte Despard gave her affection, Maud Gonne exercised the most compelling charm, and Helena Swanwick, a woman of markedly cool intelligence and self-possession, paid it due tribute. 'It is well for me', she confessed, 'that I have not spent my life within her orbit, for I have sometimes felt as if I might have committed any folly against my judgement if she had desired it.' The Maud Gonne whom Yeats had adored in frustrated agony was a marmoreal beauty of unfathomable obsessions; but less sensitive admirers responded to what might be called, a little crudely, star-appeal. She had the ability to silence a room full of people when she came through the door, and her glorious appearance was made the more moving by an evident vulnerability, described by Helena Swanwick as 'an air of gay gallantry covering tragic experience'. Wherever she went, men and women constituted themselves into a little court about her, partly to shield her and partly to share that aura of light-hearted recklessness which came from 'having thrown all she had, memories as well as dreams, into the cause she believed in'. To these courtiers she seemed to offer everything of herself, demanding only a total commitment to her cause in return. To this bargain Charlotte Despard gladly put her hand, and drove herself to the limit of her ancient strength.

Late in 1921 they had moved from St Stephen's Green in Dublin to Roebuck House, an immense Victorian mansion a dozen miles north of the city, which Charlotte Despard had purchased. It stood at the end of a short drive, surrounded by lawns and gardens and a scattering of outhouses. Among its rookery of bedrooms, billiard-rooms, bathrooms, dining-rooms, library, conservatory, kitchens and sculleries, there could periodically be found, in addition to the two elderly ladies, Maud's son, Sean MacBride, her daughter and son-in-law, Iseulte and Francis Stuart, an un-specified number of her pet dogs and a floating population of homeless prisoners, IRA gunmen and refugees from Belfast. It was said, indeed, that only the dogs were unwelcoming, 'but having faced these, any person could walk on and ask for dinner or asylum for life'.

At night the house came to secret life. Charlotte, who had lived a hermit's existence for thirty years, used to waken in alarm when she heard furtive steps on the stair and urgent, muttered conversations on the landing outside her door. Once the secret purpose of the night visitors had been explained to her, she took a small pride in not being frightened by the strange noises – 'these things affect me very little now', she bravely declared, but she awoke no less frequently.

Eighteen months earlier she had been alone in a small flat, the doyenne of Nine Elms and the moving spirit of all that happened there; now, as the owner of a vast, bustling house, she found her-self an outsider, an earnest old lady only half understanding the cryptic references to IRA activities and eagerly finding in her own breathless indignation against the government some resemblance to the hard, embittered sense of betrayal which drove the young men to make war on it. Both Sean MacBride and Francis Stuart had been imprisoned as members of the IRA, and the former was to become one of its senior staff officers and a hero to its hard-liners. Roebuck House was therefore a popular haunt for IRA men on the run, and for the same reason a favourite target for police raids. Each side largely ignored the ancient owner, who was irrelevant to the hunted and an embarrassment to the hunters. On one occasion the police, desperate for a victim, picked up

Vere who happened to be there on holiday; to their evident consternation, Charlotte Despard insisted on riding with her in the back of the lorry, and the sight of her being taken to police headquarters almost set off a riot. Like the presence of IRA men in her house, the escapade reassured Charlotte that she was in the heart of the battle against a despotic government, and for that illusion she was willing to endure much discomfort.

As a neophyte Irishwoman she had taken Maud Gonne as her guide through her new land's mazy politics, but the path of pure nationalism which Maud Gonne followed was impossible for one who did not have the experience of the past decade in her bones and its vocabulary embedded in her subconscious. Just as the lack of this heritage excluded her from the inner circle at home, so it handicapped her in public. Although she presided at the O'Connell Street meeting, and, in an emergency, spoke, such occasions were rare and, compared to her work in England, she was almost mute. When she gave voice it was in little debating clubs, where the country's future could be discussed without invoking dead heroes and acts of treachery to prove a point. Tea at the Ritz with Constance Markiewicz became a more frequent ceremony than speech-making. While Maud was summoned to west and south to help in by-elections, Charlotte visited wounded prisoners in hospital, and in moments of weakness read the English papers at the library to learn of Labour's successes in the 1924 election and to worry whether Ramsay MacDonald's administration would carry out her old dream – 'they seem to be moving towards reform, but whether to the real thing, the new order, one cannot tell'.

The extent of the sacrifice she had made to live in Ireland was brought home to her in April 1925, when her brother Jack died after a long illness. Although she had written to him periodically, he had not forgiven her, and when she made a flying visit to his hospital the doctor would not allow her to see him. A brief rally raised her hopes that there might be time for reconciliation (a little optimistically, she wrote to suggest that he might like to come over to Ireland and meet her rebel friends), but a sudden relapse ended her hopes. His death was 'a deep sorrow to me', she told Mrs Solomon, but it was a comfort 'that it cannot be long before I follow him'. Her language was the product not just of mourning but of a sapping melancholy which had settled on her.

She had cut herself off from England, but she remained an outsider by history and political temperament from the narrow-visioned circle in which she moved. Perhaps, too, she sensed the Mephistophelian aspect of her bargain with Maud, which provided excitement and a sense of purpose but at the price of compromising her cherished ideal of non-violence and winking an eye at the exploits of her friends. Republicanism, which once had seemed the high road of idealism, was beginning to look like a murky cul-de-sac.

On 16 July 1924, the most important of the internees was released, and the following day Charlotte Despard wrote:

I went with Maud to [WPDL] headquarters to find out what was to be done in the way of demonstration, and we were told 'He has been here, and will be in again in half an hour'. We waited. I was just finding Maud to remind her of her White Cross committee when, at the head of the stairs, I saw a little group; someone said 'The President', and then I was shaking his hand and saying as well as I could my gladness.

'The President' was de Valera, but the title was accorded him only by the IRA and supporters of the anti-Treaty Sinn Fein deputies – the Republicans – who resolutely refused to recognize the Free State or any government which was not that of an independent, united Ireland. This was the direct line of succession from the United Irishmen, the Fenians and the martyrs of 1916 and 1922; and for the purist Republican no other policy was required. The words of Liam Mellows, written hours before his execution by the Free State government, provided their credo: 'It is a hard road, but it's the road our Saviour followed – the road of Sacrifice. The Republic lives, our deaths make that a certainty.' They recognized no half measures in ends or means, but for a substantial part of the Republican movement the economic depression of the twenties made it necessary to search for a policy more specific than undiluted martyrology.

The harvest of 1924 was the worst since 1879, and the heavily agrarian economy of Ireland suffered severely. This local disaster, coupled with the international economic decline, sent an army of unemployed to compete with thousands of ex-prisoners for a diminishing number of jobs. The only economic theory the Republicans could put forward was self-sufficiency. It was hoped that a plethora of cottage industries might supply Ireland's wants and cure unemployment.

In common with many other Republicans, Charlotte Despard set up her own small industry, a jam factory, in the summer of 1924. Her cherished flower gardens were ploughed up for strawberries and raspberries and for two years she acted the role of business manager, labouring over accounts and trekking round the retailers to pick up orders. In season there were up to fifteen employees, recruited according to political sympathy and financial need – that is, they were all Republicans, usually ex-prisoners or Belfast refugees – and, since they were visionaries of unyielding will, the rigours of industrial relations were daunting. The van man took it as a reflection on his honesty that he should be asked to keep accounts of his transactions, and the girls who boiled and bottled the jam angrily resented any criticism of their hair in the sugar or their smeared finger-prints on the jars. From the furious rows which resounded among the seething vats and writhing steam, Charlotte retired with her head aching and her dedication bruised.

After eighteen months she was disenchanted. It was not simply that the factory required a substantial subsidy from her income to keep going, but that the entire Republican approach to the economic problem was ineffective. Few of the cottage schemes were more successful than her own, and unemployment continued to grow. Many other Republicans shared her conviction that 'we have not struck the right note in the country, more effort should have been made to find a solution to the economic distress'.

The most damaging defection was that of de Valera. When the Boundary Commission split up in disarray in November 1925, leaving the frontier between North and South as it had been, de Valera was careful to dissociate himself from the IRA's policy of restoring unity by force. Six months later he withdrew from Sinn Fein itself and set up his own political party, Fianna Fáil (Warriors of Destiny), whose purpose was to achieve the same ends as the Republicans but through political pressure from within the Dáil.

As a large chunk of the Republican movement split off to join Fianna Fáil, a smaller group began to promote the view that Republicanism's true ancestors were Wolfe Tone and the ideas of the French Revolution, together with James Connolly and the theories of the workers' republic. This slant, with its echoes of French anti-clericalism and Soviet godlessness, made uneasy those martyrologists who confused Mother Church with Mother Ireland, but it had the charm of a familiar landscape for Charlotte Despard. She resigned from Sinn Fein, abandoned the Republican debating clubs and joined the centre of left-wing thought, the Connolly Club, where Marxists met under the chairmanship of the revolutionary's son, Roddy. There at last she found people who associated the name Despard not with a suffragette, but with Wolfe Tone's comrade in the rising of 1798 by the United Irishmen; and she began to feel herself at home.

By the beginning of 1926 she was writing optimistically that 'abroad and in England, Communism is growing extraordinarily; we mean to try and start a group here; so far as Society is concerned, that is the only hope for this tortured world.' Her optimism was premature, for the mere suggestion of this at a trade union meeting aroused criticism that it was a godless faith; but she promised a lecture on communism and Christianity to show that the two faiths were reconcilable. 'I have tried to do some thinking,' she wrote during a period of quiescence forced on her by arthritis, 'chiefly on the New Order to be brought in if Communism comes to be the accepted economic gospel. I wish to show how it will express that perfect, universal love which exists, I believe, in the very meaning and basis of creation.'

Coincidentally, as she was preparing her lecture, news came from the Theosophist headquarters in Adyar that Krishnamurti had revealed himself as the avatar, the incarnation of God, for whose arrival she had worked and prayed since before the war. It was momentous information – the Coming prophesied in her writings for which she had worked and waited so enduringly. For months she pored over the reports, half expecting Krishnamurti to proclaim the New Order of Communism, but at length she was driven to reject his revelation: 'impossible to believe – if the Master Christ was speaking through him, would he not be with the people?'

Her question caught at the contradiction upon which spiritual movements since Darwin have foundered. Once the authority of the Church was shattered, it could be seen that the religious impulse was confined to a minority of the population, and in an era of mass culture it was intolerable that God's truth should only be revealed to a few. Confronted by this dilemma, most political idealists between the wars decided, as Charlotte Despard did, that the only remaining path to the higher forms of civilization which

Darwinian theory had seemed to prophesy, lay in communism. All her hopes for civilization's future now rested in that ideology.

Her physical strength had dwindled since her eightieth birthday, but she possessed considerable financial muscle. The 1926 dividend from Muir Mills was made over to Roddy Connolly to set up the Irish Workers' Party, and she purchased a printing press for its newspaper, *The Workers' Republic*. The paper's slogan was Connolly's phrase, 'Ireland free is Labour free, and Labour free is Ireland free', which, translated into political terms, meant a policy of nationalizing the banks, appropriating landlords' estates and abolishing pawnbrokers. Unfortunately, the king of Irish labour, Jim Larkin, scented a threat to his rule and, after attacking the new party in arguments and fights, set up his own Irish Workers' League. 'In the Labour world', Charlotte Despard lamented, 'it is all hideous chaos – splits, suspicions, mutual recrimination everywhere.'

Since Dublin, the centre of Larkin's power, was denied them, efforts were made to form branches in the staunch Republican areas of Mayo, Cavan and Meath. Charlotte Despard had acquired an ancient car, depressingly prone to punctures, and a one-legged chauffeur, named Michael, who drove her on political forays across the country. A visit she paid to Portacloy, a fishing village on the West coast, typified the problems of the new Party.

After Mass, she addressed a meeting in pelting rain 'on the economic side of things, putting before them the aims of the IWP'. Undeterred by their lack of response ('they do not quite grasp our position, the men here are just Republicans'), she arranged to speak to another gathering after the local fair. Eight people took the opportunity of travelling to the fair in style, and piled into her car. When the last cow had been prodded and the last horse disparaged, a crowd of small farmers, horse-copers and labourers gathered round and listened in fascinated awe to her proposals. There was nothing subtle about her theme, and a member of another audience, who heard her deliver the same speech a little later, could still recall some of her remarks after a lapse of fifty years: 'Pay no rent, pay no rates. The land is a God-given right. Farmers, to you gentlemen I say, you don't own your land. You have no call to it. Divide with your neighbour. Let Ireland be as the wild geese – fly in, fly out.' With great courtesy her audience refrained from comment, and her pleasure in the day was only marred by the necessity of sobering up Michael 'and what I felt to be a dangerous drive home'.

In the circumstances, it is not surprising that the Irish Workers' Party gained few friends but did contrive to make some powerful enemies. The Church had no doubt about its real nature, and in parish after parish the priests called their congregations together after the speaker had left, to rebuke them roundly for listening to anti-Christian ideas. In addition, by poaching in Republican areas, the IWP was in direct competition with Fianna Fáil. The alliance between the two for which Charlotte Despard had hoped was made impossible, and, when the IRA decided to throw its weight behind de Valera in the 1927 election, the IWP was left without support, soon to dwindle away for lack of interest.

Its failure brought on an almost unendurable depression. She felt that she had lived too long, and that her existence had lost its purpose. Theosophy had failed; in Britain, Labour had been betrayed by its leaders; in Ireland, communism was a dead letter. All her causes had withered away, and with them went her optimism. For the first time in her life, too, she now had to worry about money. The expense of running a large house, especially when it was full of guests, put a strain on her resources which could hardly be met while the jam factory needed to be subsidized, and the IWP ate up her dividends.

She remained, nevertheless, almost profligate in her personal generosity, feeding, housing, and at the least giving money to anyone who came to her door. A succession of wounded prisoners convalesced in the house and, after the fishermen at Portacloy had told her that lack of transport prevented them from getting their fish to market, she purchased a lorry for them. When the Dublin Poor Law, almost overwhelmed by workers requiring relief, reduced the amount to 7s 6d a week and imposed a severe work-test, she helped to from yet another association, the National Unemployed Movement, to press for more generous conditions. A massive demonstration forced the Guardians to abandon the work-test, but the rate of relief could not be increased, and to supplement it Charlotte Despard organized and contributed on a large scale to the NUM's emergency distribution of food.

To meet these expenses she had to sell capital, but it was clear that savings would have to be made. The decision was effectively taken by the jam factory foremen, who disappeared with the reserves and a week's takings, and the ailing business had to close. It was only one of a series of disasters. Michael crashed the car, which distressed her less than that in his shame he ran off and never returned. Her gardener refused to move out of a cottage which was needed to house refugees, and she was reduced to the wicked expedient of getting an eviction order from the court. All this took place in a household already made gloomy by the disappearance of Sean MacBride after a burst of IRA violence in November 1925. He was known to be in hiding, but it was hoped that he was out of the country. Then, in July 1927, Kevin O'Higgins, the Home Minister, was murdered coming out of church, and the first suspect to be arrested was Maud Gonne's son. The case was never proved, and he was eventually released, but the shock of his arrest for such a brutal crime jolted Charlotte Despard from her tacit acceptance of the IRA's violent tactics, while it intensified Maud Gonne's hostility to Cosgrave's government. This growing alienation from her friend and preceptor completed Charlotte's misery.

She was ancient now, her skin brown and furrowed, the pain in her shoulder a torture liable to be inflicted for any and no reason, and her vision too blurred for her to read on any but the brightest days. On her eightieth birthday she had written stoically, 'I must not complain about this poor old body, though I begin to feel its limitations.' When she fell seriously ill with pneumonia, the nearness of death did not disturb her, and she reflected afterwards, 'It is curious to find oneself near the crossroads and to wonder what the passage will be.' At times she positively yearned for 'the body's end'. As disasters piled up and her political causes were split by personal rivalries, she felt her sanity going. There was betrayal on all sides. Money went missing ('treachery I fear from some of those in my own house'); a leader of the National Unemployed Movement had 'played the traitor' and, she suspected, made off with her contributions; while in the IWP 'none of those who lead seem big enough for their big task', and everywhere the distress of starving people seemed a reproach to her own helplessness. 'Everything is sad and perplexing, and I have had difficulty in holding the balance of my mind.' Her handwriting had by then become a trembling, irregular scrawl. It was clear that she was approaching death or senile dementia, but from that fate she was rescued by an old friend.

Each summer she was accustomed to go to London for a month. It was something of a triumphal tour – to Nine Elms where her old home was now a municipal nursery, to Kurandai where her bungalow was part of a school for crippled children, and to the Women's Freedom League, where the celebration of her birthday was always an occasion for an outpouring of love. Compared to the obstacles and hidden reservation she knew in Ireland, these were miraculous months when all difficulties were smoothed out by the efficiency of Florence Underwood and Elizabeth Knight, and all friendship seemed as straightforward as Kate Harvey's. Venerated by the League members, and cosseted by its officials, she was swept away by emotion: 'How is it I have such friends? May I become worthy of them. . . . Thanks, thanks, for the unspeakable gift of human love.' Her eightieth birthday celebrations in June 1924 had included leading a procession, in which Dame Millicent Fawcett and Emmeline Pethick Lawrence had also taken part, all the way from the Embankment to Hyde Park to press the demand for women to have the vote at twenty-one. It turned out to be almost the last suffrage demonstration: the ceremony of her eighty-fourth birthday was a victory feast to celebrate the achievement of their ancient claim to have the vote on the same terms as men. In that triumph her old faith in the power of the spirit suddenly revived.

Trying to convey the real achievement of the suffragettes, she had once written, 'Has it struck you, I wonder, that women understand women, love women, admire women, as they never did before?' That the struggle for a purely political goal should effect such a change had always seemed to her the perfect example of the way the material and spiritual worlds interacted. Living in Ireland, where it seemed that only physical force and the power of the gun achieved political ends, that insight had gradually been buried until this moment. When she spoke at the League's celebration, the old vaulting confidence returned in familiar style:

I have seen great days, but this is the greatest. I remember when we started twenty-one years ago, with empty coffers. . . . I never believed that equal votes would come in my lifetime. But when an impossible dream comes true, we must go on to another. The true unity of men and women is one such dream. The end of war, of famine – they are all impossible dreams, but the dream must be dreamed until it takes a spiritual hold.

Only one country had dared to turn dreams into reality, and, with her morale restored, Charlotte Despard determined to test her frail strength by visiting it. A near fatal fall down the stairs of Roebuck House delayed her plans, but in the summer of 1930 she felt able to undertake her mission, and with Hanna Sheehy-Skeffington she sailed to Leningrad with a delegation from the Friends of Soviet Russia.

She had come because Russia represented the future, and she was determined to find that the future worked. In everything she saw, there was a spirit to be admired and an object lesson for capitalism. The children whom she encountered in Leningrad's kindergartens, schools and technical colleges enchanted her by their openness and lack of timidity. 'No shyness at all', she noted with approval; 'one could see that they had met with kindness only.' A little anxiously, she enquired about punishment, and gladly recorded the answer, 'Punishments are taboo. In cases of insubordination, deprival of some dainty or treat, or, for a few short hours, isolation.' Even the Red Army, she was pleasantly surprised to discover, inflicted no harsher penalty.

From Leningrad her party travelled to Moscow, where they were taken on an exhausting but, for her, inspiring, tour of factories, craft schools and rehabilitation centres for prostitutes and minor criminals. To her unbounded delight, each of these institutions was run by an elected committee, which set standards and solved problems to universal satisfaction. There was neither competitiveness, compulsion nor quarrelling, and everywhere women were elected to posts of responsibility on absolute equality with men. Having attended a church service, she 'could testify that the Soviet State is not a robber of churches', and a guide disposed of the rumour that there was still hostility to the collective farms: 'the poor peasant proprietor is being taken along gently – given really preferential treatment – ' she recorded, 'and his opposition to collective farming has quite broken down'. So, after all, idealism could be made to work, and as she watched a youth rally the accumulated joy in that fact came flooding through: 'Free, happy and rejoicing – I thought of Shelley and his

Revolt of Islam, and breathed within myself a fervent wish that this grand nation – risen from the depths of humiliation – may not have her progress retarded by the capitalists and imperialists who are bent on her destruction.'

There remained, however, one question to which she as a veteran campaigner in and around prisons required an answer. Was there any serious crime in Soviet Russia, and if so how was it punished? There was a lengthy delay before a reply was given, but just before the end of her visit, three legal experts satisfied her curiosity. 'According to Russian law there are no crimes and no punishment', she reported:

Those whose actions either endanger the new social order, or show a person to be unfit for good citizenship are, generally, isolated for certain periods. During this time of isolation they are taught and trained for the duties and rights of citizenship. The opinions of others are never forced upon them; they are encouraged to judge for themselves.

In cases of treason where the traitors were utterly incorrigible, sentences of death might be passed; 'these are very rare. Other cases, and real incurables are sent to the island penal settlement. There, but that they must not leave the island, they are free to live as they will and, practically govern themselves.' Such was the picture painted of that island, or archipelago of islands, known as Gulag, and accordingly she departed from the Soviet Union with her happiness unimpaired.

Even at that stage, three years before the Stalinist purges began in earnest, it was a travesty of the truth. If she erred in believing it, she had, at any rate, tried to find out, and by her own lights she was not to be blamed for having been deceived. 'The sin', she once wrote, 'is not ignorance but indifference.' The need to believe was overwhelming; it was the vindication of her whole life to have walked in the socialist utopia which had been prophesied by Shelley, and to discover that, as Marx and the millenarians had foretold, it would lead on to a higher stage of civilization.

Like a young girl in love, her joy could only be expressed in verse, the first she had attempted since schooldays. In quavering strokes she scratched out vast, heroic stanzas, and the contrast between the frail hand and the trenchant words can produce the same sense of unseemliness that her audiences sometimes felt,

hearing such intense passion of the furrowed lips of an octo-
genarian.

At first she wrote only to celebrate the Soviet Union:

> The People want songs! I'll sing one to thee,
> Land of vast vistas, valiant and free,
> Seeing before thee a great destiny –
> 'Tis the land of the rising sun.

> Dear comrades, dear friends, across the wide sea,
> We meet you, we greet you in sweet amity,
> May the day soon arrive when all Nations shall be
> As the land of the rising sun!

Possessed by something like a sense of grace, she awoke each
morning with a confidence in the future which no longer could be
dismayed by political or economic calamity. The unemployed and
the Prisoners' Defence League continued to demand her time, but
she now had two new political enthusiasms. She was on the
Executive of the Friends of Soviet Russia, and was a vigorous
supporter of Saor Eire, or the Republican Congress, which was
set up by the left wing of the IRA and had inherited the aims
of the defunct IWP to sequester landlords' property and national-
ize the banks. After the IRA had tried to whip up opposition to
the Free State government in November 1931, the IRA itself and
every one of Charlotte Despard's organization was banned as subversive; but, instead of the doddering confusion of earlier years
she responded with defiant verse. To 1931 she dedicated the lines:

> Cover it over, Humanity's lover,
> With a pall of deep blackness, the infamy year,
> Set wild bells a-ringing to herald its passing,
> Let no bard sing its story, no flower deck its bier.

And the New Year was greeted triumphantly with:

> Thou bringest us life – we feel it, we know it,
> Life noble and true – Life valiant and free.

She took to the hustings in the General Election of February 1932
as she had in the palmy days of 1910. Her chief targets were the
constituencies of Cosgrave's ministers, who used to find her
perched on a step-ladder beside their platform, urging their crowds
to vote for de Valera; and, however much the minister or crowd
might dislike it, out of respect for her age no one dared move her

away. Her thin voice no longer carried, but the small boys around her who gleefully yelled 'Up de Valera!' destroyed any hope of an orderly meeting. An embarrassment to her enemies, Charlotte Despard was also something of a liability to her own side, and Desmond Fitzgerald, the Defence Minister, scored a useful smear when he shouted, 'That woman there was on de Valera's platform – a member of the executive of the Friends of Soviet Russia and the Communist Party who seek to establish anarchy on the Russian model in this country in conflict with the teachings of the Catholic Church.' That line of attack could not prevent de Valera's victory at the polls, but in the end its potency was to drive Charlotte Despard from her adopted country.

When the new government ordered the release of political prisoners and lifted the ban on illegal organizations, it seemed possible that de Valera might open the way for a socialist Ireland. No longer the revered figure of the 1920s, he was still 'a straight man' in her eyes, and that, she felt, would be sufficient to enable the workers' cause to advance.

The signs were certainly favourable in 1933. From the unions there emerged a Marxist organization called the Revolutionary Workers' Group, which was led by Jim Larkin junior; and the IRA, under a socialist Chief of Staff, David Fitzgerald, and heavily influenced by Saor Eire, took a pronounced turn leftward when it declared that 'the reorganisation of Irish life demands the public ownership of the means of production, distribution and control'. To hasten matters further, Charlotte Despard rented and later bought a tall, red-brick house in Eccles Street, which became the headquarters of the FOSR and a college for working-class members of the IRA. Marxist theory and life in Russia provided the staple of lectures at first, but soon they were overshadowed by a more dramatic theme, the rise of fascism.

The menace of fascism appeared in the guise of the Army Comrades Association, an employment agency for former Free State soldiers, which in 1933 began to recruit men and uniform them in blue shirts as a guard for Cosgrave's supporters against harassment by the IRA. Politically, the Blueshirts were right wing; but the confrontation never became a classic battle of left and right, because their opposition to the IRA was dictated by history – the old enmity of the civil war – rather than by ideology. So far as there was a conflict between left and right, it took place within the IRA, but there it was confused by religion.

Nearly one million people had attended the Eucharistic Congress in Dublin in Easter 1932, and religious feeling remained intense when, in his Lenten letter for 1933, the Cardinal-Primate tainted communists as 'the enemy of God' and bluntly stated that 'there was no room for them or their blasphemies among the children of St Patrick'. In Charlotte Despard's eyes, it was an aberration as deplorable as that committed by her Battersea priest when he prayed for Germany's defeat during the war, and she granted herself the same dispensation to ignore the Cardinal's words as she had the priest's. The IRA, however, was utterly split. The right wing, under Maurice Twomey, accepted the Church's teaching, but the anticlerical left, led by David Fitzgerald, was still resentful of the Church's excommunication of the IRA during the civil war and remained unmoved.

On the streets, Catholic gangs began to attack left-wing speakers and break up their meetings. In the inflammable atmosphere a rumour spread that the Revolutionary Workers' Group had placed a consecrated wafer under the doormat of their headquarters so that everyone entering would tread on the body of Christ. Armed with knives and hatchets, a mob, in which the Blueshirts and the St Patrick's Anti-Communist League were well represented, besieged the house and set it on fire. A week later Charlotte Despard's Irish Workers' College was wrecked and looted, and for a few anxious hours she was trapped inside by the mob before escaping through a backyard. She refused to be dismayed, and her ancient fingers scratched out another long poem to commemorate the attempt to build a world where:

> . . . those who sow and reap and weave,
> Who delve and dig and mine,
> Who make this earth, our dwelling-place,
> Productive, rich and fine,
> Shall reap the harvest, call the tune,
> Shall live as free men ought,
> Enjoying the abundance
> They themselves have wrought . . .
> Can these indeed be Communists?
> By all that's just 'tis true.
> Wild people cease from cursing,
> We build that world for you.

But it was soon clear even to her that the communist world could not be built in Dublin. In April, de Valera earned her lasting contempt when he gave in to the pressure of the priests and deported a communist, James Gralton, simply for his ideology. Two months later, the Republican Congress, together with a left-wing IRA group and the newly inaugurated Communist Party led by Jim Larkin junior, assembled to celebrate Wolfe Tone's birthday at his grave in Bodenstown, but personal rivalries proved stronger than ideological sympathies and the day ended in a pitched battle. To put the seal on matters, the IRA expelled members of the Republican Congress and declared that: 'The movement which is known as Communism has become definitely associated with atheism and irreligion. Hence any good or bad in the Communist economic theory is submerged.'

To be a Catholic communist in Ireland had become impossible. Even in her own house, Charlotte Despard's political beliefs could hardly be accommodated. Maud Gonne and Sean MacBride had both joined her in the IWP, but the IRA's pronouncement made her extreme beliefs an embarrassment. When she returned from her annual visit to England she moved out of Roebuck House to Eccles Street, but in fact there was no place left to her. As a communist she was not at home in the Republican Congress, and she could not tolerate the communist leadership's hostility to the Republicans. She toyed with the idea of returning to England, where she was much in demand on anti-fascist platforms, and considered going to Spain to study how relations between the Church and socialist republicans were conducted there. In the end her mind was made up for her by Hanna Sheehy-Skeffington, who had visited Belfast at the beginning of the year. From her she learned of an astonishing development in Northern Ireland. During the winter, unemployment had risen to over 20 per cent, which produced widespread rioting in Belfast; but the remarkable feature of these disturbances had been the unity of Protestant and Catholic workers in that oppressively capitalist corner of Ireland. Trying to spread the gospel of communism, Hanna Sheehy-Skeffington had been arrested, but the sister of Lord French might enjoy a greater measure of immunity.

The call of duty presented itself clearly and, with little to keep her in Dublin, Charlotte Despard did not hesitate. She gave away her house in Eccles Street to the Friends of Soviet Russia, left

Roebuck House to Maud Gonne and, encumbered only by Lord French's portrait, Max's bust and her own picture of the Christian, communist republic that was to be, travelled north to confront the Stormont government. She was close to ninety, but, as she used to tell the younger members of the Women's Freedom League, 'I have always believed in discontent – not grumbling, which is usually selfish and individual – but a disinclination to sit down idly, knowing things are wrong.'

12

The birthday visit of its first president provided the Women's Freedom League with an annual reminder of the manifesto for psychological and political independence which she had drawn up before the war:

We ask first for enlightenment. We wish using our own capacities, seeing with our own eyes, and not with the eyes of men, to understand our true position, to see clearly what are our duties and rights. Women demand . . . of society that they share equal rights with men, equal moral standards, equal opportunities, equal pay and equal justice.

After the fight for the vote had been won, the women's movement lost sight of the importance of 'seeing with our own eyes' and left itself with no greater ambition than to see from the same viewpoint as men. Suffrage societies became societies for equal citizenship, professional organizations like the National Union of Women Teachers had no other goal than parity with male colleagues, and the hugely popular Women's Institutes were concerned with standards of living rather than self-understanding.

The reason was obvious. It was to take another decade of solid lobbying and petitioning of coalition, Labour and Conservative administrations before Stanley Baldwin introduced the Equal Franchise Bill in 1928; equal pay was not widely achieved until the last years of the League's long life; equal opportunity of employment did not come until after the League was dead; and equal morality is still in the future. Beside these, an independent consciousness seemed a luxury. Even the Women's Freedom League, an avowedly feminist group, was inclined to forget its first president's words, but each summer, after eleven weary months of inching towards equality, there would appear amongst them the withered, totemic figure of Charlotte Despard, wreathed in metaphysics as potent as the monkey skulls about a witch-doctor's waist, to present another perspective. 'The women's movement is linked by the thread of love . . . [it] has opened women up to one another,' she used to say. 'The vote may go, Parliament may go, but love will remain – spiritual love *is* the women's movement.' The spirit they aroused in each other must be spread outwards, she insisted, because '. . . that knowledge of ourselves, of our gifts, of our possibilities, is the greatest boon the gods can grant us'. As self-knowledge, in her opinion, always entailed an awareness of social injustice, she expected it to manifest itself by action for justice – but, she assured her listeners: 'Success or failure does not matter so much as the effort, the result can be left to Higher Powers. No sacrifice is meaningless.'

Beside the precise aims of equal pay for women teachers or equal sickness benefits for working wives, her goals were apt to appear diffuse, but what they lacked in precision they made up for in inspiration. It was the atmosphere rather than the content to which her audiences responded, as they leaped to their feet, applauding until the ovation cascaded into a rousing chorus of 'For she's a jolly good fellow'. The officials who ran the League for half a century, Florence Underwood and Elizabeth Knight (the secretary and treasurer until the 1930s), and later Marian Reeves and Stella Newsome, had each been drawn into the women's movement by hearing Charlotte Despard speak, and each thereafter had devoted her entire working life to the League. They at least saw it through her eyes as a crusade, a spiritual cause, which justified the service of a lifetime – if for no other reason, then, as she put it, simply because 'There is no end of fun to be got out of life with a really good cause to fight for.' In the long run, inspiration proved more potent than precision, and the dedication of its leaders kept the League alive while other suffrage societies dwindled away.

Their permanent, but secret, enemy was that Kiplingesque masculinity whose values of chivalry and paternalism had so hampered the women's movement before the war, and which still prevailed as the national ethos. Its former confidence was diminished by war, but it derived constant reinforcement from the existence of the Empire, whose values and structure were, above all else, masculine. When the equal vote was debated in the Commons, it was significant that opponents rolled out the pre-war argument that the Empire would disintegrate if women voters had a majority at home, for it recognized that women's interests were fundamentally at odds with that masculine code.

Their fear was confirmed when the League took up the issue of the exploitation of women in the Empire – whether by prostitution, child marriage or female circumcision – and in so doing flushed the secret enemy out into the open. Based on superior strength, the Empire was a pragmatic structure administered by young men who, for the most part, dealt directly with the heads of the male-dominated societies within their territories and endeavoured not to intervene too deeply in their customs. Thus, in India, the authorities turned a blind eye to the flouting of the Sarda Act which banned child marriages; and all the propaganda of the League against what it saw as an evil and barbaric tradition failed to make them take any action. In the same way child brides were auctioned in Cyprus, young girls were circumcised in the Sudan, and the daughters of poor families in Hong Kong were sold into prostitution with the tacit consent of the colonial authorities hobbled by their own code. The process is best illustrated by the response of the Hong Kong government, when prodded by the League and sympathetic MPs to take action over the scandal of child prostitutes, or *mui-tsais*, who had been sold to brothel keepers. To each prostitute it issued a card, on which was written in Chinese: 'The British Government has for its main object the love of the people. You prostitutes, your persons are your own. You can come or go away at liberty. If any extortion or oppression is imposed, you can report it to the Authorities and you will get your wrongs righted.' These excellent sentiments made no impact on the trade in *mui-tsais*, but provided a perfect demonstration of the chivalric code in action. By offering to rescue the maidens, if in distress, it satisfied the knightly ideal; but, by preserving the father's power to sell his daughter, it also sustained the paternalist authority on which the Empire itself rested. Unkindly, it might also be pointed out that, by treating the illiterate victims as free agents, it also betrayed the monumental hypocrisy which was often its salient characteristic.

Exactly the same values, although rather more expertly disguised, continued to obstruct the League's demands for legal and economic equality. The well-being of the nineteenth-century family, like that of the nineteenth-century Empire, depended on the unimpeded authority of the father, and the law of the land had always tempered its promise to protect the freedom of the weak by leaving the protection of a wife and family in the hands of the husband and father. 'Each house is a domain into which the King's writ does not seek to run', was the principle enunciated by Lord Justice Atkin in 1919. The law simply dealt with him as a district commissioner might with a tribal chief, holding him responsible for all that went on in his domain and, in return, confirming him in his power so that he could carry out that responsibility. His wife's affection was his property (but not vice versa), and he could claim damages if it was alienated. The guardianship of their children was his. Her home was his, even if they were separated. In every way, from taxation to nationality, the wife's identity was submerged in her husband's by 1200 years of case and statute law. Because the law itself reflected a dominance based on superiority in strength, wealth and sex, no substantial reforms could be made until these bases were seriously challenged. The first basis had been shaken by women's war work, while the last was not widely doubted until the sexologists published their findings in the 1950s and 1960s; but the era between the wars was when man's crucial role as breadwinner came under the severest pressure.

There was initially nothing to suggest that this would be the case. The revolution in women's war work was undone swiftly when peace came and, by the time the 1921 census was taken, the pattern of employment was precisely what might have been expected had there been no emergency. Approximately one third of the female population went out to work – the same proportion as had existed through most of the nineteenth century – while the trends towards a diminishing number of female servants and an increasing number of female office workers and shop assistants, which had begun in the 1880s, continued as though the war had never been.

Even before hostilities had ceased, the munitioneers, land girls, Wrens and other servicewomen had been laid off with a week's notice, and they were soon followed back to the kitchen or unemployment queue by the 'substitutes' when demobilized servicemen returned to claim their old jobs. In fulfilment of its wartime pledge to the unions, the government passed the Pre-War Practices (Restoration) Act, which made it an offence to employ a woman in any class of job performed by a man before the war, and in 1920 a committee under Lord Lytton, the suffragettes' friend, recommended that all women taken on by the Civil Service during the war should be combed out. As the economy contracted during the twenties and unemployment grew, organized labour pressed for the dismissal of wives from all jobs in local and central government to make room for men. The unions' view, as expressed by J. H. Thomas, the railwaymen's leader, was simply that 'married women should not work at all, that is outside the house'.

Even in the areas where women were allowed to work, barriers of pay and promotion were erected against them. Despite the Sex Disqualification (Removal) Act of 1919, the Civil Service, the Post Office and local government ensured that women were almost entirely debarred from the higher grades; and, although it could be shown that only about 50 per cent of employed males had a family to support, while 25 per cent of the female workforce maintained at least one dependant, a woman in industry or government was paid about one third less than her male counterpart because it was assumed that only a man would have others to support. Finally, she was subject to regulations such as that forbidding her to perform industrial work at night, which presumed that she was above all a wife and mother. The chivalric code was hard to escape.

Against each piece of discriminatory legislation and procedure the League launched vigorous protests and objections. It organized 'Right to Work' demonstrations against the Civil Service dismissals. It was a major force in defeating an attempt to abolish the employment of women police. It briefed sympathetic MPs with examples of inefficiency resulting from the dismissal of trained women in favour of untrained men, or from discriminatory regulations which, for instance, prevented a woman power-engineer working after 10 pm and in consequence blacked out some rural areas every night. From Charlotte Despard it had inherited a belief in absolute equality in employment, so it was equally opposed to a Bill forbidding pregnant women to work in lead-paint factories because of the threat to their health. 'We do not want the sex factor to interfere with labour,' a member said, 'only the human factor as a whole.' If pregnant women were at risk, so were men, it was argued; in the same way, if compulsory maternity leave were introduced, that too should be available to men. The League's pugnacity and lack of compromise gave it a pre-eminent position in the women's movement during the twenties.

Through its newspaper, *The Vote*, the League monitored the progress of the women's movement in Britain and abroad, using foreign sympathizers and local branches to provide a highly efficient grapevine, which won accolades from such political disparates as the Tory Nancy Astor, the Republican Hanna Sheehy-Skeffington, the Liberal Lady Rhondda, and the Labour Chrystal MacMillan. Its comments on proposed legislation were quoted in the Commons as representative of the women's movement, journalists who wanted the women's angle on political questions automatically rang the League headquarters for a quote, and *Punch* could identify women in its stories as serious feminists simply by describing them as members of the League.

There was in truth no great challenge to its pre-eminence, since the fastest-growing women's societies were, like the Women's Institutes, social rather than political, and the old suffrage societies were in disarray. Members of the old WSPU, which had virtually ceased to exist in August 1914, tried to organize the Six Point Group to press for legislation in half a dozen key areas, but, lacking public support, it soon faded. The National Union of Societies for Equal Citizenship became steadily less political in an attempt to slow the loss of members to the Women's Institutes and social clubs; one of its oldest members, who could remember J. S. Mill receiving the women's petition in 1867, concluded sadly that 'vitality is limited to a generation and to a need, and it is not transferable'.

The League itself was severely diminished, with only about 5000 members and twenty branches, but it had always been more visionary than the other societies and its members had never felt that the vote alone was their goal. It continued to spread its policies through its old strongholds in Scotland and the North of England, an especially fruitful area being the Clyde coast during Glasgow Trades Week, when the resorts were thronged with holidaymakers. For many years one of the traditional sights on Dunoon pier was Lillian Lenton, a former arsonist in the WSPU, lecturing on the inflammatory topic of equal morality – until the pubs closed, when the meeting had to end because moon-eyed patriots, staggering into the fresh air, would invariably mistake the green, white and gold colours of the League for an Irish tricolour and come flailing in for a fight. More decorously, the message of equality was conveyed at the League's dining society in London 'for men and women of progressive views', and at the Minerva Club, run by Marian Reeves for professional and university women.

Although professedly apolitical, the League had been, under Charlotte Despard's influence, more left wing than the other women's societies. This slant was continued by its next two presidents, Alice Schofield Coates, elected in 1920, who had a long career as a social worker and Labour supporter in Middlesborough, and Emmeline Pethick Lawrence, whose socialist and egalitarian views seemed Despardian. Under Alice Coates's presidency the League included Labour's demand for a minimum wage among its objectives, and members were urged to join trade unions. For much of the decade, members of the League almost monopolized the leadership of the National Union of Women Teachers, and they were prominent in other women's unions also; but the eagerly awaited Labour government proved no more sympathetic to the women's movement than Lloyd George and Bonar Law.

The League was swimming against the tide in the twenties, but a succession of reforming Acts half answered some of its demands. The Sex Disqualification Act had opened the professions, magistracies and juries to women, and with pardonable pride the League recorded the appointment of its members as magistrates, their refusal as jurors to withdraw from rape trials, and the triumph of Helena Normanton, an Executive member, in being the first woman to plead in the High Court. Other measures were welcomed; the Infanticide Act, which enabled courts to treat the crime as manslaughter if necessary, represented a signal triumph for the League's long battle; the Divorce Act removed the wife's need to prove cruelty, and made adultery the sole grounds for either partner; the age of consent was raised to sixteen, and it was no longer a defence to have believed that the girl was over that age. This last reform, which treated child molesting as a serious crime rather than the normal failing of a privileged sex, did suggest that attitudes to women were beginning to alter. The very presence of women magistrates on the bench was a deterrent to the old outlook, and their recommendations provided powerful ammunition for the first two women MPs, Lady

Astor and Mrs Wintringham, who helped to push the Bill through.

When the Equal Suffrage Bill was introduced in 1928, Stanley Baldwin felt able to claim that, 'Once this Bill is law, the last fraction of truth about inequality will have gone, gone for ever.' The apparent justification for his claim could be seen in the androgynous shape of the flapper, whose cropped hair, cylindrical body and easy command of car and plane seemed proof that women were at last the equal of men. 'How I love the modern girl with her long legs and short skirts,' Charlotte Despard insisted. 'In my day we did not dare show our ankles and we felt we had to apologise for being present.' Far from apologizing, the twenties girl marked her presence with an order for cocktails and a puff of her cigarette; she took as the model for her giddy independence Amy Johnson, who had gate-crashed the male arena of aviation by flying alone in her Tiger Moth from London to Australia. Yet the surface was deceptive. Sexually and socially, the absence of those young men slaughtered in the Great War allowed the persistence of a tomboy streak in women which would otherwise have been sublimated in adult relationships, and it had become a mimicry of male fashions and habits. Emmeline Pethick Lawrence put her finger on the problem when she said, 'The attainment of the equal vote has removed the material obstacle to freedom, but the moral and spiritual obstacles that lie within ourselves are very great.' The difference between what the feminists were aiming for and what the flappers achieved emerged in a letter from Amy Johnson herself. Thanking a member of the League for some pamphlets on the movement, she admitted that 'they have tended to make me feel more proud of being a woman, it being all my life a great grief to me that I was not born a boy'.

As the imbalance of the sexes was gradually redressed in the 1930s, femininity returned as the ideal of womanhood. Fashion dictated longer, swathing garments, and popular magazines like *Good Housekeeping* and *Woman and Beauty* offered multiple variations on the theme of pleasing men and creating a home fit for the breadwinner. Paradoxically, the decade which saw the trappings of emancipation disappear allowed women to make some genuine movement at last towards legal and economic independence, albeit for the worst of reasons. Just as the contracting economy had crippled women in the twenties, so it made victims of men in the thirties.

Unemployment averaged over 14 per cent through the decade, and the number of workless men never dropped below a million. The business of bringing up children and running a household at least gave a wife an occupation, but for the man there was nothing, and his helplessness was underlined by the introduction of the means test, which suspended the payment of unemployment benefits when there was any other source of family income. Humiliating as it was for a man, and unjust in denying him the benefits for which he had paid insurance, the means test was nevertheless a milestone in feminist history, as significant as the First World War; for by it the government recognized, *in extremis*, that the father was not the sole support of his family. Furthermore, women's jobs like packaging, clerical work and domestic service were the least affected by the slump and, when a wife brought home a pay packet while her husband was workless, much of his authority inevitably passed to her.

The abolition in 1935 of the husband's liability for his wife's debts and other mischief perhaps owed more to the notorious bankruptcy of a certain peer by his wife's extravagance than to the unemployed man's lost power as breadwinner, but the conditions were ripe for the law to relax its assumption of the wife's subservience. In 1937, wilful desertion was for the first time admitted as grounds for divorce, as was cruelty; and, in 1938, the League saw its twenty-year battle for a wife's right to choose her own nationality achieve at least the promise of success when the Home Secretary gave his wholehearted approval to the principle, although the war intervened before legislation could be introduced. However difficult its circumstances, the decade did permit some fundamental advances to be made in the legal position of women.

Tragically for the League, its treasurer, Dr Elizabeth Knight, was killed in a road accident in November 1933. For years she had been subsidizing *The Vote*, and without her money it abruptly ceased publication, depriving the League of both a source of influence and a means of recruiting members. A cyclostyled bulletin was issued instead, and for a time the League's momentum carried it forward. It continued to goad the government about equal pay, the Hong Kong authorities about the *mui-tsais*, the League of Nations about international prostitution, and the International Labour Organization about discriminatory regulations on the employment of women. The spirit remained willing, but, in the absence of its paper, the structure began to show signs of decay, and income and membership gradually fell away.

Over sixty years older than the organization she had founded, Charlotte Despard seemed like a promise of immortality. Impossibly ancient, and as frail as pressed petals, she came without fail to remind the League of goals unachieved and to present that alternative to the chivalric code which the Soviet Union had put into practice – 'From each according to his or her abilities, to each according to his or her needs.' The alternative to the knightly ideal was, she suggested, 'the Pythagorean ideal, in which the state is father, mother, brother, and sister to its citizens'. The alternative to capitalism was, as always, communism. 'And after Communism?' she was asked. 'Ah, then we will come back to ourselves, as it were.' And so the process of liberation would be complete. The failure of the Western world to grasp this simple concept provoked a caustic note to escape her: 'You know of course', she mentioned to a journalist, 'that this world is the lunatic asylum for other planets?'

In the past it had always been Mrs Despard's fate to be placed by public estimation on the borderline between sainthood and idiocy, but now, as Mussolini postured in Italy, as the Nazis swallowed up the Weimar Republic and as Franco's Falangists challenged the Spanish republic, she began to reap a wider acclaim than she had ever known. When she spoke in Trafalgar Square on an anti-fascist platform, she was cheered as resoundingly as in suffragette days. When she warned a *Daily Mirror* reporter that discrimination against women was in danger of losing them all the gains that had been made, it was plastered across the entire front page: ' "We must fight" says suffragette of 91.' The first woman Cabinet Minister, Margaret Bondfield, said: 'If I have won any laurels, I am proud to lay them at the feet of Mrs Despard.' The secretary of the Communist Party, Harry Pollitt, proudly proclaimed that 'she has done more for Communism than any of us'. And her old friend Lilian Baylis, now manager of both the Old Vic and Sadler's Wells, knelt at her feet before the crowd at her ninety-third birthday party, and kissed her hand. Twenty-five hundred people signed a roll of homage to her, the names representing the alarming variety of her interests: the suffragettes included Teresa Billington Greig and Sylvia Pankhurst; the politicians, George Lansbury and Nancy Astor; the communists, Harry

Pollitt and Paul Robeson; the vegetarians, Bernard Shaw and Stafford Cripps; there were members of railwaymen's, caterers', laundryworkers' and teachers' unions, and a host of friends, from Margaret Bondfield to Kate Harvey.

It was an impressive list, but the missing names themselves constituted a roll of honour. Emmeline Pankhurst had died in 1928, Millicent Fawcett in 1929, Annie Besant in 1933 – while she, who had been born before any of them, lived on. 'They pass and I remain,' she mused, 'and indeed I sometimes wonder why.' It was rarely for long, however. She mourned deaths briefly, even that of her old favourite, Carrie, in 1935, and preferred instead to dispense nuggets of wisdom about life. Invariably the reporters asked the secret of her great age, and repeatedly she passed on the recipe: 'If you want to live the happiest and fullest life, live with the people.'

When she returned to Belfast, it was to be again with 'the people', the poor who were crammed into long rows of terraced brick houses, but whose labour built and sustained the towering stonework of commerce and government. To them she dedicated the poems which still came scrawling from her pen:

> Long, long in grim darkness you've silently waited,
> Now to the Red Dawn your banner's unfurled.
> Bear it on boldly, who dares to withhold you?
> Forward! and onward! yours is the world.

Outside at the garden gate, Dawson Bates's policemen stood on guard, and inside the house she and Molly Fitzgerald, her secretary, plotted the downfall of Bates and Stormont and capitalism itself. Peering closely through dim eyes, she still studied her pamphlets from the Theosophist Society and from the Friends of Soviet Russia, melding their different sentiments into yet another speech for yet another meeting of the unemployed. Her vision of the Law of Love, or the communism, or the Christianity 'which will one day rule the world', still led her on unheeding through the contradictions, and still seemed to put her beyond the reach of age. 'Do you feel at all old with your grandchildren about you?' she wrote to a Despard nephew. 'I don't . . . I have never been quite so well.' But in the end the contradictions trapped her.

Although her heart was with 'the people', they had little interest in her or in her ideas. Indeed apart from her doctor, John O'Prey, who shared her concern for the poor, she had little personal contact with Ulster people. The Protestant working class thought her living proof of the secret alliance between Stalin and the Pope, but even the Catholic working class found her espousal of godless communism and her contempt for de Valera's banana republic beyond comprehension.

In an attempt to make closer contact she moved in 1935 from the Newtonards Road to a small house in Glenburn Park, a mixed area nearer the centre of Belfast; but the gap was more than geographical. A small incident illustrates the problem. To raise morale among the unemployed, she decided that it would be helpful to have a brass band, such as miners and millworkers had in the North of England, and at considerable expense she purchased the necessary instruments. At first there was huge enthusiasm, and the band could be heard practising in back rooms and be seen marching in the street; then gradually its discordant noise grew fainter, and after a short time a number of barely used cornets and tubas could be seen gleaming in the pawnbrokers' windows. It was a small parable of what happened to her speeches on the revolution of the workers. People might see that the goal was desirable, but just at the moment there were more pressing needs, and, as music was sacrificed for a hungry child or a heavy thirst, so workers' solidarity crumbled in the face of sectarian division.

In the summer of 1935 the worst riots yet broke out in Belfast, and the brief working-class unity of 1933 evaporated as Protestants raided Catholic areas in what the latter called 'the pogroms'. Even Charlotte Despard's home, though guarded by the police, was not considered safe, and the situation was made worse because she had staying with her Ronald Kidd, a reporter for the National Council for Civil Liberties, who was investigating abuses of the Special Powers Act. His enquiries attracted the attention of Protestant hooligans, and two years after being threatened and abused by Catholics in Dublin, she suffered the same fate from the other side in Belfast. A little wearily she decided to move out of the city.

In the last years of her life the contradictions finally and tragically destroyed her. Living on the income of the French and Despard trusts, she had always been the beneficiary of the capitalist system she hated, just as she had continued to value her friendships among

254

the class whose power she hoped would be overthrown; but now the system and the class had their revenge.

The unwitting agents were her two companions Molly Fitzgerald, the impulsive, idealistic girl, who had been a secretary in Dublin, and Jack Mulvenna, the former publican, who had been expelled from the IRA for his membership of the Republican Congress. They were both in their early thirties, vivacious, friendly and staunchly left wing, and, although they were officially her secretary and chauffeur, Charlotte never referred to them except as 'my dear friends'. She fed off their youthful energy, particularly Molly's enthusiasms, and their Irish accents gave her the impression that she was still in touch with 'the people'. Yet there was a price to be paid, for they were both extravagant with her money, and her fortune was less than in the past.

A few of her friends thought the bargain worthwhile. Others, notably Marian Reeves, suspected them of exploiting her generosity. But her relatives were unanimous in believing that Aunt Lottie had fallen into the clutches of scheming rogues; they were, after all, not only the wrong age for an old lady's companions, but so obviously the wrong class.

In 1937 she moved out of Belfast to a bungalow built for her on the clifftop above the small town of Whitehead, and to pay for it she was forced to borrow £2500 from the bank. She still drew the interest on her marriage settlement, but Max's fortune had dwindled by now to less than £5000. Her extravagance in Dublin, culminating in the gift of Roebuck House to Maud Gonne, had accounted for much of it, but in addition the loans to her brother Jack had never been repaid. She had only once dared ask him about the debt, a few weeks before the attempted assassination, and that near-tragedy, followed by their estrangement, prevented her ever returning to the matter. It was, therefore, largely from a sense of justice that she asked the trustees of her marriage settlement, who were Jack's two children, to make available some of the capital to pay off her debts. Suspecting the money would be misused, the trustees refused to make it available, and thus, eighteen months later, when a further £1100 of debts had been run up in her name, Charlotte Despard was made bankrupt.

By then she was beginning to fade away. As war approached, dividends were frozen or reduced, and under the mental stress of falling income and mounting bills she became confused and a little senile. The old pain in her back redoubled its bite, and she spent entire days in bed, drugged against the pain and unable to move. A Belfast priest, Father McCloskey, who was able to accommodate her communist ideas, and a Belfast doctor, Dr O'Prey, came to talk to her and give her pain-killing tablets, but locally she was hardly known. On a fine day the neighbours might see her hobbling down the road towards the bay or in her garden looking blindly across the Irish Sea towards the Isle of Man. A nurse sometimes came up the hill from Whitehead when the pain became critical, but otherwise few local people entered the house. It had in a way been tainted before it was built, for the Belfast CID, knowing who would live there, had once conducted a thorough search of the foundations for arms. In a small Unionist town like Whitehead, there was scant liking for Republicans.

Quite abruptly the fire of public affection which had warmed her was doused. The outbreak of war in September 1939 cut her off from England, and her choice of friends branded her an outcast in Whitehead. In the last days of her life, the compassion, anger and enthusiasm which had been the very breath of Charlotte Despard seemed to drain away, leaving a forlorn, decrepit figure at the centre of a sulphurous scandal.

In September 1939 she made a new will, leaving the vast bulk of her estate to her two companions, and six weeks later she fell down a flight of stairs late at night. She cut her head and dislocated a hip, but for three days she lived on in hospital. Then on 9 November she died, without having regained consciousness.

There was hardly a doubt in local people's minds but that she had been pushed. Nevertheless the evidence presented to the inquest pointed to an understandable accident. A ninety-five-year-old woman, who was subject to dizzy spells and dosed with sleeping pills, would have been all too liable to stumble as she made her way along a landing darkened because of the wartime blackout. Reluctantly the jury recorded a verdict of accidental death. There still remained the matter of Charlotte Despard's estate. Technically the creditors should have been paid off, and the residue left to Jack Mulvenna and Molly Fitzgerald, but in legal circles it was an open secret that 'no Republican would get a penny from the estate of Lord French's sister'. So it proved, for when the case was eventually settled, in 1951, Molly had died and legal fees had drained away the last of Maximilian's fortune.

One part of the will was carried out. She had asked to be buried in Glasnevin Cemetery, the Republicans' resting-place in Dublin, and despite the protests of the creditors' assignee, who declared the expense to be unjustified, Jack Mulvenna ensured that her wish was fulfilled.

On a bleak, rain-scoured morning, the hearse carrying her coffin left Belfast followed by two cars. Half an hour later when they reached Lurgan there were five vehicles in the cortège; at Newry just north of the border, there were a dozen, and at Dundalk, the first town inside the Republic, there were twenty; others joined at Drogheda; and from every town along the slow, cold journey her body called out mourners until it came to Dublin at the head of more than fifty cars. The coffin rested overnight at St Joseph's Church, while a steady stream of the poor passed through to pay their last respects to their champion, and the following day a crowd of over two thousand people assembled to accompany it to the cemetery. Her pall-bearers were a judicious choice from all the warring factions she had failed to unite in life: Peadar O'Donnell, once of the Republic Congress, Roddy Connolly, once of the Irish Workers' Party, Sean MacBride from the right of the IRA and Frank Hugh O'Donnell from the left, Sean Murray, head of the Communist Party, and Mick Price, the bitterly anti-communist chief of staff of the IRA. At the graveside, it was Maud Gonne – 'Cathleen ni Houlahan', the spirit of Ireland – who stood beside the heaped earth to make the peroration:

Throughout her life she was like a white flame in the defence of prisoners and the oppressed. As President of the Prisoners' Defence League, she left her home to work all over the country for human liberty, and I, like many men alive today, owe my life to her. Because of her work the people of Ireland loved her, and especially the poor of Dublin, and to all of us her death is the loss of a great light.

It was a good funeral, and its sorrowful, theatrical mourning would have been relished by the Irishwomen of Nine Elms whose intimacy with death had first drawn Charlotte Despard to her life's work. Yet it was not quite her style to make so much of the body's demise. Of her crowded career exactly half had been compressed into the years surplus to her allotted span, and she had lived her old age as though life were just beginning. Long study of things mystical and of news from the other side had made her almost callous about 'passing-on', and when she thought of death, it was in Shelley's words:

> Death is the veil which those who live call life;
> They sleep, and it is lifted.

The only death she feared, and wished always to mourn loudly and angrily, was that of the spirit – which poverty and cruelty caused.

From the vantage point of Nine Elms, she had seen clearly the spiritual murder committed by nineteenth-century capitalism, and quite simply found it so intolerable that, as the *Manchester Guardian*'s obituary put it, 'no personal sacrifice and no break with the past [was] too great in seeking a remedy'. Others fought as unwearyingly, and perhaps more effectively for reforms, but no one conducted the battle on quite so long a front as hers, which stretched from the institutionalized brutality of the Poor Law to the discrimination of the Northern Ireland government.

In course of time the graveside at Glasnevin Cemetery was where the Women's Freedom League virtually ended also. The war hastened the erosion of its membership and, although some of its most notable battle honours came in the years following 1945, it was living on its past.

A peculiarly mean government attempt to pay war-wounded women two thirds of the compensation given to men was defeated after three years of lobbying and badgering by the League's penultimate president, Mrs Mavis Tate MP. In 1948, a generation after the League first took up the question, legislation was passed allowing wives to choose their own nationality, and in 1956 the League celebrated a victory, in importance second only to the vote, when the government announced that it would introduce by stages equal pay for the women in the Civil Service and in education. The Equal Pay Committee had united all the women's organizations since 1944, and on its dissolution the League lost its best means of influencing Parliament. In the rising affluence of the 1950s, the material battles of women seemed to have been won; as mothers, they were immediate beneficiaries of the Welfare State, as wives they could go out to work as a matter of course, and unmarried women had an unprecedented choice of careers.

The old voice of masculinity still rang loud in the land, but the Commonwealth could never give it the confident bark that Empire once had. The League still pressed for its old equalities, of pay in the private sector of industry, and of moral standards in the treatment of prostitutes, but no one was listening. Perhaps if they had not lost hold of the importance of 'seeing with our own eyes' they might have found new adherents. In the new phase of the women's movement which was to break in 1963 with the publication of Betty Friedan's book, *The Feminine Mystique*, that theme answered an unrealized need in many women who had achieved material equality.

When the Women's Freedom League celebrated its Golden Jubilee in 1957, many of the pioneers reassembled – among them Teresa Billington Greig, Alice Schofield Coates and Muriel Matters Porter – but there were no longer any young members, and no local meetings were being held. When the League's head-quarters were moved in 1958 from 144 High Holborn to the Minerva Club, which Marian Reeves ran, there were suggestions that the time had come to dissolve. Many years earlier Charlotte Despard had advised: 'Better close down at once rejoicing as you have every right to do in the victory you have gained, than creep on from month to month, a little society not attracting the strongest and best women.' That time had clearly come, but the League hung on for another three years.

In September 1961 the last president, Marian Reeves, undertook a trip to Dublin to inspect the condition of the first president's resting-place in Glasnevin Cemetery. A few days after visiting the grave, she died, and with her the League also ended.

On 16 October 1961, the *Guardian* carried the following report:

In the coming week its remaining 150 members will receive the last bulletin that the Women's Freedom League will ever issue, one that publishes the news of the passing at a special conference of a final and fateful motion, 'That the Women's Freedom League should disband'. Thus ends one of the great women's organisations of the century.

BIBLIOGRAPHY

Personal papers, corresponence and diaries: in the Belfast Public Record Office, the Fawcett Library and family possession.

Personal papers of the Despard family: in family possession.

Unpublished notes of Teresa Billington Greig; in Fawcett Library.

Minutes of Kingston Poor Law Union 1892–4.

Minutes of Lambeth Board of Guardians 1895–1903.

Minutes of Nine Elms Board of Education 1899–1914.

Women's Freedom League: Conference reports 1908–1933.

   National Executive Committee reports 1908 and periodically thereafter.

   Various documents.

   The Vote, 1909–33.

FAMILY BOOKS

Charlotte Despard, *Chaste as Ice, Pure as Snow*; London: Tinsley, 1874.

Wandering Fires, London: Tinsley, 1874.

A Modern Iago, London: Griffith & Farran, 1879.

Jonas Sylvester, London: Sonnenschein, 1886.

A Voice from the Dim Millions, 1888.

The Rajah's Heir, London: Tinsley, 1890.

and Mabel Collins, *Outlawed*, London: Drane, 1908.

'Women's Franchise and Industry' (pamphlet) 1908.

'Women in the Nation' (pamphlet) 1909.

'Women in the New Era' (pamphlet) 1910.

'Theosophy and the Women's Movement' (pamphlet) 1913.

Gerald French, (ed.) *War Diaries, Addresses and Correspondence of Sir John French*, London: Cassell, 1929.

The Life of Field-Marshal Sir John French, London: Cassell, 1932.

Edward Lydall, *Enough of Action*, London: Jonathan Cape, 1949.

Anon. *The Trials of the Late Colonel Despard*, London: Mudie, 1803.

George Despard, *The Patagonian Mission Justified*, London: Nisbet, 1860.

Charles Oman, *The Unfortunate Colonel Despard*, London: Arnold, 1922.

SOCIALISM

Charles Booth, *Life and Labour of the People of London* (Vol. 5), New York: Kelley, 1902.

G. D. H. Cole, *British Working Class Politics*, London: George Routledge, 1941.

Philip Henderson, *William Morris*, London: Thames & Hudson, 1967.

James Klugman, *The History of the Communist Party of Great Britain*, London: Lawrence & Wishart, 1968.

S. Ramsey, *Historic Battersea*, London: Rangecroft, 1913.

Sheila Rowbotham, *Women, Resistance and Revolution*, London: Allen Lane, 1972.

Hilda Scott, *Women and Socialism*, London: Allison & Busby, 1976.

P. B. Shelley, *The Complete Poetical Works of Shelley*, London: Clarendon Press, 1904.

Chusicki Tsuzuki, *The Life of Eleanor Marx 1855–98: A Socialist Tragedy*, London: Oxford University Press, 1974.

Clara Zetkin, 'Social Democracy and Women's Suffrage' (pamphlet) 1906.

WOMEN'S SUFFRAGE

Maud Arncliffe, *The Child*, privately published.

Teresa Billington Greig, *The Militant Suffrage Movement*, London: Frank Palmer, 1911.

Margaret Bondfield, *A Life's Work*, London: Hutchinson, 1948.

George Dangerfield, *The Strange Death of Liberal England*, London: MacGibbon & Kee, 1966.

A. G. Gardiner, *Pillars of Society*, London: Nisbet, 1913.

James Hunt, *Suffragettes and Satyagraha* (monograph), 1976.

J. S. Mill, *The Subjection of Women*, London: Longmans, 1869.

David Mitchell, *The Fighting Pankhursts*, London: Jonathan Cape, 1969.

Women on the Warpath, London: Jonathan Cape, 1966.

David Morgan, *Suffragists and Liberals*, London: Blackwells, 1975.

Stella Newsome, 'The Women's Freedom League' (pamphlet), London: WFL, 1959.

E. Pethick Lawrence, *My Part in a Changing World*, London: Gollancz, 1939.

Millie Polak, *Mr Gandhi, the Man*, London: Allen & Unwin, 1931.

Andrew Rosen, *Rise up Women: The Militant Campaign of the Women's Social and Political Union, 1903–14*, Routledge & Kegan Paul, 1974.

Ethel Snowden, *The Feminist Movement*, London: Collins, 1913.

Helena Swanwick, *I Have Been Young*, London, Gollancz, 1935.

H. G. Wells, *The New Macchiavelli*, London: Allen Lane, 1911.

Mary Wollstonecraft, *A Vindication of the Rights of Women*, London: Allen Lane, 1906.

Almroth Wright, 'The Unexpurgated Case Against Women's Suffrage' (pamphlet) London: Constable, 1913.

M. Wynne Nevinson, *Life's Fitful Fever*, London: Black, 1920.

PACIFISM

G. Bussy and M. Tims, *The Women's International League for Peace and Freedom*, London: Allen & Unwin, 1965.

John Graham, *Conscription and Conscience*, London: Allen & Unwin, 1922.

Mary Lutyens, *Krishnamurti the Years of Awakening*, London: Murray, 1975.

Arthur Marwick, *Clifford Allen*, London: Oliver & Boyd, 1964.

J. M. Rae, *Conscience and Politics*, London: Oxford University Press, 1976.

Bertrand Russell, *Autobiography* (Vol. 2), London: Allen & Unwin, 1968.

James Webb, *The Flight from Reason*, London: Macdonald, 1971.

MISCELLANEOUS

M. E. Chamberlain, *Britain and India*, London: David and Charles, 1974.

Maurice Collis, *Way Foong*, London: Faber & Faber, 1965.

Joseph Goldring, *The Nineteen Twenties*, London: Nicholson & Watson, 1945.

M. G. Schenk, *The Mind of the European Romantics*, London: Constable, 1966.

Martin Seymour-Smith, *Sex and Society*, London: Hodder & Stoughton, 1975.

George Watson, *The English Ideology*, London: Allen Lane, 1973.

IRELAND

Basil Chubb, *Irish Government and Politics,* London: Oxford University Press, 1970.

Tim Pat Coogan, *The IRA*, London: Fontana, 1971.

R. M. Fox, *Rebel Irishwomen*, Dublin: Progress House, 1935.

Samuel Levenson, *Maud Gonne*, London: Cassell, 1976.

Dorothy MacArdle, *The Irish Republic*, London: Gollancz, 1937.

Nicholas Mansergh, *The Irish Question*, London: Allen & Unwin, 1965.

C. Markiewicz, *Prison Letters*, London: Longmans, 1934.

Sean O'Faolain, *Constance Markiewicz*, London: Jonathan Cape, 1934.

W. B. Yeats, *Autobiographies*, London: Macmillan, 1966.

INDEX

268